Uprising

Will Emerging Markets Shape or Shake the World Economy?

George Magnus

A John Wiley & Sons, Ltd., Publication

This edition first published 2011
© 2011 George Magnus

Registered office
John Wiley & Sons Ltd, The Atrium, Southern Gate, Chichester, West Sussex,
PO19 8SQ, United Kingdom

For details of our global editorial offices, for customer services and for information
about how to apply for permission to reuse the copyright material in this book please
see our website at www.wiley.com.

The right of the author to be identified as the author of this work has been asserted in
accordance with the Copyright, Designs and Patents Act 1988.

The opinions and statements expressed in this book are those of the author and are
not necessarily the opinions of any other person, including UBS. UBS accepts no
liability whatsoever for any statements or opinions contained in this book, or for the
consequences which may result from any person relying on any such opinions or
statements.

Library of Congress Cataloging-in-Publication Data

Magnus, George.
    Uprising : will emerging markets shape or shake the world economy / George
Magnus.
        p. cm.
    ISBN 978-0-470-66082-9 (hardback)
    1. Economic development–Developing countries.   2. Investments, Foreign–
Developing countries.   3. Developing countries–Economic policy.   4. Developing
countries–Foreign economic relations.   I. Title.
    HC59.7.M244 2011
    337.09172'4–dc22

                                                                    2010034792

A catalogue record for this book is available from the British Library.

Set in 10.5 on 15 pt Monotype Janson by Toppan Best-set Premedia Limited
Printed in Great Britain by TJ International Ltd, Padstow, Cornwall

To My Mother

Contents

Acknowledgments

The financial crisis that began in 2007 has been shocking in every sense of the word, and the consequences will be felt for many years to come. The enormity of this phenomenon dawned on me in March 2007, and I have explored and examined its dynamics at length for UBS clients and in the media ever since. The book about it I intended to write, however, barely got off the ground when I was persuaded to think about a different kind of crisis book, one that looked at the implications of the crisis for emerging markets.

For this, I have to thank Ellen Hallsworth, Commissioning Editor with John Wiley & Sons in the UK, who planted the idea and then offered me a continuous and regular menu of suggestions and corrections that were invaluable in helping me to develop the structure and the narrative.

My purpose is to re-examine the claims made and prospects for major emerging markets in the wake of the crisis. There is, inevitably, a substantial focus on China. But because the global economic system we have grown up with these last 25 years is in flux, we have to put to one side the linear, spreadsheet-type projections which still abound, and consider the strengths and weaknesses of emerging markets anew, seen through a global, as well as a local, lens. I have had the fortune to be able to look to and consult with several people whose expertise and knowledge have filled many gaps.

I'd like to thank several colleagues at UBS Investment Bank: Terry Keeley, formerly Global Head of Sovereign Relations, whose sharp mind is now considering a new challenge outside UBS; Jonathan Anderson, Head of Emerging Markets Economics, whose prolific work and ideas are an inspiration; Paul Donovan, Senior Global Economist, whose irreverent view about economic research and conventional economic thinking is always refreshing; and Geoffrey Yu, foreign exchange strategist, whose youthful perspective and knowledge are a match for any more seasoned analyst.

Julie Hudson, Head of Socially Responsible Investment Research at UBS, gets very special thanks for contributing almost everything I now know about the challenge that climate change poses to emerging markets and their policies. She went to considerable lengths while pursuing a literary venture of her own.

I'd also like to thank Mark Steinert, Global Head of Research, and Larry Hatheway, Chief Economist, who supported my previous book on demographics, for their encore with this book. UBS takes its research product very seriously, and they have again allowed me to combine my research and client work with this project.

Two emerging market gurus took the time to digest and comment upon my work, offering me their particular insights into China, Asia and emerging markets in general. Guy de Jonquieres, formerly Asia editor of the *Financial Times*, and now Senior Fellow at the European Centre for International Political Economy, and Simon Ogus, a former colleague at UBS in Hong Kong, now running his own consulting firm, DSG Asia, gave me a lot of food for thought, and the benefits of their rich experience.

And since one of my recurring ideas through the book is that, over time, the quality of institutions matters more than, say, Gross Domestic Product or any cyclical phenomenon, I am grateful to Ed Gottesmann of Gottesmann Jones and Partners LLP, and David Ereira, Partner at Linklaters. These wise lawyers not only tried to straighten out my thinking about the role played by political and legal institutions in economic development, but also inadvertently stimulated me to ponder generally on the respective roles of lawyers and economists in trying to fix the world.

To all of these people I owe a debt of gratitude in helping me reflect on and refine the content of this book, and it remains only to say that I take full responsibility for errors and omissions.

They all made up different parts of an informal team, but as authors are apt to insist invariably and correctly, that team is never complete without spouses and partners. In my case, then, Lesley, my wife, had to put up with my disappearances for extended periods chained to the laptop in my office at home, my impromptu outbursts on often esoteric economic issues at moments that could have been better-timed, and with my sometimes single-minded focus on the book that caused me to hear, but not listen to what was being planned at home. But she also read my drafts, asked me poignant questions, and was, as ever, my rock, love and close companion.

Introduction

Not everything that counts can be counted, and not everything that
can be counted, counts.

(attributed to Albert Einstein)

Tens of thousands of people poured spontaneously into Tiananmen
Square on a July night in 2001 to celebrate the decision by the
International Olympic Committee to award China the Olympic
games in 2008. Former Chinese premier Li Peng watched with
pride as workers and students danced the conga and sang patriotic
songs. Ironically, those same songs had filled the square eleven
years earlier when the same Li Peng declared martial law and sent
the tanks in to crush the pro-democracy protests. This was 2001,
however, and although China had already been making enormous
economic progress for a decade or so, it was in the process of
moving into top gear.

In 2008, then, the Olympic games provided the backdrop for the
much-heralded demonstration of China's modern image and self-
confidence, which took place with great fanfare and to wide acclaim.
The games symbolised China's economic success, coincided with
the fifth consecutive year of double-digit economic growth and

were the perfect hors d'oeuvre for the 60th anniversary of the founding of the Peoples' Republic in 2009.

Unfortunately, the games were sandwiched between two earthquakes, both of which served as a reminder that awesome economic achievement and serious political shortcomings were on two sides of the same coin. A geological earthquake that killed about 70,000 people struck in May in the province of Sichuan in central China. In the aftermath, there were allegations about the lax enforcement of building codes and political corruption. The decision to build a reservoir behind a major dam, which burst just a mile from the earthquake's fault line, exemplified a system in which government takes place without challenge or openness to debate and dissent. These issues are hardly unique to China, but they form part of the mosaic of political and institutional weaknesses that I will argue compromise the country's capacity to achieve sustained, linear and rapid economic growth as widely anticipated.

In October, a financial earthquake struck, following the collapse of the US investment bank, Lehman Brothers. This brought the world economy to the brink of an economic Armageddon, unrivalled since the Great Depression of the 1930s. Although this was first and foremost a Western crisis, it had a significant impact on China and, indeed, on all emerging markets. The idea that emerging markets would 'decouple', or remain aloof from the economic contraction in richer economies, proved wide of the mark.

In China, the authorities misread the signals in the form of the rising number of bankruptcies of small and medium-size enterprises, a fall in exports for the first time in seven years, and sharp declines in the output of electricity, automobiles and steel.

Yet China's subsequent response was impressive. In November, it announced an economic stimulus programme of 4 trillion yuan were the perfect hors d'oeuvre for the 60th anniversary of the founding of the Peoples' Republic in 2009.

Unfortunately, the games were sandwiched between two earthquakes, both of which served as a reminder that awesome economic achievement and serious political shortcomings were on two sides of the same coin. A geological earthquake that killed about 70,000 people struck in May in the province of Sichuan in central China. In the aftermath, there were allegations about the lax enforcement of building codes and political corruption. The decision to build a reservoir behind a major dam, which burst just a mile from the earthquake's fault line, exemplified a system in which government takes place without challenge or openness to debate and dissent. These issues are hardly unique to China, but they form part of the mosaic of political and institutional weaknesses that I will argue compromise the country's capacity to achieve sustained, linear and rapid economic growth as widely anticipated.

In October, a financial earthquake struck, following the collapse of the US investment bank, Lehman Brothers. This brought the world economy to the brink of an economic Armageddon, unrivalled since the Great Depression of the 1930s. Although this was first and foremost a Western crisis, it had a significant impact on China and, indeed, on all emerging markets. The idea that emerging markets would 'decouple', or remain aloof from the economic contraction in richer economies, proved wide of the mark.

In China, the authorities misread the signals in the form of the rising number of bankruptcies of small and medium-size enterprises, a fall in exports for the first time in seven years, and sharp declines in the output of electricity, automobiles and steel.

Yet China's subsequent response was impressive. In November, it announced an economic stimulus programme of 4 trillion yuan

Introduction

Not everything that counts can be counted, and not everything that
can be counted, counts.

(attributed to Albert Einstein)

Tens of thousands of people poured spontaneously into Tiananmen
Square on a July night in 2001 to celebrate the decision by the
International Olympic Committee to award China the Olympic
games in 2008. Former Chinese premier Li Peng watched with
pride as workers and students danced the conga and sang patriotic
songs. Ironically, those same songs had filled the square eleven
years earlier when the same Li Peng declared martial law and sent
the tanks in to crush the pro-democracy protests. This was 2001,
however, and although China had already been making enormous
economic progress for a decade or so, it was in the process of
moving into top gear.

In 2008, then, the Olympic games provided the backdrop for the
much-heralded demonstration of China's modern image and self-
confidence, which took place with great fanfare and to wide acclaim.
The games symbolised China's economic success, coincided with
the fifth consecutive year of double-digit economic growth and

($590 billion), equivalent to 13% of GDP. With a strong emphasis on infrastructure and property projects, it was intended to turn around the slowdown in economic growth, which slipped below 5% in the year to the final quarter of 2008. It also encouraged state banks to make loans on a scale that had barely been rivalled before. China set an example to many other emerging economies and, by the spring of 2009, most emerging countries in Asia and Latin America had started to respond in a strong, positive way. A potential economic crisis had been averted successfully, but perhaps only by a whisker.

These two stories illustrate a dichotomy to which I will return throughout the book. On the one hand, China and other nations with strong central authorities are indeed capable of vigorous economic success, and very effective in the implementation of quick and large-scale policy responses when necessary. On the other hand, strong central authorities that operate without accountability and strong political and social institutions lack transparency and a capacity to change and adapt responsively. One of the major themes in the book is that the West's financial crisis sparked a major change in the structure of the world economy, and that China's capacity to also embark on structural change voluntarily is weak, unless it is specifically geared to the long-run interests of the Communist Party's grip on power, as was the case, for example, in the 1980s. The consequences for China, and indeed for countries in the West and for international relations, could be far reaching. It is appropriate, therefore, to think about the financial and economic crisis, not as bad luck or just an accentuated business cycle, but as a take-off point for outcomes that are more judgement than prediction.

Like most financial crises, this one was preceded by the excessive accumulation of debt, and of the leveraging of banks' balance sheets. Like many crises, this one involved housing-related loans and securities, predicated on the assumption that house prices could only rise. Unlike other financial crises since the end of the Second World War, however, this one was global in scope, and had the United States at its epicentre.

Fixing the banking system and arriving at the point where the overhang of debt has been destroyed or restructured is likely to take several years. Further, since governments have assumed substantial obligations to and liabilities of the private sector, the debt problem has also embraced the public sector. This too poses large risks to the economic stability of the US, Japan, the Euro Area and the UK, and will entail years of painful budgetary adjustment.

The severity and significance of the crisis and its legacy effects for Western economies is an essential part of the background to this book, but not its principal focus. Rather, this is to examine whether the crisis has acted as a lightning rod to accelerate the rise to economic and political dominance of Brazil, Russia, India and China (known as the BRICs[1]) and other emerging nations and, implicitly, the decline of the West. The BRICs are the nucleus of a resurgent expansion in the economic position of developing countries, whose share of world GDP has risen from about 15% in 1990 to 35% today, and is expected to continue rising in the next decade.

The BRICs comprise the apex of a developing country triangle, so to speak. This is not so much because they are the wealthiest, but because they are the most populous, with strategic significance and regional power status, and, in China's case, a potential global power.

It is partly for this reason that the emerging markets focus of this book is quite heavily on China. It is also because China is really the only emerging country to have increased its weight significantly in the world economy over the last 20 years. Brazil and India are dynamic economies but they don't account for a significantly higher share of world GDP than in the past, even though India's size will certainly increase its weight in the future. And Russia is a more sophisticated economy in many respects, but is essentially an oil and resource power with global geopolitical, but not economic, significance.

Below the apex, you find countries such as Singapore, Hong Kong, Taiwan and South Korea, also known as Newly Industrialising Economies because of their relatively advanced economic status and high standards of living. Many economists and investors already pigeonhole these four regions as developed, rather than emerging or developing. In the book, I shall use the term 'emerging' to refer to those countries that show the largest economic potential and that are of interest to investors today, while 'developing' countries comprise the rest or is used as a generic term.

In the still narrow part of the emerging triangle, then, you will next see countries such as Mexico, Argentina, Poland, Turkey, Indonesia, Thailand, Malaysia and Vietnam. After that, in the broadest part of the triangle, you will see oil-producing countries, such as Saudi Arabia, Iran, Mexico and other members of the Organisation of Petroleum Exporting Countries (OPEC). Some of these countries are quite rich when you look at income per head, but they are mostly one-trick ponies – that is, they are essentially energy economies. You will also see other emerging countries, such as Chile, Colombia, South Africa, Egypt, and many of the countries in Eastern Europe and central Asia. Across the base of the triangle, you will find the remainder of the developing world, comprising poorer and or smaller nations and most of the countries in Sub-Sahara Africa.

The growth in emerging and developing countries' share of world GDP in the last 20 years has been significant for inhabitants who have either experienced a rise in their standard of living or been lifted out of relative poverty, but the importance goes further. For investors, financial entities and multinational companies, it has meant new opportunities to cash in on new trends in economic development, as those in the West start to look tired or become shrouded by rapidly ageing societies. At the top of the food chain, though, economic power is the basis for political power. This is about rising prosperity, but only when mixed with a large population, and other factors that contribute to the use of leverage in the pursuit of influence and political power. The debate about the BRICs and emerging markets nowadays celebrates these developments as exciting, which they are, but also as inevitable and unstoppable. I want to give the reader pause for thought about this latter assertion, if not the basis to disagree.

This is not to dispute history. Developing country exports already amount to about $6000 billion, or nearly two-fifths of the global total, and the rise of emerging market companies has been meteoric. In 1990, there were barely two dozen companies head-quartered in emerging nations with individual sales over $1 billion per year. Based on 2008 revenues, there are now about 560, and 111 of them had sales over $10 billion. Three companies – Petrochina, China Petroleum and Gazprom – had sales in excess of $100 billion. If you could get out your ruler and draw the future in straight lines, the size and importance of emerging market companies would increase, they would figure in the largest companies beyond the energy focus of the three just mentioned, and there would be plenty of examples of what we could call reverse foreign direct investment, such as the Indian steel company Tata's purchase of UK producer Corus in 2007.

There is a strong conviction that we are all bystanders in an inevitable and world-changing shift in the structure of global power. The long-awaited decline of the West now seems to many people to be in full swing. When President Barack Obama visited his opposite number, Hu Jintao, in Beijing in November 2009, many observers were struck by the symbolism of the leader of a battered and highly indebted US going to meet the leader of America's main geopolitical rival, and its most important creditor.

Books abound proclaiming the rise to dominance of China, Asia or emerging markets in general. Some titles speak for themselves, for example, *When China Rules The World*, *China's Megatrends*, *The Next Asia*, *China Shakes The World*, and *The Emerging Markets Century*. The ideas behind these titles are not new, for historians and philosophers have wondered for a long time whether the world might one day change course, with the West in persistent decline, and China – and maybe India – reverting to the position of global dominance that they once held for a couple of millennia. The debate today is really about whether the financial and economic crisis is acting as a catalyst to speed up this process. What I call here 'Uprising', though, is more a questioning of the idea that the last two centuries of Euro- and US-centric history have simply been a historical aberration.

There is little question about a shift in economic power, which has broad significance. It is driving a realignment of political and national interests that is reshaping the world. Before the crisis, the tensions between advanced and developing nations played second fiddle to the rising tide of global prosperity. It was assumed that, one way or another, global democracies would stick together somewhere under an American umbrella, while others would stand firm behind China. The crisis seems to have changed this perception because it has been seen as a failure of the type of capitalism and globalisation championed by the US over the last 25 years. Political leaders in emerging markets have had important reservations in the past about the so-called Washington Consensus, which captured an approach to economic policy and structure, emphasising the primacy of markets, the minimisation of the role of the state in the economy, and the intrusion of US-dominated international financial institutions into the sovereignty of nation states. Now, the world seems to be splitting more between 'rich versus poor' on matters such as trade, finance and climate change, as opposed to along lines of political structure. Emerging market democracies, such as India, Brazil, Turkey and South Africa, identify increasingly as developing nations rather than as democracies. Many look to the Chinese model, not the tarnished US version, even if they retain respect for some of what the US stands for and also have reservations about China's policies and its posturing about emerging market solidarity. There is no BRIC or emerging market bloc, as such, and many emerging markets have competing national and geopolitical interests among themselves. Among the BRICs, for example, China and India are rival continental powers, and Brazil and India don't always see eye to eye with China over exchange rate and several trade issues. Emerging markets may find themselves confronting the US and the West, therefore, on a variety of topics with great ambivalence, but more chaotically than coherently.

Developing countries did dig their heels in over negotiations with the West before 2009, over trade liberalisation in the context of the Doha Round of talks. These negotiations started in 2001, and were still nowhere near an amicable conclusion in 2010. As the financial crisis rumbled through the global economy, the BRICs, especially China, were already engaged in the scramble for access to energy and other natural resources in the Middle East, Africa and Latin America. In response to the crisis, they coordinated policy responses, placing the blame firmly on the US. They have become more vocal in the debate about how to reform and restructure global financial institutions and regulation, and the role of the US dollar in global finance. They formed a united front at the Copenhagen climate summit in December 2009, and refused to accept the proposal that greenhouse gas emissions of poorer nations be capped at lower levels than those of the US and Europe. There is little question that the developing nations are now in a position to supplement their public reservations about US and global capitalism with action or, at least, a refusal to go along with a Western agenda.

Yet the debate about the decline of the West and the rise of China and other emerging markets has assumed feverish proportions. Such fever tends to blur sensibility and leads to muddled, and possibly dangerous, thinking. The West has had a *fin de siècle* moment, in which the economic growth drivers of the last 30 years have broken down, or at least been compromised. Its reputation has suffered too, for its claim to economic and financial leadership now looks tenuous at best. We should not underestimate the structural change or time that will be needed to reboot our crisis-affected economies, if indeed that is possible.

At the same time, however, it would be dangerous to imagine that China and other emerging economies can carry on as before the crisis, in the mistaken belief that nothing has changed, and that the crisis had nothing to do with them. There is little doubt that their economic outlook for decades is potentially robust, and many companies relish the prospect of tapping the world's next billion consumers. Emerging markets might well be the economic powerhouse of the next decades of the 21st century, but this is by no means inevitable.

Far too often, the trajectory of emerging markets is portrayed by protagonists in a naïve, linear fashion that doesn't accord to historical outcomes. Instead, the future is really about political economy, not economic forecasting or the models that drive confident assertions that the future has already arrived. History, politics and institutions all matter deeply to the future of emerging markets even though, in Einstein's parlance, they cannot be counted.

Politics are pivotal in this debate. Domestic political issues and debates arising from the consequences of the financial crisis and the need for reform are liable to increase in importance as China grows and modernises rapidly. These go to the heart of the nature of the Confucian state.

Confucianism was adopted as the state philosophy over 2000 years ago, giving a moral authority to a legal and administrative structure based on a regimented citizenry, standardisation of rules and regulations, and a strong central authority. Central to Confucianism is that government should be in the hands of moral people, that the purpose of government is the welfare of the people, and that since morality can be taught, only people educated in morality should rule over others. These ideas permeate the Communist Party and its factions, although not always uniformly. Nevertheless, when China talks about 'harmonious development' in the economy and society, the harmony refers to shared beliefs imposed from above, and represents a kind of religious orthodoxy that may have shed most of its Marxism but that typifies China's history. One of the negative effects, though, is the suppression of independent legal and judicial institutions, and creative ideas that challenge the government. This is a motif to which we shall return, but there are economic consequences. Consider, for example, that the state can build the world's fastest and most efficient railway network, and as many airports as there are towns and cities, but if it doesn't tolerate dissent over environmental, cost and building issues, the long-term economic practicality of such projects could be limited.

Rapid economic development is also being accompanied by a sharper focus on social and political unrest. China's human rights record, which has been a constant sore in relations vis-à-vis the West, was underscored by the imprisonment in December 2008 of Liu Xiaobo, a human rights activist, who received an 11-year sentence for 'subversion'. This was only one example of an escalating official campaign against activists and human rights groups, whose protests against the government have become increasingly troublesome – over, for example, corruption, land evictions in the name of commercial and infrastructure development, the environment, and unemployment. In 2010, strikes and suicides brought industrial unrest and massive pay hikes to numerous factories in southern China, where the country's manufacturing hub is located.

These were not isolated incidents. The government has acted for years to suppress protests over taxes, land rights and wages, and to stifle activists pursuing reform of human rights, land rights, and struggling for environmental protection and against corruption. Although there are no official data, there may have been about 90,000 incidents of social unrest (many involving deaths) in each year between 2006–2009, ranging from individual protest to spontaneous and unorganised outbursts of public rage[2]. The latter, now known as 'social venting incidents' differ from others in that participants don't have material issues to present to the government, but are venting resentment and anger at government powers and the better off in society. Freedom of expression and the right to dissent are not part of the Communist Party's version of modern China. This could now start to have much larger implications than simply the suppression of domestic protest.

There are also important international policy issues that are likely to remain significant. Foremost among these is China's exchange rate regime, over which the US and China have locked horns for several years, but increasingly so since 2009. Other emerging countries, such as Brazil and India, may be less vocal, but they too complain that China's exchange rate policies are stealing their capacity to benefit from global demand. The exchange rate regime, though, is only the tip of the iceberg, beneath which lurk even more complex issues including how and how quickly China should reform in response to the crisis, and whether it should have any responsibility to do so.

The threat in January 2010 by Google, the Internet titan, to quit China because of alleged attacks by (government) hackers on its e-mail service and growing controls over the Internet in the country, reflect demands for a more prominent cybersecurity policy, in which 'netizens' might be prevented from colluding in any possible 'colour' revolution, such as the Orange Revolution in the Ukraine, and the Green Movement in Iran. But they may also have wider implications for companies doing business in China, for the kind of business they are willing to do, and for the technology that companies are willing to bring to China. The drive towards 'indigenous innovation', in which government procurement contracts and other regulations are being tweaked to favour potential national champions and local companies, could compromise China's access to foreign know-how and its contribution to national productivity growth.

The Google story, though, sitting alongside other developments involving human rights, freedom of expression, and control over information has a still larger significance in this, the information age. For as long as China was essentially a customer for global goods and services, its incorporation into the global economy was seen as a win-win for everyone involved. Western governments and think tanks were critical of China's authoritarian structure, but were willing to believe that economic integration and rising prosperity would bring forward further liberal political and economic reforms eventually.

China's status, however, has changed. Rather than being a customer, it is now a competitor, and a major creditor. China trades economic and financial favours with strategically important countries in the developing world for political leverage, but it does much bilaterally, not as part of a multilateral system. It is taking advantage of the Western financial and economic crisis to assert its greater weight in the world. The failed Copenhagen climate summit, for example, spawned bad feeling, with the West viewing China as an obstacle to global climate cooperation, not a partner. The human rights and similar issues to which the West previously objected but essentially tolerated, are now portrayed as instances of an authoritarian society that only wants to play in the global economy by its own rules.

We can see here the emergence of a familiar great power problem. This revolves around two processes that are essential for global stability and order. The new kid on the block has to be willing to integrate into the global economy without causing serious strains and to balance its domestic and external policy obligations. The established powers have to accommodate the new kid in the global power structure, by accepting the new order, and also compromising where necessary.

Arms control, nuclear non-proliferation, climate change, global ageing and health, adequate food and water supplies, and greater diffusion of technology rank among the world's greatest challenges over the next two to three decades. These tasks call for high and complex levels of international cooperation, and a willingness by all parties to surrender some sovereignty in their common interests. None of this will happen, however, if advanced and emerging nations, championed by the US and China, cannot figure out how to cooperate economically in the aftermath of the crisis. Economic nationalism and the erection of trade barriers and other obstacles to economic integration threaten not only further major economic turbulence, but also a much more fractious and hostile environment for international relations generally.

To avert such an outcome, it is important that the US and China, in particular, acknowledge why the financial crisis happened and what role they played in bringing it about, even if inadvertently. In the US, the Congress and other institutions are at least holding hearings on banking and regulatory matters, debating openly what went wrong and how to avoid such a crisis in the future. Some people have been embarrassed publicly and been forced to resign, some have gone to gaol. In China, by contrast, we hear nothing, and not even the slightest thought that Chinese economic and financial policies may have had some role to play in creating the crisis.

The crisis as a catalyst

The 2008–2009 crisis involved a near collapse of the world's financial system, precipitated a global recession, and led to the sharpest decline in world trade for almost 80 years. Global banks may have incurred around $2500 billion in losses, and Western governments were forced to intervene in unprecedented and spectacular ways to stabilise the banking system and keep their economies from collapse. According to the IMF, support of all types for the financial sector has amounted to about half the GDP of all advanced countries, and as much as 80% of GDP in the US and the UK[3]. These programmes include loans and guarantees that will eventually be repaid or run off, but the eventual cost of saving the financial system may be as high as 15–20% of gross domestic product (GDP) in the US and the UK, and between 5 and 15% of GDP in several other large advanced countries.

It is still unclear how the United States, Japan, the United Kingdom and other European countries will emerge from the crisis, or what their economies might look like in five to ten years, for there can be no going back to the economic and financial conditions of the boom that lasted from the early 1980s to 2007. The United States and other Western nations have been holed below the waterline by the crisis. It will take years to repair the financial system and trust in financial institutions and products, and to build a new model for growth based on high employment, innovation, and low carbon intensity. In the process, they will have to confront the legacy effects of the crisis in the form of soaring public borrowing and indebtedness, and the enormous budgetary and other economic and social consequences of ageing societies.

Moreover, the crisis demonstrated the weaknesses and dangers in the Western, laissez-faire model of financial globalisation that had been developed in the prior two decades, and which many emerging markets had criticised as being relatively hostile to their interests. Good governance, according to Thomas Friedman, harnesses creativity, but in a variety of spheres, including finance, trade, energy, the environment and education, the US and the West have been found wanting[4]. Further, the crisis generated a change in thinking in the West about the relative merits of markets versus government in finance and economic development. It is hardly surprising that China's state-directed economic model has acquired many sympathisers, especially in developing nations.

Emerging markets also went into recession or experienced a surprisingly sharp economic slowdown. At first, there was concern that the anticipated 'decoupling' of emerging markets – that is, their capacity to remain aloof from what was occurring in the rich world – had failed. However, they bounced back relatively quickly and, in some cases, all the stronger, reaffirming the proposition that they had become sufficiently mature and independent, economically, to detach themselves from dependency on the West. In fact, most emerging markets bore few, if any, of the hallmarks of financial excess that had spread throughout the Western financial system, and entered the crisis in a far stronger financial position and with healthy government budgets. To a significant extent, this was because most Asian emerging markets, though not China or

India, had been through a period of intense financial crisis between 1997 and 2001, and had already had several years within which to repay or restructure debt and reorganise their economies and public finances.

As the financial crisis erupted, governments in emerging countries were able to rally to the global recovery cause, implementing large economic and financial stimulus programmes. The largest by far was in China. The second biggest was in Singapore (3 percent of GDP), but the significance of emerging market action was emphasised by the coordinated response. Indonesia, South Korea and India, and Argentina, Brazil, Mexico, Chile and Peru were among many nations that also contributed to the task of stabilising the global economy. This was no act of altruism, but a response to the global meltdown and a strong expression of national self-interest.

Moreover, while the fate of the global financial system was still hanging in the balance, the first heads of state meeting of the so-called Group of 20 countries (G20) was called in Washington DC on 15 November 2008[5]. It met again in London in April 2009, and confirmed or announced a series of coordinated economic and financial measures to combat the crisis, and to work towards economic stability. In May, Russia hosted the first official BRIC summit meeting.

At the Pittsburgh G20 leaders' meeting in September 2009, it was announced that the G20 would henceforth replace the narrower G8 group of countries (Canada, France, Germany, Italy, Japan, Russia, the UK and the US) as the main body for coordinating economic policy. The G20 countries have also agreed an increase in the quota shares for emerging countries in the International Monetary Fund and the World Bank (at least 5%, and at least 3%, respectively) from 2011. These quotas determine subscriptions into the institutions, access to finance from them and, importantly, voting rights. These rather esoteric details of global financial governance are important, since they reflect the increasing voice and influence of emerging countries in the world economy.

BRICs in the wall of the future

The idea of China, and perhaps India, dominating the world economy in the decades to come is nothing new. The economist Angus Maddison, for example, demonstrated often and at great length, how robustly China and India compared with European and other economies for over 2000 years before the start of the 19th century. As I shall explain in the next chapter, several economic historians argue that the world is now reverting to a structure that obtained long, long ago. While the Byzantine, Roman and Ottoman empires, for example, can all be said to have shaped the world, China and India dominated the world economy. Many are familiar with – and nowadays many travel – the Silk Road. This term, coined by the German scholar, Baron Ferdinand von Richthofen in 1859, centuries after it had faded into obscurity, described a complex network of trade and commercial trails that ran from China through central Asia, then forked north through Russia to the Black Sea, and south via India to the Arabian Sea, ending up in Turkey, North Africa and Europe.

Today, the old Silk Road is enjoying a renaissance. Caravan trails have been replaced by modern merchant fleets and jumbo jets. Trade in silk, spices, gold, pottery and grains has been replaced by trade in hydrocarbons, petrodollars and financial assets, Chinese consumer products, labour and technologies. China has again established a Sino-centric economic system, first in, but subsequently beyond Asia, and is building commercial and political ties with Russia, central Asian republics, Iran, Saudi Arabia, Brazil, and several smaller countries in Africa. Some of these ties are overtly related to access to raw materials and markets, others are simply to stymie or pose a counterweight to the influence of the United States[6].

In the last 10 years, China has strengthened financial and commercial links with many countries in Asia and the Middle East, often based on Islamic finance products and conditions to fund infrastructure and project finance deals. It is also a key member of the Shanghai Cooperation Organisation, founded in 2001 with Russia, Kazakhstan, Tajikistan and Uzbekistan. Designed originally to deal with disputes, terrorism and separatist threats, it now includes India, Pakistan and Mongolia, along with observer status for Iran, and fosters energy and economic cooperation among members and strategies to deter or contain America's presence in central Asia. Although the trade and investment deals announced by China and other BRICs over this period run into hundreds of billions of US dollars, their growing involvement in Sub-Sahara Africa from a very small base has been particularly noteworthy. Since 2009, they have agreed deals including foreign investment, concessionary loans, aid and grants amounting to around $13 billion with African nations, including Nigeria, Angola, Mozambique and Tanzania, and in 2007, China played a key role in helping Sudan to restructure its foreign debt.

Predictions abound about the number of years it will take the BRIC economies to exceed the size of the major advanced economies. China is expected to overtake the US some time between

2016 and 2026; India will overtake Japan and the UK by 2020–2030, and Brazil and some other countries, including Mexico and Indonesia, will overtake the major European countries and Japan by 2050. According to one report, the US will still be the largest economy in 2030, but very closely followed by China. Japan will be half as big as both, followed by India, Germany, the UK, France, Brazil, South Korea, Italy, Canada, Mexico, Russia, Turkey, Indonesia, Saudi Arabia and South Africa. The share of advanced economies in global GDP will fall by 20% to 52%, while the share of emerging markets and other developing countries will rise by the same amount to 48% (measured in real terms, that is, adjusting for inflation)[7].

Yet what do these projections and all this 'counting' mean? What do they depend on? What difference does it make if your GDP is large, but if the quality of life and living standards for most citizens are relatively low? China and India are still relatively poor countries, with per capita incomes just a small fraction of those in the exclusive group of rich nation trade partners. In 2008, 76 countries in the world had a per capita income of $15,000 or more, but half of these were oil producers or small islands, and principalities with tiny populations. Within the other group of 38 countries, 22 were Western nations, the remainder being Russia, nine emerging markets in Eastern Europe, and Israel, plus South Korea, Taiwan, Singapore, Malaysia and Hong Kong. It may take generations, with many setbacks on the way, for major emerging markets to raise per capita incomes to a level comparable with OECD countries today.

In the uncertain times unleashed by the crisis, we might ask many other penetrating questions. For example, what would become of Asia's manufacturing supply chains and the emerging countries' dependence on exports to Western consumers if globalisation faltered, for example, as protectionism proliferated or, possibly, if the US and other major advanced nations succumbed to a crisis over public debt? Alternatively, what if the US were able to reinvent itself, as it has on many occasions in the past, blazing a trail towards a green economy and a new wave of productivity-enhancing innovation. How would that leave the catch-up debate? How would developing countries fare if international institutions, such as the G20 and the IMF, were to prove impotent in the face of resurgent nationalism? If oil prices rose to $200 per barrel for any reason, Russia, Mexico and other oil exporters would benefit, but how would the oil importers, including China and India, cope?

We do not know which way China's state capitalism will turn if economic growth and the demand for social and political reforms collide. Elsewhere, we cannot foresee whether Russia's version of state capitalism will be able to manage a serious demographic crisis, whether its dependency on energy and natural resources is a curse in disguise, or if it might become more fearful of large and powerful neighbours. It is hard to judge if India's strengths in technology and its democratic institutions will help to turn it into the next Asian Wirtschaftswunder (economic miracle), or simply skim the surface of deeply embedded economic and social divisions and constraints. Brazil needed a series of serious crises until 2000 before it turned towards constructive reform and more competent macroeconomic governance, but the still waters of populism run deep.

Even as we confront these glacial and ponderous developments over the medium and long term, the urgent issue of unbalanced trade, commonly known as 'global imbalances', which lay at the heart of the financial crisis, remains unresolved. I will argue that fault for global imbalances cannot be restricted to the US alone, and that if China and other major emerging markets fail to recognise their part in the causes of unbalanced trade, there is a high risk that the seeds of the next crisis will take root all too quickly.

In any event, the breakneck speed of economic catch up over the last two to three decades is most likely to slow, not least as most emerging countries encounter stronger demographic constraints from about 2030 onwards, when their age structures begin to resemble Western nations today. In the case of China, these will become much more evident in the next decade. Moreover, faster ageing in all emerging markets is going to occur at levels of per capita income far below those achieved in advanced economies at the same stage. The phrase 'growing old before they grow rich' is not a cliché for nothing, not just because of much lower levels of income but also because of much weaker social security systems and financial infrastructure.

As demographics clip the contribution of labour to economic growth, technical progress will become increasingly important. While many emerging markets are increasingly able to acquire new technologies, this isn't the same as innovation or commercial exploitation. Only a handful of rich countries have the edge here, and it's one they are likely to retain for decades.

I will argue, moreover, that sustained economic and political success resides in several important attributes, including macro-economic policy competence, a willingness to engage actively with the outside world, and the high levels of innovation and educational and scientific attainment that contribute to technological progress. But it resides in these areas only to the extent that they are nurtured by the sound quality of institutions, the need for which increases with economic development and as economies become more complex. The quality of institutions comprises good governance, the rule of law, protected property rights (including intellectual), a robust and independent legal system, sound structures that raise and allocate capital efficiently and distribute income equitably, and a political–economic framework that promotes creative enterprise and encourages debate and disagreement. As technical progress and economic reform feed off each other, the political elite has to be prepared to 'rock the boat' if necessary, and allow challenges to conservative and vested interests.

Many major emerging markets have made great strides in these areas, but while the quality of institutions has improved much in the last decade or so, it may take a generation to develop them more fully, assuming the political will and capacity to do so exist. From this standpoint, it is evident that China is the emerging markets' biggest conundrum, and that is why, in a way, it commands so much of the focus of this book. It boils down to whether the need for strong, sustained economic growth can be realised without new major political reforms or more intense social unrest. And what if this was not possible, or took too long to happen?

The plaudits for emerging markets over the last 20 years are deserved, but the caveats, as outlined above, should not be overlooked. High-powered economic performance may indeed be attributable to radical improvements in macroeconomic, structural and financial policies in the last decade or so. To that extent, the 2008–09 crisis may have represented little more than a short shock.

On the other hand, much of the emerging markets' performance in recent years occurred on the back of what we might call the 'bad bits' of late 20th century globalisation, that is, a global credit expansion sustained by low international interest rates, unbalanced trade and unsustainable credit flows. And when the financial crisis erupted, remember that the BRICs, and most emerging markets apart from Eastern Europe, were in rude financial health. After the Asian crisis in the late 1990s, they worked hard over a decade to build up high levels of private and public savings, and strong balance sheets, that stood them in good stead after 2007. Now, some emerging economies, including China, are pursuing the type of credit policies that could end up weakening their ability to contain and resist financial turbulence in the future. Money, finance and complex banking arrangements are what make economic performance exciting, unpredictable, and occasionally irrelevant. We should have learned that much by now, but people have a strong tendency to neglect or ignore the role of money and financial phenomena, always with regret in the end.

Which of these two hypotheses is right? Was the financial crisis a short and now unimportant shock for emerging markets, or does it have deeper, if not immediate, consequences for them? Both have substance, depending on the length of the time horizon over which one is looking.

But even this is to view the issue of the emerging market uprising through too narrow a lens. Financial services companies, investors and the media focus on short- to medium-term business cycles, and on things that can be counted, such as GDP, and a myriad of high frequency economic indicators. However, a true understanding of the position of emerging markets in the global economy, and their future prospects requires a deeper focus on less quantitative matters, such as structural change, and the capacity to improve the quality of institutions, encourage people to use their imagination, and exploit innovation. Economic extrapolation plays a subordinate role here to history, culture and geopolitics.

In the crisis-affected countries of the West, it is said that China, India and other major emerging markets are shedding their 'emerging' status as they come to dominate a new world order. However, we have been here before. In 1956, Soviet Communist Party leader Nikita Kruschev yelled at Western ambassadors in Moscow, 'We will bury you', and many believed him. America's industrial decay in the 1970s was supposedly irreversible in the face of a European renaissance. In the 1980s, Japan's economic muscle-flexing and its ability to 'buy the world' were seen as final proof of the country's great power status, and the relative decline of the US. In 1989, the unification of Germany ushered in a chorus of concern that this would lead to a resurgent Germany which would undermine the European Union, and thereby destabilise the world. These examples highlight the risks of linear extrapolation and of focusing on the things we can count. They also illustrate the danger of ignoring institutional and geo-political context.

Belief in the inevitability of China's rise to dominance requires a deep level of misunderstanding about the problems China is going to have to confront in the next several years, as well as about the strengths in flexibility, decision-making, and technological prowess that some Western nations, especially the United States, could yet deploy as the financial crisis fades and economic behaviour changes. The simple answer to the question as to whether China is now primed to take over is to repeat the words attributed to former Chinese Communist Party leader Zhou Enlai (1898–1976), who is supposed to have responded to a journalist's question about the impact of the French Revolution on world history by saying 'It's too early to say'. The honest answer is to acknowledge two things. First, over time and in an open global economy, emerging markets should continue to catch up the West economically. For some, like China and India, the future may be economically bright and politically empowering. Second, however, none of this is in the least bit preordained, according to the certainties embraced by those who claim, sometimes self-servingly, that it is.

The future is about structural change and reform, and the political aptitude and willingness to embrace both. Ultimately, this will determine whether China and emerging markets are more likely to shape the world, or just shake it.

Chapter One

Back to the Future?

Once upon a time, China, India and other Asian and Middle Eastern countries did shape our world, and for many centuries China was the biggest economy and most populous country on the planet. Before 1500, China was, by all accounts, a great power, and even though other dynasties and empires in Asia and the Middle East existed before or emerged subsequently, China retained a prominent, if not dominant role for at least another 300 years. In 1820, China still accounted for about a third of world output.

The years 1500 and 1800 are often referred to as global 'tipping points'. The former corresponds roughly to the surge in European maritime and navigational zeal, not least following Christopher Columbus' voyage to the Americas, while the latter more or less identifies the point at which China's relative decline, compared with Europe, turned into absolute decline and effective obscurity on the global stage.

After the beginning of the 19th century, China went into an economic decline that continued into the first three decades of the People's Republic. It is of no small consequence to ask how and why this decline occurred, bearing in mind that China had once been decades, if not centuries, ahead of Europe in the development of agriculture, industry and social organisation. The purpose of this chapter is to see what lessons can be drawn as we ponder whether or not today's uprising is taking us back to a long-forgotten global system. In other words, have the last two hundred years of Euro-centric historical focus and economic development simply been a short aberration in over 2000 years of economic and political history?

This is important for two reasons. First, it isn't only China among the world's emerging nations that is making waves in the global economy. The balance of economic power is clearly shifting towards Asia, including the heavily populated countries of India and Indonesia, and the manufacturing hubs of South Korea, Taiwan, Malaysia and now, Vietnam. Second, the contemporary debate focuses on simple economic measures, such as GDP growth, exports, financial flows, and infrastructure development as signposts of the rapid emerging market 'catch-up' relative to the US, Europe and Japan. It is, however, underlying geopolitical, demographic and institutional characteristics and trends which will be far more important for how economic power will be configured in the global system of the future. In thinking about how China may shape or shake the world, it is worth going back to the future and to the time when the balance of power lay in the Orient, and when Europe emerged to dominate the global system.

Once upon a time

In the West, we pay scant attention to the way the world used to be organised and structured. We learn about the Roman Empire but few people are aware that in the first century the Han dynasty in China, straddling two hundred years either side of the birth of Jesus Christ, had achieved a comparable level of development to the Roman Empire[1], or that China, then more of an empire than a country, was even then the largest economy in the world.

We learn about life in the Middle Ages, the succession of kings and queens, the Crusades, the Black Death, the siege of Vienna and other events, but often without proper geopolitical context. Little, if any, attention is paid to the development of Chinese, Indian and Arab civilisations. Normally, in this whirlwind tour of how we got to where we are today, we move swiftly on, as it were, to Columbus and then, by way of the exploits of 16th century Portugal, 17th century Netherlands, and 18th century Britain, to the Industrial Revolution and European hegemony.

The Euro-centric version of world history neglects the fact that, for centuries, Europe comprised a collection of interesting but warring and unremarkable societies on the periphery of an inter-connected and multi-polar global system. China's Ming and Qing dynasties (1368–1911), and the empires of Persia (Safavid, 1500–1722), India (Mughal, 1526 to mid 19th century), and the Ottomans (1299–1922) were of far greater significance than Europe before the Industrial Revolution[2].

In contrast to these civilisations, which were spread over large landmasses and unified by secular or religious leaders, Europe was handicapped by its geography. The ice and large water masses to the north, west and south, the vulnerability to invasion from the east, and the internal geography of mountain and river systems all contrived to make and keep Europe geopolitically incoherent and 'balkanised', literally, into competing states.

The demographics of Asia and Europe offer some insights into their economic development, not least because of the paucity of other economic data, but also because bigger populations typically meant bigger production and bigger armies. The population of Europe in 1000 is estimated to have been about 40 million compared with about 170 million in Asia, which corresponded to roughly 60% of the world's total. By 1750, Asia's population had grown to 600 million, or about 68% of total population, outpacing Europe's population increase which reached about 140 million.

Angus Maddison estimates that China and India accounted for about a half of world GDP, and twice that of Europe for the 600 years until about 1700. By 1820, both countries were still one and a half times as big as Europe[3]. The higher level and faster growth of population in Asia contributed to the higher level of output overall, but in terms of output per head, the two large Asian countries had begun to slip behind Western Europe during the 15th century, possibly earlier.

Thomas Malthus, an English 18th century scholar, proposed that rapid population growth would be self-correcting because it would outpace food production, and that famine and war would result[4]. If he had been right even then, however, China and India would not have been able to support a fourfold expansion in population and nearly treble output per head of population over this period. Even if we are sceptical about economic statistics from long ago, the evidence of continuous, if erratic, progress in the development of agriculture, trade, industry, urbanisation and culture, leaves no question that China was the most advanced civilisation in the world.

By the end of the 19th century, however, something had changed and China began a lengthy period of upheaval and secular decline. In 1900, it represented little more than 13% of world GDP. Following the Russian revolution, the Chinese Communist Party was formed in 1921, first collaborating with but then fighting the Chinese Nationalist Party, or Kuomintang, which captured Beijing in 1928 and set up a government in Nanjing. Both sides were preoccupied with the Japanese occupying forces during the Second World War, but after the Japanese surrender, the Communists took up arms against their nationalist foes.

By the time Mao Zedong led the Communist Party to power in 1949, China's world population share had fallen to 20%, and its world GDP share had fallen to 5%. China experienced several sequential and disorienting political shocks, including collectivisation and cooperativisation in agriculture (1955–1956), the Great Leap Forward, or forced restructuring of industry and agriculture that resulted in terrible famine (1958–1961), the Cultural Revolution, or revolutionary campaign to purge China of liberal bourgeois forces (1966–1969), and subsequent political instability until 1976. Throughout this period, China stood still economically, and did not stir until sweeping reforms were introduced in 1978.

So, what happened? If Asia had been the dominant part of a global system for many centuries, why did it falter, going first into relative, and then absolute decline? Why did the Industrial Revolution, which transformed Europe and then America, happen in an unknown village called Coalbrookdale in Lancashire in northern Britain, not in the Yangtse delta, which was China's most populous and dynamic region? To answer these questions could fill several books, and provoke endlessly heated and complex debates among economists and historians[5]. Here, I can only sketch out the very broadest of contours of the shift in power from the Orient to the West. Yet this search for answers reveals important insights into our understanding of today's uprising in China and other emerging markets.

The role of geography, ecology and maritime adventure in economic development is important, but doesn't tell us anything as far as China's booming factories and America's financial woes of today are concerned. On the other hand, the role played by demographics, technology and institutions, including legal and judicial structures, in driving economic and political development remains as potent today as ever.

A change of heart

Western thought sometimes views China as a giant landmass that has traditionally been inward looking, and economically and technologically backward. The historical evidence does not support this observation, at least not consistently. According to data compiled by Professor Angus Maddison, Asia constituted the lion's share of the global economy for millennia, and China's economy was always at its heart[6].

In the first millennium, China had already made many advances that Europeans would only make much later, for example, in the use of farm cattle and farm implements, the exploitation of crop rotation and new varieties of rice, the production of iron and salt, and textiles and water-powered spinning machines. China had private ownership, basic property rights (though only for its gentry), productive agriculture, and openness to trade. For a long time, the caravan trails of the Silk Road took spices, silk and cotton out of China, while new crops and payments for trade in silver travelled in the opposite direction. China was the leading producer and exporter of porcelain ceramics, silk, zinc and cupronickel (for coinage), and occupied a dominant position in trading cotton and silk textiles, gold, copper and tea.

Under the Ming Dynasty (1368–1644), China was a populous and agriculturally fertile country. Its inland waterway system was run by a well-educated Confucian bureaucracy. It invented movable type printing technology in the 11th century – some 400 years before Gutenberg introduced it to Europe. It was a country of huge libraries, extensive trading networks, and flourishing industries. China's iron industry produced about 125,000 tons a year (a level of output far larger than in Britain in the early stages of the Industrial Revolution), not least to supply an army of a million.

China invented the magnetic compass, and built huge ships. In 1420, the Ming navy had 1350 combat vessels, including 400 floating fortresses, and 250 ships designed for long-range sailing[7]. Apart from guns, munitions, printing and ships, China also became a world leader in metallurgy and transportation. From what can be discerned from the time, China had a strong edge over Europe in matters of culture, mathematics, engineering, and navigational and other technologies.

Despite China's unquestioned achievements and economic status, history records some interesting developments that go some way in explaining why China was prone to autarky and closing doors to engagement with the outside world, and unable to generate the spark for an industrial revolution. For example, China pioneered the use of coke in iron ore production several hundred years before Abraham Darby succeeded in the same venture in Britain in 1709. However, just as Darby's ironworks started to boom, the blast furnaces and coke ovens in northern China were abandoned, as the country succumbed to internal rebellions, wars and, later, the commercial intrusion of foreigners. The iron ore industry would not be revitalised until the 20th century, but other aspects of Chinese economic advancement were also compromised during the 18th and 19th centuries. China's canal system was allowed to decay, the army was starved of adequate equipment, astronomical clocks were disregarded, and printing was restricted to scholarly works and not used to disseminate practical knowledge widely or encourage criticism[8].

Consider also China's maritime exploits. In the 15th century, several decades before Vasco da Gama found a route to India, the Chinese mariner Zheng He sailed (1405–1433) to Arabia, East Africa, India, Indonesia and Thailand trading gold, silver, porcelain and silk for exotic animals and ivory. His initial 'treasure fleet' consisted of 317 ships – the largest of which was 400 feet long (compared with Christopher Columbus' 'Santa Maria' which measured 85 feet) – and 27,000 crewmen. Indeed it was the largest fleet assembled for a single voyage until the 20th century[9].

As in industry, so it was in exploration. Just as Europeans began to set sail around the world, China's ships were increasingly docked, as a conservative Confucian bureaucracy, which did not care for conflict, and was suspicious of merchants and traders – and prone to confiscate their property – viewed maritime and naval activities as unimportant or contrary to the interests of the state.

Zheng's maritime expeditions spread Chinese knowledge, products and people as well as his own diplomacy and influence, to other lands. At home, however, the bureaucracy became nervous that foreigners would become so in awe of China's power and magnanimity to those who acknowledged its symbolic suzerainty, that they would extract economic and political advantages that would be costly, and perhaps ruinous. The Chinese authorities felt they were self-reliant and self-sufficient, and were suspicious of foreign influence. They closed down the open-door policy to the outside world, and the door would not open again in a meaningful way until Deng Xiaoping celebrated Zheng's exploits and the Ming Dynasty's engagement of the outside world in a keynote speech in 1984.

In any event, internal political struggles between factions of the Chinese court eventually culminated in the destruction of the fleets, a ban on the building of ships with more than two masts, breaches of which became a capital offence, and even on ocean-going voyages[10]. China's institutional behaviour clearly compromised its capacity to exploit maritime and other technology for the purposes of economic development. Such behaviour, however, was not the only reason that economic advantage slipped away.

People power

The significance of anecdotes can be overstated, but they conform to political and institutional patterns that run through Chinese history and economic development.

Demographics also play a vital part in economic development. After all, more people mean more workers, and more output. More skilled people mean a higher quality of output and higher productivity. On this basis, China should have had a big advantage over Europe.

The much larger population in China did mean there were more mouths to feed and, consequently, Chinese farmers and households might have had a smaller agricultural surplus to invest. Once basic survival needs had been satisfied, there would have been less produce or money available to save and invest. In Europe, however, the reverse should have happened, where smaller families and lower fertility rates would have resulted in larger surpluses. But if these demographic differences had been really important, Chinese and European economic development would have parted company long before it actually happened.

Moreover, because European populations were much more heavily concentrated in smaller geographic areas, it is possible that the real wages of workers rose faster than in China, where labour was much more plentiful, spread out and cheaper. In other words, higher real wages in Europe could have helped to accelerate and sharpen the incentive to find mechanised and labour-saving devices. In turn, these would have raised the amount of capital per worker, and hence productivity growth. It's a theory, and one of many that have been proposed to explain China's tardiness in economic and industrial development compared to Europe. As I have pointed out, however, China was no laggard when it came to economic achievement until a mere 200 years ago, and held its own in the global economy, even if Europeans were doing a fair bit of catching up until then.

The lie of the land

Geography played an important role in shaping economic and political fortunes. The milder and wetter northern European climate may have conferred advantages that were not as robust in China's more arid and hotter climate. It could have offered Europeans greater protection against disease, drought and natural disasters. It could have helped to sustain more fertile soil which, in turn, allowed spare agricultural land to be used for animal grazing, the deployment of animals for industrial purposes, and food production. That said, China's cultivation of, for example, rice and beans (as opposed to wheat in Europe, for example), its use of horses in agriculture, and its development of water supplies and waterways for transport and irrigation testify to a comparable, if different, path of agricultural development.

The European climate certainly forced citizens to confront a phenomenon that was less pressing in China – flooding. Eventually, the need to overcome flooding would encourage innovations that led to the steam powered pump and, later, the more generic and industrial use of steam power that would spur the Industrial Revolution in northern Europe.

There are, however, more important geographic factors that shaped China's and Europe's progress. Europe's more complicated geography was an integral part of its political fragmentation. There were no great landmasses to enable armies to establish control, and no broad and silty river areas, such as existed in China, India, and Egypt, to be exploited by mass agriculture. And there were large mountain ranges and forest areas that kept populations separate. Political fragmentation made it much harder to establish a unified system of political control, and encouraged the creation and development of decentralised authority. In turn, this meant there was no monolithic structure, especially of an orthodox or fundamentalist nature, that could determine or alter commercial and industrial development. While the Church or the Romans may have attempted to rule by proclamation and edict, they were unable to do so in the systematic ways of Ming China or, for that matter, other regional empires in Japan and the Middle East. Centralised authority had many advantages in terms of being able to organise social and economic functions and get things done, but equally its raison d'être served also to restrain economic development. Asia's empires all faced internal strife and external enemies at various points in their histories, but unlike European states, they held together for long periods of time. This was largely thanks to bureaucracies that were centralised, sometimes despotic, and always conservative or orthodox in their outlook. The benefit of centralised authority was the greater stability of the administrative elite, but against this, the emphasis on the maintenance of traditional ways of life and values, and the desire to impose regularity, common standards, and uniformity restrained initiative, dissent, innovation and commerce. Government and society in Asia were, in effect, indistinguishable. The role of Confucian values and political structures in China has already been discussed, and simply warrants a reference here to the capacity to excel in oversight, conservation and consolidation, but not innovation[11].

The mighty civilisations of China and India were large, relatively stable, and successful but their empires were also rather isolated, with a high tendency towards stagnation. Like Europe, they had to contend with both internal strife and external threats, but they lacked the more intense pressures experienced by Europe's warring nation states to innovate, and steal a technological march on their neighbours[12]. Power structures in China and other empires developed, and survived shocks, and did so with great success. Eventually, however, isolationism and conservatism were to cost them their place in the world order.

Standing on the shoulders of giants

There is a fascinating argument that European economic ascendancy was bought, or possibly even hijacked, as its explorers, navies
and merchants forcibly clambered on to the shoulders of the giant
Asian economies. Christopher Columbus was not the first person
to set foot in the Americas, but he is credited with the discovery,
even though he did so accidentally, having estimated incorrectly
the circumference of the Earth. He was actually looking for a faster
route to the East Indies than the journey by land through Arabia
and central Asia. If successful, he thought, Spain would gain access
to new markets and, importantly, a comparative advantage in the
trade in spices and other products, hitherto run by Arabs and
Italians. In the 10th to the 15th centuries, the city-states of Venice
and Genoa, for example, had become well-established industrial
and wealthy trading centres, forming a bridge between Europe and
the East. However, Columbus' exploits, and six years later, Vasco
da Gama's circumnavigation of the Cape, were important contribu-
tors to their decline.

European navigators had strong interests and incentives, as well
as advanced scientific and navigational know-how, to 'globalise', as
we might call it nowadays, or to bring Asia into their masters' commercial orbit. The discovery of the Americas bestowed unexpected
new riches of gold, silver and other precious metals upon Europeans,
who used their wealth to build and finance trade in goods with Asia,
trade in slaves with Africa, and increased access to new and bigger
markets in Asia, and rising prosperity at home.

In effect, the Americas provided the capital for Europeans to
compete with, and infiltrate what was already, a Sino-centric economic system in Asia, with a long commercial reach. They did so

often using armed force, and later through a full-blooded colonial system, though not in the case of China. The combination of wealth, guns, ships, and a drive to explore and expand, were key determinants of Europe's ability to climb on to the shoulders of Asia's eastern giant, and then to reach for global hegemony[13].

Even as China's relative decline began, Adam Smith, grandfather of economic thought, noted in his book, *The Wealth of Nations* (1776), that,

> 'Even those three countries (China, Egypt and Indostan, the wealthi-est, according to all accounts, that ever there were in the world, are chiefly renowned for their superiority in agriculture and manufac-tures......China is a much richer country than any part of Europe.'[14]

Smith knew, though, that change was afoot. He claimed that the discovery of America and the sea passage to the East Indies via the Cape of Good Hope had been two of the most significant events in the history of mankind, and that they were 'game-changers' for the world order that favoured Europe. The significance of the Americas lay in the enrichment provided by the discovery of gold, silver, precious metals and new markets. The faster route to India and the Orient allowed Europeans to capitalise by, in effect, buying a place at the global economic table, and implanting themselves into the profitable trading routes inside Asia, and between Asia and Europe. Backed by force and driven by the search for riches, spices and exotic Asian products, Europeans created global trading com-panies and penetrated the Asian economy.

Seventy-two years later, in the opposite ideological corner, Karl Marx and Friedrich Engels argued in the Communist Manifesto that these two events had breathed life into the rising European bourgeoisie. They had encouraged the development of commerce, navigation and industry, thereby helping to fuel Europe-wide revolution against feudal societies. For Marx, these stimuli to the development of capitalism in Europe were pivotal to its industrialisation.

Innovation, imagination and institutions

Something is still missing, because we still don't know why continuous and broad-based technological innovation succeeded in Europe and not in China.

Economic development happens as a result of the application of more labour, more capital per worker, and what economists call total factor productivity (TFP). This is the extra growth that occurs when you mix labour and capital together in an efficient and optimum way. We don't actually know all that much about how to measure TFP properly even today, let alone how to assess its role in centuries gone by. What we do know is that it's very important. TFP can come from having good infrastructure, top quality education and training systems, efficient organisation of work and management, a strong bias towards innovation, and research and development, sound economic and financial governance systems and, importantly, robust institutions that facilitate change and improvement.

Great powers, in other words, cannot become, let alone stay, great just because they are good at trade, or have copious reserves of rice, wheat, coal, oil, or money. They need to be able to foster and exploit continuous technological innovation. Their citizens, scientists and leaders must have the imagination to (excuse the cliché) dream. They must have high quality institutions to protect the property rights that exist in every human interaction, and also to secure transactions, and safeguard contracts. Property rights may refer specifically to property, such as a house, in the narrow sense, but are generally defined to encompass rights to physical property, natural resources including land, intellectual property rights, including knowledge and information, and the services of labour. Courts normally determine how property rights are created, altered, transferred or infringed, and adjudicate in the event of disputes.

In Europe, for example, the ending of feudal constraints on the free purchase and sale of property paved the way for major changes in social class relationships, This gave rise to the subsequent development of free labour, trade and merchant capital. Eventually these led to new forms of entrepreneurship, and a raft of institutional innovations such as non-discretionary legal systems, accounting and book-keeping, access to credit and insurance, new organisational and management techniques, and family systems that facilitated capital accumulation[15]. I shall return to this theme in the concluding chapter.

The German sociologist, Max Weber, argued that the principal, though not sole, catalyst for European economic and industrial success was the impact of Protestant religious belief from the 16th century onwards, as it pertained to values regarding work, initiative, investment and knowledge. In effect, a devout Protestant would live a life of disciplined self-denial and hard work, both of which God would approve. As a result, people would conform to a culture based on both, which, in economic terms, amounted to the 'capitalist spirit'. The Protestant work ethic was, therefore, the driver of an unplanned, autonomous and uncoordinated mass movement that defined and shaped the development of capitalism.

Weber contrasted Protestantism to religions practised elsewhere that were based on mysticism, myth and magic. Indeed, Weber and his followers have attributed, controversially, Asia's failure to compete with Europe to Asian societal norms and culture, including Confucianism itself. Specifically, in China, the state was the defining form or social organisation, and had strong vested interests in uniformity and continuity.

Weber's thesis, first published in 1904, has been heavily criticised, mostly from an ideological and conceptual standpoint, in particular by those who deny that religion has got anything to do with economic progress. A more quantitative way of approximating the impact of Protestantism on economic development, compared with other factors, also asserts that religion had no particular role to play[16]. In one respect, at least, Weber had a point. There was no plurality of power in China. The corollary of a rigid, conservative, and ideologically orthodox economic and political system was an inability to reconcile its own codes and dogma with the freedom to enquire, experiment and improve – except at the risk of posing threats to the State.

China's bureaucracy, craftsmen and peasants were hardly backward when it came to technical progress, but they did not revolutionise China in the way that their peers in Europe did. In general, Asian empires were good at invention, often long before Europe, and adept at exploiting knowledge, based on experience. Thus, if you discovered on-the-job, as it were, how to do something better or more efficiently, that would count as progress. The knowledge of how you do things is important, and vital to invention.

This is different, however, from the exploitation of knowledge based on scientific experiment, which is the knowledge of why things happen or work, and of how to improve their effectiveness. This is about the innovation of products and processes which, in Europe, comprised the deliberate and conscious act of conducting science-based research. For example, during the 16th and 17th centuries, Europeans recognised the ability of human beings to transform the forces of nature, and developed crucial products such as telescopes, microscopes, clocks, watches and other precision instruments. In general, these were essential to empirical methodology, and specifically, they had a direct influence on navigational skills and the ability to penetrate distant oceans[17]. They made maritime travel less unpredictable as well as more practical. Once the momentum of technological advance had begun, it spread far beyond to armaments, agricultural science, botany, metallurgy, engineering, astronomy and medicine.

Scientific discovery and experiment were at the heart of European industrialisation. As an autonomous method of intellectual enquiry, science detached its proponents from the social restrictions that were imposed by organised religion, for example in the Arab world, and from the political restrictions imposed by centralised authority and orthodoxy, such as in China. In Europe, the Church was not exactly in the vanguard of progressive research, but the diffusion of power in Europe, as opposed its centralisation in other empires, was enough to stunt the influence of religious authority. Latin may have helped too, since it facilitated adversarial discourse in which advances in the physical world could be tested and demonstrated. New inventions and rapid technical progress were catalysts for the transformation of knowledge and of society, and contributed to an array of social and legal changes that, in turn, changed the region's institutions in ways that were more conducive to modernity.

That was then

There is no single explanation for the fact that China and other ancient civilisations were not the first to industrialise and take the path to modernity. It is a long and complex story, taking in everything from mountain ranges and river systems, to birth rates and social organisation, maritime exploits and the discovery of gold and silver.

We should reject the notion that some sort of religious superiority lay behind the Industrial Revolution and capitalist development in Europe, partly because Protestantism didn't stop other civilisations and cultures from joining in. The idea, however, that the West had or has some sort of inherent cultural advantage is one that resurfaces periodically. As recently as the 1990s, after the collapse of communism in Russia and Eastern Europe, some were convinced that the only possible model for human organisation in the modern age of communications and industrialisation was one based on market economies, and limited, pluralist and democratic government[18]. This was pure hubris, or alternatively a version of cultural triumphalism, which was patently wrong and a demonstration of arrogance.

Since the financial crisis, Western thinkers have become more introspective and cognisant of the ways of other countries. Yet there is much in Western culture and institutions that will help us to adapt, to be creative and reinvent ourselves, even if not all Western countries are able to live up to this billing. If that were to be true over the next two to three decades, the reasons would almost certainly lie in flexible institutions, the primacy of the rule of law, and the ability of societies, even if under extreme duress, to challenge the status quo, undertake structural reform, and innovate. It would stand in stark contrast to the experience of Japan, where a strong bureaucracy and a national pre-occupation with social consensus and cohesion have prevented the country from taking the kind of risks that are essential if the deep consequences of the 1990 financial bust and simultaneous rapid ageing are to be controlled and overcome.

And that is probably the main lesson from history. China's ancient political structure, the culture of its bureaucracy, the legal system, and the overall quality of its institutions were simply not up to the task. They had a negative impact on the country's willingness and ability to consider radical change, and embrace technical progress across a broad range of activities. A large bureaucracy, as opposed to a developing and dynamic legal system perpetuated a culture of conservatism and uniformity, when experiment, change and openness to external ideas were required.

How then should we assess China's prospects, and those of other emerging nations in the second decade of the 21st century? Although the Chinese Communist Party's commitment to full-blown Marxism is now history, has China changed so much, compared to its past?

Further afield, does India's democratic model function in a far more cumbersome, but ultimately more efficient and sustainable, manner? And as Brazil, Mexico, and Chile plant seemingly stronger democratic roots, could they too look forward to greater political stability and the capacity to manage economic cycles more successfully than in the past? After all, these countries are hardly simple export junkies. India is about world-class service-producing industries, and Brazil is about natural resources, oil, and a deservedly good reputation in manufacturing, including of short-haul aircraft. Mexico is quite diversified across agriculture, energy and manufacturing, relatively rich, and exposed to a wealthy northern neighbour.

Good institutions matter. Consider, for example, that the Asian Tiger economies (South Korea, Taiwan, Singapore and Hong Kong) recorded extraordinary economic growth and development and became benchmarks for the developing world. Hong Kong is a bit of an outlier in this group, because its ascent was not driven by a strong central authority, it had good judicial though not strong political institutions, and it didn't rank as well on educational achievement – and still doesn't. But there's no question that as a group, they achieved something quite special.

At the beginning of the 1970s, their demographic structures, labour force and savings characteristics, and incomes per head were comparable to those of the major countries in Latin America. The Tigers went on to become developed nations to all intents and purposes, whereas Latin American countries remain emerging, at best, but for the most part developing countries.

The main difference is that the Tigers developed strong political institutions, encouraged openness in their economic structures, made rapid strides in educational attainment, and became able to acquire and utilise new technologies – all under the watchful eyes and management of a strong centralised authority.

It's a good cat so long as it catches mice

China has employed the same Tiger model, with rather more emphatic central authority, but with a twist. After the Cultural Revolution had laid waste to the economy, China endured a lengthy power struggle in which Deng Xiaoping eventually

returned to the pinnacle of the Communist Party following Mao
Zedong's death in 1976. Deng had fallen out with Mao and been
sent to work in a tractor factory, while his family had been targeted
by the Red Guards who caused his son severe and permanent
injury. Many years before, at a party conference in Guangzhou,
Deng is reported to have said, 'I don't care if it's a white cat or a
black cat. It's a good cat so long as it catches mice.' This has been
interpreted as revealing Deng's belief that productivity was ultimately more important than ideology, per se, but whatever he
meant at the time, there is no question that it was he who in 1978
set China off on the road to economic success. And in this sense,
he clearly demonstrated that China could break from its past, could
pursue political reform on a grand scale, and could be receptive to
outside ideas and influence.

Deng's reforms, which consigned many post-1949 orthodox doc-
trines to history, aimed to modernise agriculture, industry, science
and technology, and the military. He wanted to create a socialist
market economy with limited private competition, which was open
to foreign investment, and responsive to and engaged with the
global market. To this end, the reform programme introduced
significant changes in the organisation and structure of farming and
industry, and sought to emphasise higher agricultural productivity,
the development of light industry – or what we could call 'toys and
textiles' – and the promotion of export-led growth. In these ways,
China would generate the revenues that would be ploughed back
into technological advances and capital spending that would, in
turn, drive the economy forward. How right he was.

For about ten years, China's agricultural sector experienced an
extensive transformation – for the first time since the disastrous
collectivisation of the 1950s. Rural incomes rose, based on a sus-

tained rise in agricultural labour productivity, and farmers were allocated some property rights so that they were allowed to retain a larger proportion of their available surplus for consumption, savings, and investment. This also reflected the pattern of modernisation in, for example, Japan, South Korea and Taiwan, where industrialisation went hand in hand, more or less, with increases in rural welfare.

Since the 1990s, however, the rural sector has been left behind by even greater and more rapid industrialisation, as the focus has shifted from light to heavy industry, such as steel, cement, iron ore, metal fabrication and automobiles. Since two thirds of China's workers are employed in rural areas, it is essential for economic stability and social tranquillity that the countryside be allowed to catch up. I use the phrase 'be allowed' because the solution lies firmly in the hands of the political elite of the Communist Party, and its ability to engage in new structural reforms, and challenges to the economic status quo.

Deng's reforms and the industrialisation push in the 1990s demonstrate that the Chinese Communist Party can be pragmatic and flexible. The country's achievements in industry, exports, education and science since the reforms began in the 1980s have been nothing short of remarkable. The historian Paul Kennedy wrote over 20 years ago,

'While the material constraints upon China are great, they are being ameliorated by an economic expansion which, if it can be kept up, promises to transform the country within a few decades.'[19]

Except for the 1989–1991 period when economic growth collapsed and the authorities acted to clamp down on accelerating inflation, and on the social unrest captured by the Tiananmen Square protests, China has realised Kennedy's condition. From 1991 until 2004, spurred by the elevation of foreign trade and foreign direct investment as the lynchpins of China's growth model, China's economy grew by 8% per year. From 2005–2007, it grew by 11% per year. Despite the temporary shock of the crisis, bankers, business folk and economists assume as gospel that this sort of performance will continue for many years to come.

Under constant supervision and management by the State, and with labour and capital markets still controlled, the development of market forces and the ambition to modernise have propelled China to become one of the largest economies in the world. Once again, it is the hub of a strong Sino-centric global trading system, and a global creditor, customer and competitor. It is an integral member of the United Nations, was admitted to the World Trade Organisation in 2001, and will be an increasingly influential voice in the affairs of the International Monetary Fund and the World Bank, as voting rights in these institutions shift in its favour (and that of other emerging markets) following the decisions reached in 2009 by the G20 countries. It has become a key participant in climate change discussions and goal-setting, and it has used its position to extend its influence on and relations with other major emerging and developing countries, including India, Brazil, Iran, Saudi Arabia and several oil and resource-producing countries in Africa.

The past and the present are what they are: it is the future that is open to question. China's success has been based on the vigorous attempt to balance enterprise and initiative with a state-centric determination to direct its citizens towards the fulfilment of cherished national goals. Maintaining this balance will be a challenge

of increasing significance in the post-crisis world, and requires four conditions to hold.

First, because of its centralised authority and role, the legitimacy of China's Communist Party – the social contract, if you will – depends on its ability to deliver continuously rising prosperity to its citizens. Most people define this as steady and stable 8% economic growth per year. If it cannot capitalise on continuous boom, and always avoid the bust, renewed social and political instability is possible.

Second, and also because of the structure of power, the Chinese leadership has little margin for error in the conduct of its strategic economic policies. It has to make the right choices and do the right things all the time. By its own admissions, China has become a rather unbalanced economy, in which the coastal provinces, urban dwellers, heavy industry and exports have prospered, and overshadowed the growth in the rural sector, domestic demand and social security. The trouble is that the factions that hold sway in the Chinese Communist Party have strong vested interests in the status quo, even if there is debate among intellectuals and others about the need for change and reform. Moreover, much economic and industrial power in China resides with local governments, which can resist or frustrate Beijing's policies for reform. A failure to redress homegrown imbalances in the next several years poses risks not just to China's growth rate but also existential threats to itself, and to the global economy.

One of the major reasons for the financial crisis was – and remains – structurally unbalanced trade. China is no innocent bystander in this, and needs to take responsibility for its role in this imbalance through appropriate economic, financial and exchange rate policies. It isn't. If it continues to behave and perform as though the

global economy hasn't changed, simply waiting for the status quo ante to be restored, it will run huge risks of economic and financial instability, and be the target of rising protectionism. In fact, there are worrisome signs that China is unwilling to change its economic behaviour and strategy in the global economy, and to take global responsibility. This intransigence could end up worse for China than many currently envisage.

Third, the institutional capacity to adjust will also be tested by China's demographics. China is the fastest ageing country on Earth, and its working age population will start to fall from around 2010 onwards. By 2050, China's demographic characteristics will be inferior to the US on all measures. It has financial resources a-plenty, and the State is in a good financial position to be able to expand social and old age security, but unless it acts soon, it really will become old before it gets rich.

Fourth, the ability to acquire new technologies is being facilitated by the factory-type production of graduates in engineering, science and computing, as rising investment in human capital continues to lift the barriers to economic development. School enrolment and educational attainment levels are high. But acquiring technology or copying it isn't the same thing as innovation. The capacity to innovate, and to reach for the most advanced global technological possibilities, exploiting them for commercial gain and social transformation, still seem to be a long way off. For the foreseeable future, this still seems to be a happier hunting ground for the US and possibly some European countries with a penchant for creativity.

As a general point, and provided that globalisation does not falter, there seems to be little doubt that China and other major emerging markets are poised to continue to catch up the West in

economic terms. It's also almost inevitable that they will leverage that economic strength for political influence and power.

There are, however, two big caveats. First, the extraordinary growth of the last decade is most unlikely to be repeated. Second, catching up is quite a different proposition from China ruling the world, or an Asian century. The longer-lasting ramifications of the 2008 financial crisis and its aftermath have still to play out, especially as they affect the structure of the global economy. Demographic and climate change challenges will become increasingly pressing, and many economic and financial policy errors, and business cycle and political shocks lurk in the next decade or two. The acid test for China and other nations will surely be the responsiveness of governments and whether and how political structures and economic institutions change in a timely way.

China is now, on some measures, the second largest economy in the world, and has recently overtaken Germany as the world's biggest exporter. It is the hub of an Asian and global manufacturing supply chain, and whereas its reputation was once limited to toys and textiles, it can now boast of being a leading supplier of electronic goods, solar panels and wind turbines. It is also one of the world's leading creditor nations, with about \$2500 billion in foreign exchange reserves. India started to reform and modernise later than China, but is a specialist in technology and information services rather than manufacturing. It is also a much more closed economy, with exports accounting for about a fifth of GDP, or half as large as China. Brazil is a potentially exciting prospect, having emerged over the last 20 years from a long period of political and financial instability. Better governance and reformed institutions have allowed Brazil to prosper, and develop strengths in oil exploration, commodity exports, agri-businesses, and manufacturing. In some ways, it is strange that Russia is considered a BRIC. Investors think its vast oil, gas and mineral reserves will serve the country well in an environment of possible resource scarcity. But that's about all it has got (apart from nuclear weapons), and it has a large, if falling and rapidly ageing, population. That said, energy is a vital resource and tool of foreign policy and diplomacy in modern times, and no one disputes Russia's geopolitical significance.

The preceding snapshot serves to remind us that emerging markets are anything but a homogenous group of countries. The title of this chapter asks 'Who are those guys?' In the 1969 film, 'Butch Cassidy and the Sundance Kid', Paul Newman and Robert Redford are observing their relentless pursuers from afar. Newman says 'I couldn't do that. Could you do that? Why can they do it? Who are those guys?' In this chapter, then, I will discuss this dis-

Chapter Two

Who *Are* Those Guys?

Whether or not you buy the argument that the shape of the world economy is gradually reverting to a structure that existed hundreds of years ago, there is no question that the last 20–30 years have witnessed an exhilarating, if sometimes erratic, transformation of emerging markets. The original Asian Tiger economies (South Korea, Taiwan, Singapore, and Hong Kong) had already become well established as leading economies in manufacturing and trade by the 1980s. Several major countries, including China, looked to them as an example of how to integrate into the global economy and derive the benefits of rising prosperity, and implemented political and structural reforms accordingly. In the absence of reforms, it is unlikely they would have been able to take advantage of the extraordinary economic opportunities offered by the acceleration in globalisation after 1989, and the longest period of rapid global economic growth in a generation.

parate group of countries, how and why they became increasingly significant in the global system, and some of their principal attributes. I will also provide a simple guide to how best to assess the weight and significance of emerging markets in the global economy, because many of the optimistic predictions made for emerging markets are based on what most of us would consider dubious measurement propositions.

Economists are continuously bringing forward the point at which they believe the GDP of the BRICs will overtake that of Japan, the Euro Area, and the US. If China were to grow by 10% per year, and the US by just 2%, the two countries' GDP would cross over in the mid-2020s. Aside from the US, China's GDP is already bigger than any other country except for Japan, and that milestone is likely to have been passed by the time this book is for sale. India is expected to overtake major EU countries during the 2020s, and Japan by the end of that decade, while Russia and Brazil are about 5–10 years behind India. The implications of these projections, if accurate, are momentous. They are on a scale that is comparable to the emergence of America and Germany in the late 19th century.

The rise of the BRICs, as the largest emerging market economies, will increase the economic significance of other developing countries because of growing interconnectedness arising from closer trade, investment and political relationships. What economists call South-South trade, or trade between developing economies, amounts to around 10% of world trade but it is likely to increase steadily. China, for example, has taken strong initiatives in the trade and diplomatic spheres since the 2000s to build closer commercial ties with Brazil, Iran and Saudi Arabia. In the case of Brazil, some limited trade will be paid for in Chinese Yuan, a very

preliminary indication that China might one day consider abolishing controls over the international use of its currency. China's growing ties with several countries in the Middle East, Africa and Latin America, as I highlighted earlier when discussing the renaissance of the Silk Road, are driven by the need to secure long-term access to oil and other raw materials.

At the same time, the relative economic position of advanced nations is expected to decline, notably as the economic size of emerging markets increases. This is not simply a question of the relative decline of the West, but possibly absolute decline for some countries because of the coincidence of some troublesome trends, including rapid ageing, financial stress, and an at least contemporary blindness as to where and how sustainable economic growth might ever resume.

Western nations must now confront the negative economic and financial consequences of rapid population ageing, and other painful and costly developments associated with the financial crisis and other economic shocks. Many observers look to Japan as the laboratory experiment for what might lie in store. As recently as 1989–1990, Japan was thought to be using its economic strength to 'buy up the world' as a means towards a global economic and political renaissance. A major financial crisis and four recessions later, Japan's relative economic position and population are declining, rapid ageing is underway, public debt stands at 230% of GDP and is still rising, economic growth is running at an underlying rate of barely 1%, and it has not yet really managed to address properly either the weaknesses in the financial system or the deflation in the economy. Were it not for its still strong trade with China and the rest of Asia, it would be in an even more precarious position. If Japan is a prototype for the West in the next 20 years, we 'ain't seen nothin' yet'.

develop, but who probably didn't hatch one GDP forecast between them.

In 1952, a French demographer, Alfred Sauvy, published an article in a magazine, *L'Observateur*, in which he coined the term 'Third World'. He drew parallels with the Third Estate pamphlet published at the time of the French Revolution ('Qu'est-ce que le tiers état?'), suggesting that if the developed nations were the modern equivalent of the nobility, and the Communist world were the clergy, then the rest of the world represented the 'exploited, ignored and scorned' who would ultimately hold sway. Sauvy has been shown to be more or less right. There was indeed an uprising of developing nations, which after the Second World War were able to devise political institutions not only to demand and achieve independence from their prior colonial or imperial masters but also to sustain mass political engagement thereafter, though not always with the same success.

Many countries, though, lacked the economic basis on which to sustain the mobilisation of public opinion, and to fulfil the aspirations of citizens. The fact that so many developing nations failed to achieve any sort of economic 'take-off', even after independence, testifies to this shortcoming. For many of today's poorest countries, it is still the case. Or think about the revolutionary zeal in China that led to the creation of today's Chinese state but failed to produce an economic awakening. Worse, and as I pointed out in Chapter 1, it led to turmoil, culminating in the entrenchment of rigid conservative and bureaucratic rule during the Cultural Revolution.

Just before the end of the Second World War, in 1944, our second thinker, the geographer and strategist, Nicholas John Spykman had a book published posthumously, *The Geography of*

All these predictions, however, lack something crucial: context. They take no account of political and policy developments, and do not incorporate the universal aspects of ageing populations. They don't recognise that there are just as likely to be negative economic shocks in major emerging economies, which may retard development, as there might be potentially positive technological ones in the US, for example. They give no quarter to the quite likely prospect that globalisation will not be the same in the next two decades as it has been over the last two.

Further, they do not take into account the dubious meaning of GDP in the context of the climate change challenge that all countries will face. Wang Yang, the Communist Party chief of Guandong province in China put this well when he said 'some of our GDP figures are very "good looking". But they do not mean the growth of social wealth, but are instead achieved with a waste of social wealth. ... Chasing after growth without considering its quality, results in air pollution, pollution in water resources. We create GDP by polluting the environment. Then we create GDP again by dealing with pollution'[1]. We could go further. You can have high growth today by consuming resources that are finite, but this is simply to borrow from tomorrow's growth which, by definition, will be lower. It follows that a GDP view of the world economy today and over the next 20 years should be viewed with much scepticism.

From Third World to emerging markets

The idea that emerging markets would become a global phenomenon is not new. Consider, for example, two thinkers who foresaw in general how the world's economic and political order would

Peace. Looking at Asia, he highlighted the concept of the rimland (as opposed to the heartland), comprising the countries nowadays pigeon-holed as the Pacific Rim. He emphasised that their population characteristics, natural resource endowments, and industrial development potential pointed to outcomes of great significance. He argued that whoever controls the rimland rules Eurasia, and whoever rules Eurasia controls the destinies of the world. His geopolitical focus was prescient in ways not even he could have imagined at the time of his death. His perspectives can be seen in US, Soviet Russian and Chinese foreign policy developments during the Cold War and since. US economic policy towards 'friendly' countries in Asia did indeed shape the world.

One of America's principal goals after the Second World War was to facilitate the rebuilding of a devastated Japan. To generate the foreign currency needed to buy energy and raw materials, Japan had to produce things for export. Thus began Japan's industrial export cycle, starting with textiles and light industrial goods, and moving on to machinery, steel, chemicals, automobiles, audio equipment and so on. To help Japan on its way, the US purchased much of its exports, the total volume of which rose fourfold between the mid-1950s and the mid-1960s, and even faster in the following 20 years.

This export model served as the economic development template for the Asian Tigers after the 1960s, a time when GDP and living standards were little different from those of much of Africa. Later, it was copied by Malaysia, Thailand, the Philippines, Indonesia, China and, most recently, Vietnam. Asian economies were able to organise and manage the inputs for rapid economic and societal growth – and, importantly, engage with globalisation – in ways that other developing countries, including India, Latin

America, the USSR and formerly communist Eastern Europe didn't or couldn't until the 1990s.

The key to success was export development, a process that was encouraged by the US. In 1975, Robert McNamara, the former US Defense Secretary and then head of the World Bank, said that Asian leaders should 'turn their manufacturing enterprises away from the relatively small markets associated with import substitution toward the much larger opportunities flowing from export promotion'[2]. Fittingly, the US provided economic, financial and trade assistance and, crucially, access to the US market.

While the Tigers were being monitored closely by professional economists in the 1970s, that particular decade was good for emerging markets in general, only because it was a period of high inflation around the globe, marked by substantial increases in oil and other commodity prices. China was counting down to a major turning point of its own, namely the sweeping agricultural, corporate and banking reforms that were initiated by Deng Xiaoping in 1978[3]. These would eventually release China to follow the path to economic modernisation and industrialisation, which in turn would act as a catalyst for even faster and deeper economic integration in Asia, and between Asia and the rest of the world.

The 1980s and 1990s, however, were much more disappointing for emerging markets as shown in Table 2.1.

Commodity prices came down significantly as the global fight against inflation gained momentum, and the entire period was punctuated by a succession of financial crises, beginning with a debt and banking crisis across Latin America, and ending with the financial crises that ripped through Asia, Russia, Brazil and Argentina.

By the end of the 1990s the acceleration in globalisation was in full swing, aided and abetted by the information and communi-

Table 2.1 Economic growth in developing countries over the last 40 years

	1970s	1980s	1990s	2000–07	2008	2009
Asia	6.2	7.1	7	7.4	6.2	4.4
Asia-ex China	6.1	6.3	5.6	5.6	4	1
Central/Eastern Europe	6.1	2.1	1.3	4.9	3.5	−4.8
CIS	4.2	3.3	−5.2	7.5	6.2	−6.6
Latin America	6.1	2.2	2.9	3.7	4	−2.8
Middle East	8.2	0.9	4.2	5.2	5.8	−1.4
Africa	4.2	2.6	2.2	5.2	4.9	1.4
All developing countries	6.1	3.5	3.4	6	5.4	0.8
% per annum in 2005$ terms						

Source: IMF, World Bank

cation technology revolution. Economic performance in developing countries improved across the board, and even more challenged countries in Sub-Sahara Africa expanded at about 5–6% per year, the strongest and most sustained period of economic growth since the end of the Second World War.

The globalisation of emerging markets

Looking back to the events of 1989, it is clear that they did not mark the end of history or represent anything close to the final triumph of global capitalism as alleged by many at the time. Notable among them was the author Francis Fukuyama, whose 1992 book

The End of History and The Last Man argued that ideological struggle had largely ended with the balance of argument settling permanently on the side of liberal democracy. The fall of the Berlin Wall, though, did mark an inflexion point, after which hundreds of millions of workers and companies around the world became part of an interconnected global market economy, and took their positions in a rapidly advancing globalisation.

The effective labour force in the global economy increased fourfold between 1980 and 2007. Most of the increase, half of which was accounted for by East Asia, occurred after 1989. The rise in the number of people of working age (15–64 years) in emerging markets, the vigorous expansion of trade and investment between emerging markets and developed countries, and within the emerging markets, and sustained increases in immigration all contributed to this development. The Chairman of the Federal Reserve, Ben Bernanke noted, 'The emergence of China, India, and the former communist bloc countries implies that the greater part of the earth's population is now engaged, at least potentially, in the global economy. There are no historical antecedents for this development'[4].

Although that statement is true, the world had been globalised before, from the late 19th century to 1914. The British Empire, and the emerging economies of the time, especially the United States and Germany, presided over a rapid expansion in world trade, and movements in capital and immigration. As with other periods of globalisation, before and after, the key driver was the death of distance. The opening of the Suez Canal in 1869, faster and more powerful steamships, the development of railway systems, and the technological improvements in iron and steel production and telephone and telegraph technologies contributed to a sharp decline in transportation, industrial product and communication costs.

In modern parlance, although the physical distance between Berlin and Beijing is fixed, to all intents and purposes it diminishes with ever-faster and cheaper forms of transportation and communication. The current globalisation phase spans advances in telecommunications, powerful computing, mobile telephony, and relatively cheap air and ship transportation, all of which serve to lower costs and enhance speed and access to information.

Ben Bernanke emphasised the extraordinary feedback loops between globalisation and emerging markets. As I've explained, exports matter a lot in economic development. They comprised only 10% of developing countries' GDP in 1960, but this proportion had doubled by 1989, and now stands at about 37%. There are some exceptions, for example, India, Brazil and Argentina where the relative size of the export sector is much smaller. Yet for many economies, including Singapore, Hong Kong, Malaysia, Slovakia, Vietnam, Hungary, Taiwan and Thailand, the export share of GDP is much higher.

Between 1980 and the start of the crisis, world exports rose from less than $1000 billion to $15,800 billion. In the last decade, the volume of exports of goods rose by 6% per year, twice as fast as the overall growth in GDP. Excluding the trade that the 27 member countries of the European Union conduct with each other, China's share of world exports in 2008 was 11.8%, far above that of other emerging countries. South Korea's share, for example, was 3.5%, Hong Kong and Singapore each had shares of about 3% though the bulk of their exports are re-exports, Taiwan's share was 2%, and the only other shares of note were those of oil exporters such as Russia, Saudi Arabia, Mexico and the United Arab Emirates, which all had shares of between 2% and 4%.

The value of exports of commercial services rose by 12% annually between 1980–2007, or roughly the same rate of growth as the value of goods exports. Developing economies accounted for a 20% share of the $3700 billion of services exports, but most of this was attributable to the Tigers ($271 billion), and to China and India with sales of $137 billion and $100 billion, respectively.

Foreign direct investment inflows amounted to a record $1700 billion before the crisis. Developing countries, which received a paltry 10–15% of these flows before the collapse of the USSR, received about 40% in 2008, at the top end of a range of 20–40% that has persisted since 1994.

Before the crisis, the consensus was that world trade and investment would simply keep on growing, almost without interruption. Today, the balance between assertion and hope has moved towards the latter, because wrenching structural changes lie in wait in both advanced and emerging economies. The model we have lived with for the last 30 years, based on export-led growth in emerging economies and an infinite capacity on the part of the US and other western nations to import, consume and run large external deficits, has been shown to have deep flaws.

Yet optimism abounds that emerging countries will be the driving force in the global economy, and continue to gain output and export shares at the expense of the rich world. Many people reason, with some justification, that their population growth, young age structures and urbanisation will create the next billion consumers, just as similar conditions in the West created the first billion. This is pure and simple demographics. Western baby boomers became high-spending, high-saving consumers in the period 1980–2000, but the leading edge of the boomer generation is now on the path to retirement and unproductive activity. And low or weak fertility means that their offspring generations will be smaller – and more indebted, incidentally. By contrast, the working age population in developing countries will increase by 1 billion between 2010–2030, and the 30–55-year-old age group will increase by almost 600 billion. But it isn't just the numbers that could make the difference, but also the fact that their average incomes 'should' rise too.

Take Brazil, with a per capita income of $4000, and Italy, with a per capita income of $17,000 as the benchmarks for a relatively poor and relatively rich country, respectively. According to the World Bank, the proportion of middle class people in developing countries, with per capita incomes between the two, is expected to double to 16% by 2030. In China, this socio-economic group is expected to rise from 56 million in 2000 to over 360 million, while Brazil's middle class is predicted to rise by a third. Meanwhile, the proportion of poor people in developing countries, with per capita income below that of Brazil is expected to fall from 82% to 63%[5].

History teaches us, though, that it is incorrect and dangerous to see globalisation and geopolitics in purely linear form. Losing the economic and political benefits that the era of industrialisation brought to Britain was, despite the perceptions of America and Germany, unimaginable in 1914, and yet in three decades they were gone. In a further example of the pitfalls of extrapolation, the World Bank also looked at the world economy in 1900 and, allowing for the kind of economic and financial shocks that had been experienced between 1870–1899, it tried to model some scenarios for what the world might look like in 1949. The lowest predicted level of GDP in the US, UK, Germany, France and Italy turned out to be 13% higher than the actual outcome.

The only thing we can say with certainty is that the world has become much more uncertain. The aftermath of the financial crisis will play out for many years, and may be accompanied by more aggressive protectionism in trade and capital flows. There could be new financial shocks, not least perhaps in some emerging economies, including China. Western governments may find that they cannot finance their bloated budget deficits except by imposing controls over the movement of capital and foreign exchange. The consequences of global warming for the world economy, the environment and food and water supplies, and the costs to mitigate risk could have significantly perverse effects. The main point is that we cannot take globalisation for granted.

Emerging companies

In 2007, a former senior World Bank official, Antoine van Agtmael, who coined the term 'emerging markets', published a book entitled *The Emerging Markets Century*, in which he predicted that the output of this disparate group of countries, including the relatively more advanced group of South Korea, Taiwan, Singapore and Hong Kong, would overtake that of the developed countries by 2030–2035.

He wasn't making a pitch for how the global balance of power might change. Rather, his principal purpose was to highlight the implications of economic catching up for stock markets and investment opportunities, and he argued that leading companies based in the BRIC nations and in South Korea, Taiwan and Mexico were making rapid strides in technological competence and business practices. To validate his point, he noted that nearly 60 of the

Fortune top 500 global companies were already based in emerging nations, and that the big stock market plays in emerging countries were not simply dependent on picking out the companies specialising in natural resources and dependent on cheap labour.

In 2009, there were 91 emerging market companies in the Fortune 500, including 37 from China, 14 from South Korea, eight from Russia, seven from India and six each from India and Taiwan. There were eight emerging market companies in the top 50, with sales in excess of $100 billion, and two – the Chinese oil companies Sinopec and China National Petroleum – recorded sales of $208 billion and $181 billion, respectively. Nearly all of the top emerging market companies, however, are in the oil and gas sector. The only exception was Samsung in 40th place, with sales of $110 billion. Nevertheless, in electronics, Samsung is the second biggest company, and the Taiwanese company, Hon Hai (which makes the iPhone), is the eighth largest. State Grid in China is the world's biggest utility. The Mexican company CEMEX is the fifth largest company in the building materials sector. In shipping and trading, steel, engineering and construction, emerging market companies, mostly from China, can be found in the top 10.

In the entertainment and technology spheres too, emerging markets have come to play an increasing role. According to UNESCO (United Nations Education, Scientific and Cultural Organisation), India was the largest producer of feature-length films in 2006, with 1091 films. The Indian movie industry has gone global in recent years. Known colloquially as Bollywood, though this refers to the Mumbai-based Hindi language part of the industry, India is now thought to have the largest movie industry in the world in terms of films produced and tickets sold. India is followed by Nigeria with 872, compared to 485 for the US. China produced 330 and South Korea, 110.

According to Internet World Stats, there were 1734 million internet users in 2009, three quarters of whom were in 20 countries. Within this group, China had 330 million, India 81 million, Brazil 67 million, South Korea 37 million, and Iran 32 million. Indonesia, Mexico, Turkey, the Philippines, Vietnam and Poland occupied other top slots. Emerging markets typically have relatively low internet penetration rates (internet users as a share of the population). This is partly because of high population numbers, and partly because of other factors associated with under-development, for example, large rural sectors, lower educational attainment levels, affordability and availability of new technologies and so on. But the rates of usage are rising, and a handful of emerging countries have almost developed country penetration rates, for example, South Korea and Poland where internet users are about 77% and 52%, respectively. Typically, though, emerging market penetration is about half as big.

China is already the biggest producer of solar panels, and has declared that it wants to generate power increasingly from renewable energy sources. Brazil is a major producer of aircraft and of modern energy exploration equipment, and India's role in information, nuclear, and automobile-engineering technologies is renowned.

Emerging markets have already taken major positions in the production of steel, cement and other basic materials, and of low-end manufacturing production, for example, textiles, toys and other consumer goods. However, they are steadily moving up the so-called value chain, producing goods and services of higher quality that embrace modern technologies. Doubtless, they will consolidate and expand their share of world output of consumer electronics and more sophisticated manufactures in the future.

It is not clear whether van Agtmael's view about stock market investments in emerging countries will come to pass, or even to what extent the stock market values of emerging market companies over time bear any relation to the economic performance of the countries in which they are based. Just think back to the railroad boom in the United States in the 19th century and the impact it had on economic development. But by the 1870s, 40% of the bonds issued by railroad companies were in default, and many companies went bankrupt. Or more recently, consider the economic boost that came from the information and communications technology boom, despite the failures and losses of many information and telecommunications companies in the dot com bust. Many of today's emerging country stock markets typically include a relatively small number of quoted companies, and the earnings of many of these are strongly correlated with exports and commodity prices. It is quite possible, therefore, for the stock prices of these companies to rise (or fall), irrespective of the health or weakness of the local economy. According to Jonathan Anderson at UBS, one US dollar invested in emerging market stock market indices at the start of 2003 would, by 2009, have been worth $4.80 in Latin America, $3.30 in emerging Asia, and $3 in emerging Europe, but only $1.70 in the Asian Tigers[6]. This is not what would have been expected judging by economic growth alone.

So, having world-class companies can mean that investors can make a lot of money, if they pick the successful ones over time. And the arrival of world-class companies testifies to the impressive role and impact of emerging markets in the world economy. In and of itself, though, this says little about whether emerging markets are going to 'have their century'. It just means that as more emerging countries spawn more listed and successful companies, investors have a larger and potentially more exciting universe of stocks in which to invest.

The fact that the Fortune 500 list is dominated for the most part by Western companies in virtually all the 42 sectors cited tells two stories. First, the domination by Western companies could take decades to be threatened, if at all. Second, these companies generate a growing share of their revenues from selling goods and services that emanate from the steady expansion of corporate supply chains in Asia and in other emerging markets. When it comes to marketing, branding, and selling worldwide, emerging market companies have much to learn and a long way to go, even if a handful now rank among the global elite.

Emerging demographics

Since I have already stated that demographics are important in economic development, it is appropriate to consider the basic population and demographic characteristics of the developing world ahead of a more detailed assessment later.

The United Nations reckons world population to be around 6.9 billion. Only 1.2 billion of these people live in advanced economies. As shown in Table 2.2, the most heavily populated emerging countries are China and India with 2.5 billion people between them, but Indonesia, Brazil, Nigeria, Russia, Mexico and the Philippines also figure prominently. There are some population heavyweights, such as Pakistan and Bangladesh, with 185 million and 164 million people, respectively, as well as many countries with populations in the 40–80 million range, such as Ethiopia, Egypt, Democratic Republic of Congo, Myanmar, Tanzania, Kenya and Sudan. These countries, as well as richer oil-producing countries,

Table 2.2 Major emerging markets population 2010 (millions)

Malaysia	27.9	Vietnam	89
Poland	38	Turkey	75.7
Ukraine	45.4	Philippines	93.6
Argentina	40.7	Mexico	110.6
Ukraine	45.4	Russia	140.4
Colombia	46.3	Nigeria	158.3
S Korea	48.5	Brazil	195.4
Thailand	68.1	Indonesia	232.5
S Africa	50.5	India	1214.5
Iran	75.1	China	1354.1
		World	6908.7

Source: UN Population Division

don't qualify as emerging markets in the widely accepted sense, at least not yet, while other less populous countries, such as Chile, Czech Republic, Hungary and Israel do.

An important economic and geographic characteristic of both emerging market populations and developing countries generally is the speed at which they are becoming urbanised. Since the first billion consumers in modern times were largely to be found in the cities of the United States, Europe and Japan, the next billion, potentially, will be doing their consuming in emerging market cities.

The urbanisation rate in higher income developing countries has risen from 31% in 1980 to about 48%, and demographers expect this proportion to rise to 60–70% over the next 20–40 years. In the poorest countries in the developing world, the urbanisation rate is still only about 30%. The significance of urbanisation lies in the movement of people from low productivity and low-income agri-culture and rural-based activity to higher productivity and higher-income factory, office and construction jobs. Larger urban populations generate demand for housing and real estate, and an array of social, leisure and government services.

Consider the rise and size of emerging cities, which are already more substantial than many Western cities. In 1990, there were six Western cities in the world's biggest, defined as a population over 10 million (see Figure 2.1).

In 2005, the only 'Western' cities among the top 20 with populations over 10 million were Tokyo, New York, Los Angeles and Osaka. Mexico City was the second biggest, and Sao Paolo, Mumbai, Delhi, Shanghai and Calcutta took up the next positions (Figure 2.2).

By 2015 to 2020, Tokyo will still have the largest population among 21 cities with populations in excess of 10 million. New York will be seventh, Los Angeles twelfth, and Osaka twentieth. The remainder will comprise Dhaka, Mumbai, Delhi, Mexico City,

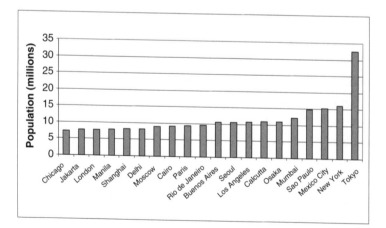

Figure 2.1 Biggest world cities 1990
(Source: UN Population Division)

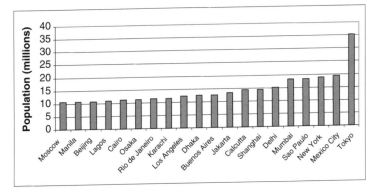

Figure 2.2 Biggest world citites 2005
(Source: UN Population Division)

Jakarta, Calcutta, Karachi, Lagos, Shanghai, Buenos Aires, Metro Manila, Beijing, Rio de Janeiro, Cairo, Istanbul, and Tianjin, southeast of Beijing.

Emerging economic weight

Being populous doesn't necessarily translate into economic success. Having one or more large cities may signify rapid economic development and modernity, but may also mask a high degree of urban squalor, and considerable poverty in the periphery of the country. Consequently, emerging markets are defined mostly with reference to their GDP and income per head of population. It should be noted that South Korea, Taiwan, Singapore and Hong Kong are still often included as emerging markets for analytical purposes, but by most measurements these regions emerged long ago.

Table 2.3 shows that in 2008, world GDP amounted to about $60,000 billion, of which 28% was accounted for by developing countries, half of which originated in the BRIC economies. China,

Table 2.3 GDP 2008 ($ billions)

	$ billion	% share
US	14204	23.6
Euro Area	13565	22.6
China	3860	6.4
Brazil	1613	2.7
Russia	1608	2.7
India	1217	2
Mexico	1085	1.8
Korea	929	1.5
Turkey	794	1.3
Poland	527	0.9
Indonesia	514	0.9
Rest of world	20196	33.6
World	60115	100

Source: IMF

of course, was the biggest single contributor. The developing nation share of world GDP is dominated by Asia which produces about 40% of the total, with most of the remainder coming from Latin America, Eastern Europe and central Asia.

We can also see by looking at Figure 2.3 how the developing countries' share of world GDP has evolved, looking at the statistics in terms of both current US dollar prices and in 2005 US dollar prices – that is, allowing for inflation and exchange rate changes. Looked at in terms of current US dollar prices, the emerging market share of world GDP declined between 1960 and 1992, and stalled again at the time of the Asia crisis in the late 1990s. The secular decline can be traced to the failure of emerging countries as a whole to keep up with the rapid advance of industrialised

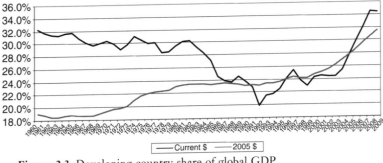

Figure 2.3 Developing country share of global GDP
Source: IMF, World Bank

countries, and to periodic financial crises and inflation in the emerging world.

Adjusting for inflation and exchange rate changes, though, the share of developing countries shows a rather different picture. Now, the emerging share of world GDP is shown as much lower in the 1960s and 1970s. Then it stabilises in the 1980s, and from the 1990s onwards it begins a sustained increase until now.

These alternative measures of the weight of emerging markets in the global system yield a slightly different version of recent history, but they end up in more or less the same place.

PPP beauty contest

There is another view about economic weight, however, which is far more contentious. It is worth emphasising what it is, because it is used often as the basis for the assertion that emerging markets are actually larger than recognised, and will overtake the biggest Western economies within the next 20 years. I shall explain why these are highly dubious propositions.

A problem arises because the prices of goods and services around the world, notably in developing countries, differ significantly, using market exchange rates to convert local prices into US dollars. The price of a Starbucks coffee, for example, or a taxi ride, an internet connection, a haircut or a Big Mac from Bogota to Beijing and from Stockholm to Sydney varies enormously. This is despite the fact that it's mostly the same product or service. The food, cooking facilities and products, and packaging that go into a Big Mac are the same everywhere. True, some things are bound to vary, for example, labour costs, rent and advertising, but I'll come back to that a little later. For now, just assume that a Big Mac is a Big Mac, but sold at significantly different prices around the world. So, when we count GDP in Indonesia or in Italy, we are counting many identical goods and services, but valued totally differently – higher in Italy, of course.

Economic theory says that, in the long run, the prices of goods and services in developing countries should converge on those in richer countries as they themselves become richer. Rising labour costs in poorer countries will push up the prices of goods that are sold largely within emerging economies, such as haircuts, and rising productivity will lower costs and prices in goods sold overseas. As these processes occur, the exchange rate in emerging markets will tend to increase in both nominal terms, that is, measured against the US dollar, and in real terms, allowing for inflation. Eventually then, using the example above, Indonesia's exchange rate will rise and the 'accounting' anomaly today will disappear.

This is a very slow process, however, and several countries, including China, peg or attempt to restrict the movement in their exchange rates. To correct for this, different exchange rates are calculated and used, according to a methodology called purchas-

Table 2.4 GDP in PPP terms 2008

	$ billions	% share
US	14204	20.4
Euro Area	10899	15.6
China	7903	11.3
India	3388	4.9
Russia	2288	3.3
Brazil	1976	2.8
Mexico	1541	2.2
Korea	1358	1.9
Turkey	1029	1.5
Indonesia	907	1.3
Poland	672	1
Rest of World	28105	40.3
World	70000	100

Source: World Bank

ing power parity (PPP). Most forecasts that are made about how large the emerging countries are now or will be in 10 or 25 years are based on the PPP measurement of GDP, which flatters their size. This is shown in Table 2.4.

The PPP calculation inflates the size of individual countries, and their contribution to global economic growth. In PPP terms, world GDP is nearer $70,000 billion, and the developing country share is about 43%. Asia represents nearly half this amount, while Latin America, Eastern Europe and Central Asia account for about 19% each. China is 11% of world GDP using PPP measurement, but about 6% based on market exchange rates. India is 5% of world GDP on the former basis, but only 2% on the latter.

The simple way to understand this exchange rate problem is to imagine, as Jonathan Anderson at UBS has suggested, there are only two countries – the US and China – and only two products – DVD players and haircuts[7]. Now, suppose in the US the price of each is $10, and that in China the DVD player costs RMB10, and the haircut costs RMB1. When you trade DVD players, the exchange rate is a market rate of 1:1 (or RMB10/USD10). But US GDP, defined as comprising DVD players and haircuts, is $20, and China's is RMB11, giving an exchange rate of 0.55:1 (or RMB1/USD10).

So on this basis, China's exchange rate is 45% undervalued, compared with what it would be if all goods and services were traded and priced similarly. And it just so happens, that 45% is precisely the extent of undervaluation of the RMB today, when we look at the actual RMB exchange rate against the US dollar of about RMB6.8 and the PPP rate of about RMB3.7.

This isn't just an academic debating point. Using market exchange rates, the Intergovernmental Panel on Climate Change has estimated that the per capita income of advanced economies, which was 38 times as large as that for emerging Asia in 1990, would only be 1.5 times as large by 2100, reflecting the conventional economic catch-up hypothesis. The purpose of the prediction was to show what the CO_2 emissions implications would be from that catching-up. However, using PPP, emerging Asia will become twice as big as the advanced economies by the end of the century. If the PPP theory has legs, then this should have a significant bearing on the calculations about CO_2 emissions and, therefore, on who should pay how much to help the global economy respond to global warming.

Economists tend to favour the use of PPP so as to reflect better consumer purchasing power across a broad range of goods and services – and therefore economic size – in emerging markets. On this basis, the weight of the BRIC economies in the world, for example, is 22%, slightly larger than the US share of 20%. However, it should be noted that this is a theoretical construct only, and while PPP exchange rates are more stable than market exchange rates, and adjust for the under-valuation of developing country exchange rates, they are devilish to calculate.

Further, they give misleading or inaccurate information when measuring trade and capital movements, monetary developments, asset markets, savings, and the relative importance of consumption and investment. They switch the focus away from inappropriate exchange rate regimes that result in the inefficient allocation of resources and, therefore, from real economic issues that countries have to overcome. In any event, no one settles transactions using PPP exchange rates, and no one holds a bank account denominated in PPP money.

The bottom line, so to speak, is that emerging countries have lower prices – which economists try to correct for by using PPP exchange rates – for the simple reason that they are poor. It is perplexing that professional colleagues, financial wizards, and political sycophants cannot get their minds around this simple fact, when asserting that China's (2010) GDP is nearly $9 trillion rather than $4 trillion. If we were to look at the developing world in terms of PPP, every single country except for Israel, Venezuela and the United Arab Emirates has a deeply undervalued exchange rate as depicted in Figure 2.4.

Every country, therefore, would theoretically have to increase the value of its exchange rate to compensate, including both surplus countries, such as China, deficit countries such as India, and an array of fellow travellers from Vietnam and Bangladesh to Pakistan and Bolivia.

Eventually, the richer that emerging countries become, the closer their market exchange rates will approximate to their theoretical

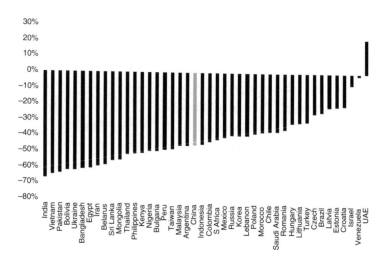

Figure 2.4 PPP exchange rate relative to actual exchange rate, 2009 (% difference).

Source: UBS, IMF

PPP rates. There is no reason, however, for us to dwell further on this theoretical construct, or its relevance to assessing the weight of emerging markets in the global economy. Note again that low prices in emerging markets aren't a freak observation. They are low because the economies are poor.

A propos poverty, income per head of population is a useful indicator of economic welfare. It doesn't tell us anything about income distribution or the quality of life for most people, but it does, nonetheless, serve as a broad benchmark of wellbeing. Some countries with small populations and large oil and gas sectors fare exceptionally well in the income per head league table. According to the World Bank, Norway had the largest gross national income per head in 2008 at over $87,000, while Qatar, Kuwait, and Brunei with a combined population of less than 5

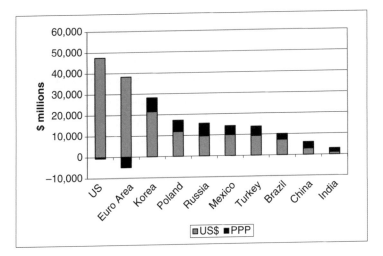

Figure 2.5 Gross national income per head
Source: World development indicators, World Bank, July 2009

million, are much higher up the list than any major emerging market or developing country.

Figure 2.5 shows that there is little to choose between the market and PPP values for income per head in the US and the Euro Area, and even in the case of the latter, it amounts to a rounding error, given the size of income per head. By comparison, the income per head in major emerging countries is far lower, even though the effect of using PPP is to increase it by $3000–4000 in China, Mexico and Turkey, and by slightly more in Russia, Poland and South Korea.

Using PPP probably reflects better what people sense when making infrequent visits to major emerging cities, such as Shanghai or Mumbai. The sight of yet more luxury shopping malls and construction sites, flashy bars and foreign cars, and widespread and efficient internet connectivity almost seem to make economic growth a spectator sport. Strong as these impressions are, they are as biased as the PPP income measures they appear to confirm. With few exceptions, they take no account of the cities' slum-dwellers and rubbish heaps, or the much poorer hinterlands and rural villages where most people live and work. They reveal nothing about living standards, wage levels or whether average citizens can even afford the goods they produce and are sold in downtown shops.

Playing catch-up

In the last 20–30 years, China and India have staked a strong claim to economic and political leadership roles. In a more regional context, so have Brazil, Russia and South Africa. The development of a Sino-centric supply network in Asia, the broader expansion of manufacturing output in emerging economies, and the scarcity premium reflected in oil and other commodity prices that favours Russia and other raw material producers, comprise the dominant developments of the last decades. Assessing how far emerging markets have come turns out to be no mean feat. We should bear several things in mind.

First, no emerging country has realised strong and sustained growth without committing to a full engagement with and integration into globalisation, in which exports play a leading role. What might happen if it were no longer possible for emerging countries to rely as much on exporting cheap goods and services to the West?

Second, rapid development cannot occur with a large pool of domestic savings, which can be channelled into investment and capital accumulation. China's households and companies, for example, save almost 50% of GDP. In order to channel those savings smoothly and efficiently, a system of property rights, market incentives and financial intermediation is required. Moreover, persistently excessive levels of national savings mean that China has to end up with large external surpluses. What might happen if institutional and structural change in China didn't happen or happen fast enough, such that China's external surpluses were sustained?

Third, demographics matter because a steady increase in the size of the population of working age generates the labour input to drive the development of manufacturing and service-producing industries. A surfeit of labour, however, is only potentially positive for economic development if the bulk of the labour force finds gainful and productive employment. This too speaks to the quality of governmental and social institutions, as well as the capacity of companies to create jobs. Although China will face the challenge of rapid ageing soon, along with South Korea, Singapore and Hong Kong, Russia and Eastern Europe, the rest of the developing world (except for Africa), will have to meet the challenge too, most probably from the 2030s onwards.

Fourth, as recent crises have shown, excessive public and private sector debt can bring an economy to a grinding halt sooner or later. Financial crises are not terminal, but they are liable to set back economic progress for some time, and may exacerbate political instability. The economic expansion in developing countries in the 1960s and 1970s, for example, was accompanied by rising government budget deficits, too much credit creation, and an unsustainable build up in foreign borrowing to finance growing balance of payments deficits.

The oil price shocks of 1970s precipitated a 20-year wave of economic and political catastrophes in which inflation surged and currency values collapsed. They initially affected many countries in Latin America and Africa, then the USSR, and between 1990 and 2002, China, Mexico, Asia, Russia, Brazil, and Argentina.

Fifth, sustained rapid development will only occur in the presence of the factors that produce economic 'bang for the buck', or what I referred to earlier as total factor productivity. This comprises the effects of political stability, good governance, and sound institutions. Some emerging markets have recorded impressive gains in the most favourable circumstances for global growth since the end of the Second World War. The challenge, though, is not to get to some arbitrary finishing line, but to strive continuously to adapt as political and economic circumstances change. In the aftermath of the financial crisis, many emerging markets have responded well, but the acid test of adjustment still lies ahead, as I will explore in the next two chapters.

Sixth, the dissemination of new technologies and nurturing of the knowledge-based economy is a critical ingredient for sustained economic success, but only the BRICs, and that is mostly China and India, have really penetrated the upper echelons of leading technology nations. Moreover, the gap between the richer and emerging economies in the most sophisticated technologies remains very large. Acquiring and copying modern technologies is well within the scope for the more sophisticated emerging markets. The trick is to establish and master a culture of innovation.

Getting these six ducks into line is not an easy task. It requires a focus on structural characteristics and developments, many of which are slow moving and transcend the measurement of GDP, manufacturing supply networks, and visitor impressions of modern cities, impressive though they may be. Later in the book, I shall examine some of those structural phenomena, and look especially at the demographics and technological capabilities of emerging markets, as well as the issues that are presented by climate change.

In the next two chapters, though, it is time to turn to the effects of the financial crisis and the global recession on emerging markets, and the extent to which they are contributing and vulnerable to a world economy, in which trade and finance have become significantly unbalanced. Globalisation has bestowed upon them many economic benefits, but also responsibilities, which are sometimes unclear, sometimes spurned. If the major emerging markets are able to adapt and adjust to their more powerful positions in the global economy, they should expect sustained economic development, losing the word 'emerging' in the process. If they do not, or cannot, a more turbulent economic – and therefore political – future awaits us all.

Chapter Three

To Armageddon and Back

The financial crisis that erupted in 2008 took the global economy to the brink of an economic – and probably political – Armageddon. Several major banks and the world's biggest insurance company collapsed, and many financial entities found that they could no longer borrow to finance themselves and were on the verge of bankruptcy. Had this been allowed to happen, there is no question that the world economy would have plunged into a depression unparalleled since the Great Depression of the 1930s.

Many politicians in emerging markets, mindful of how their countries had been criticised in the past for financial cronyism and fraud by Western governments and international institutions, drew attention to comparable characteristics in the US and other Western banks and financial systems. A Chinese Foreign Ministry spokesperson, Jiang Yu, said that when economic crises had occurred previously in Latin America, East Asia and Russia, Western economists had attributed them to failures in the countries or regions themselves. Referring to suggestions that the causes of the crisis lay, to some extent, in flaws in the global financial system, including in China, she insisted that the current crisis originated in developed countries and it was inappropriate to deflect the blame by looking for causes elsewhere[1].

And in a famous remark about the financial crisis, Brazilian President Lula da Silva used a visit of UK Prime Minster Gordon Brown in 2009, to say 'This crisis was fostered and boosted by irrational behaviour of some people that are white, blue-eyed. Before the crisis they looked like they knew everything about economics, and they have demonstrated they know nothing about economics'[2]. The Brazilian president was effectively saying 'it's your crisis, not ours'.

Because the crisis did erupt in the West, it is fitting that we take a bit of a detour from emerging markets in order to understand more precisely what it was all about. It is only by doing so that we can then double back to the origins and causes of the crisis, and put the above statement by the Chinese Foreign Ministry spokesperson into a proper perspective. China and other emerging markets that thrive by generating large export surpluses are very much implicated in the financial crisis, and it is only if this is understood that those who manage the global system will be capable of mending it so that the world is insulated better against any reoccurrence.

The great economist, author, diplomat, public servant and raconteur, J.K. Galbraith, published a wonderful short book in 1990, called *A Short History of Financial Euphoria*. At 96 pages, this book is mercifully light on detail and statistics, but it is a superb guide to what was to happen to our Western bubble, and why. Indeed, its relevance to the future is timeless. In one of many killer and poignant statements, Galbraith says that the 'speculative episode always ends not with a whimper but with a bang'. He goes on with 'the euphoric episode is protected and sustained by the will of those who are involved, in order to justify the circumstances that are making them rich.' And we might say today, 'didn't they just?'

Although the crisis started in the real estate and banking sectors, it quickly became apparent that all financial institutions were at risk, including insurance companies, pension funds, hedge funds and private equity funds. Moreover, the credit crunch starved nonfinancial companies of cash flows and credit lines, and the ensuing recession drove down their sales and revenues. Stock prices collapsed, with the S&P 500 index, for example, falling from above 1500 in October 2007 to 686 in early March 2009, effectively suggesting that large swathes of corporate America would go bankrupt in a major recession. The same developments occurred on other stock markets which, together with commodity markets, buckled. Government bond yields dropped to record low levels as people flocked to what they regarded as the best risk-free asset of all. Not even cash was deemed safe if your bank was about to go bust.

The sharp recovery in global stock markets after March 2009, and the emergence of most nations from recession during the year, were entirely due to exceptional policy measures adopted by governments and central banks from October 2008 onwards. These included substantial liquidity injections into financial markets and banks, vast purchases of private and government debt instruments by central banks, financial rescues and nationalisations, and a dramatic rise in government borrowing, partly to stimulate faltering economic growth, and partly to accommodate the sharp decline in government tax revenues. Western nations were obliged to recognise the impotence of markets, and to deploy the forces of Big

Government to combat the crisis. This was the only way to lay the foundations for stability and, hopefully, economic growth in the future.

Emerging markets shook off the worst aspects of the crisis faster and more impressively than Western nations. China stood out as a particular stalwart. The reason that emerging markets bounced back quickly was that, at the time, their banking systems were in good shape. This meant that they were able to respond forcefully to the crisis by lowering interest rates, boosting government spending, and taking advantage of a sharp increase in US dollar lending programmes provided by the Federal Reserve.

Emerging markets did not escape the crisis unscathed, however. Indeed, several among them demonstrated an unexpected vulnerability to the massive global shock, necessitating the direct action that they took. The reason for this was, and remains, an economic structure that makes them excessively dependent on exporting to Western economies. In sustaining that structure, emerging markets pursue inappropriate economic, financial and exchange rate policies, which implicate them in the global trade imbalances that lie at the heart of an unstable world financial system. It is important, therefore, to understand how the crisis unhinged the West, and why the aftermath now poses major risks and challenges not just in Western nations, but also in emerging markets.

How the subprime minnow became a monster

In early 2007, very few people had heard of an esoteric US mortgage-financing programme called subprime lending, which began around 1993. For the next decade, it accounted for about 9% of new mortgages. In the following three years to 2006, it accounted for about 20% of new mortgages. Subprime financing was the practice of lending money to borrowers who were at the high end of the credit risk spectrum. The practice entailed not only lending to uncreditworthy borrowers, but also lending imprudent multiples of income, often without confirmation or documentation of details needed to ensure that the loans were affordable and could be serviced and repaid. Borrowers were offered interest-only mortgages, so that eventual repayment was entirely dependent on continuous increases in house prices. They took advantage of 'teaser' interest rates that were low for a year or two but were then reset at higher rates when the initial period expired, and pay-option loans, where they could choose how much to repay on a monthly basis.

US house prices reached their highest levels in the summer of 2006, but later that year local news reports started to draw attention to a drop in prices and a rise in mortgage delinquency problems in some cities and states. In one of two zip codes in the city of Memphis, for example, over 40 percent of mortgages taken out between 2004 and 2006 were categorised as subprime. In Mississippi and Louisiana mortgage default rates already topped 10%, but this was all too easily attributed to the havoc created by Hurricane Katrina, America's most expensive and deadly hurricane that devastated New Orleans and wrought havoc across the Gulf of Mexico in August 2005.

Those who began to view subprime as a potential can of worms were assured that subprime mortgages accounted for just 7% of the entire US mortgage stock, and that some rise in mortgage delinquencies and defaults was inevitable after the Federal Reserve had raised short-term interest rates from 1 percent in 2004 to 5.25 percent in 2007. Anyway, how could some minor local difficulties in US mortgage markets derail a global economy that was enjoying an unprecedented period of economic expansion?

By late 2006, however, the pace of defaults and foreclosures or home repossessions in the subprime sector was rising quickly. Dozens of subprime lenders collapsed, including the country's second biggest institution, New Century Financial Corporation. The housing finance problem spread like wildfire It affected not only those entities which made loans to borrowers directly, but also financial institutions all over the world that had eagerly bought mortgage loans which had been pooled and financially engineered as tradeable securities, normally with very high credit ratings and carrying the imprimatur of the world's major credit rating agencies, Standard and Poor's and Moody's Investor Services.

In 2007, the subprime market started to decline even faster. Investors and banks had to book losses. Worse still, it became increasingly difficult to value the securitised assets they owned because the market for them had ceased to function properly or, in some cases, dried up completely. With this transparency gone, lenders and owners of securities had real cause for worry, because whilst they could make allowances for the *risk* that there might be a loss, they could not deal with the *uncertainty* of not knowing whether their assets were worth anything at all.

Uncertainty in turn caused lenders to suddenly become highly risk averse. They cut back their credit lines, and charged borrowers, including other banks, significantly more than was customary for access to credit. And that's how it all started. Subprime had graduated from a little-known US mortgage financing practice to a monster financial shock, and it started to affect financial institutions and countries that had little, if anything, to do with mortgage financing.

In July, two hedge funds collapsed which belonged to the investment bank, Bear Stearns, which had investments of $1500 billion at the end of 2006, mostly in subprime. A month later, the French bank BNP Paribas froze two funds offered to investors, after large losses attributable to subprime, heavy withdrawals by investors, and an acknowledgement that the bank couldn't value the assets that were left.

By September 2007, normal borrowing and lending behaviour in world financial markets was badly disrupted, banks began to hoard cash, and the rate of interest charged by banks to one another soared. Banks started to fret about the build-up in other loans that were deteriorating. These included other securitised assets, for example those backed by credit cards and automobile loans, and traditional loans to companies and to consumers. The problem was partly that falling asset prices undermined the collateral against which the loans were pledged, and partly that borrowers were becoming increasingly hard pressed to honour and service their debts. Some loans were so-called leveraged loans that were linked to the activities of private equity companies and to merger and acquisition transactions conducted during the boom, in which debt was used to acquire assets that were now plunging in value. Financial institutions were confronted by a double whammy – the value of their assets was falling sharply or couldn't be determined, and they couldn't borrow on acceptable terms, or at all. In short, the crisis was generating an immediate threat to their liquidity, and casting a dark cloud over their solvency.

By the beginning of 2008, contagion in the financial services industry was rampant, and a full-blown credit crunch had begun.

In February, the UK's fourth largest private lender Northern Rock, which had relied on inter-bank loans to fund most of its mortgage lending, and which had had witnessed the first bank run in the country since the 19th century, was nationalised. The list of major banking casualties then started to mount. In March, Bear Stearns collapsed and was folded into the US bank JP Morgan Chase. In September, the US government nationalised the country's two giant mortgage lenders, Freddie Mac (Federal Home Loan Mortgage Corporation) and Fannie Mae (Federal National Mortgage Association), which guaranteed half of the entire $12,000 billion stock of US mortgages, the US investment bank Merrill Lynch was sold to Bank of America amid fears that its liquidity had dried up, the insurance giant AIG had to be rescued in a form that was tantamount to nationalisation, and the US investment bank Lehman Brothers collapsed. The global financial system went into deep-freeze, precipitating fears that another Great Depression was imminent.

A 'Minsky Moment'

In March 2007, I published the first of a series of financial crisis research papers, entitled 'Have we arrived at a Minsky Moment?'[3]. By the closing months of 2008, it had arrived. But what on earth was or is a Minsky Moment? Named after the American economist, Hyman Minsky (1919–1996), it was designed to convey the point at which a systemic financial meltdown threatened to bring down good, as well as bad borrowers and lenders, precipitate an economic depression, and necessitate the widespread intervention of the State and its institutional apparatus.

Minsky had shown how and why the volume of debt expands over long periods of economic expansion and stability. Importantly, he also showed how and why the confidence with which people and companies acquire debt grows. He demonstrated that the process of debt accumulation moves through three stages. The first two are relatively benign and contribute to economic expansion in positive ways. If borrowers can service their debts, repay their loans comfortably out of current income, and have assets whose future value is likely to exceed their liabilities, credit enables the economy to expand in an orderly and effective fashion. In the last stage, however, or what Minsky labelled the Ponzi stage, the debt cycle starts to become increasingly unstable. Lenders become overly aggressive in their lending practices, and borrowers may end up borrowing far too much. Most importantly, borrowers end up having to borrow simply to remain up to date on their current debt obligations, and to pay for future obligations. Anyone who has borrowed money to pay interest payments on a credit card with a large outstanding balance is engaged in a Ponzi scheme.

Minsky named this stage after Charles Ponzi, an Italian immigrant who arrived in the United States in 1903, and who set up pyramid-type investment schemes that paid returns to existing investors out of the subscriptions made by new investors. Upon his arrest, he got three years in prison. Ponzi wasn't the first to do this, nor the last. In 2008, Bernard Madoff, former Chairman of the NASDAQ stock market, confessed to an identical scam. A year later a judge sentenced him to 150 years in prison on various counts pertaining to securities fraud, money laundering and perjury.

While financial scams and attempts to cheat investors come to light in every financial crisis, they were not Minsky's principal concerns. His focus was on how the workings of the capitalist system, itself, and of complex debt structures in particular, were prone to lead eventually to financial instability – sometimes on a massive scale, necessitating unusual intervention by public authorities to stabilise the financial system and the economy.

There had actually been a dry run of a Minsky Moment in September 1998, when the US hedge fund, Long Term Capital Management, failed soon after the Russian state defaulted on its external debt. The Federal Reserve provided emergency liquidity to financial markets, organised the orderly unwinding of the hedge fund's assets and positions, and cut interest rates as it sought to stop a financial failure from becoming a systemic problem.

Minsky died over a decade before the financial crisis of 2007–2009, but his insights into the anatomy and prognosis of financial crises were prescient. He demonstrated that the crisis was not a random event, nor was it bad luck. Rather it was the culmination of a sustained debt cycle that had begun in the 1980s, gathered momentum in the 1990s, and reached its mania stage between about 2002 and 2006.

Real estate is often at the heart of financial crises, and housing offers a classic example of why this is so. Rising home prices encourage more people to borrow more in order to acquire homes, or buy larger properties. Teaser and interest-only mortgages enable people to borrow more money than they might normally be able to afford, in the belief that, over time, rising home prices will bail them out. As long as prices keep rising and people can afford their monthly mortgage payments, there is no problem. However, if property prices suddenly go into reverse, and people start to lose their jobs or have their incomes reduced for other reasons, the entire structure of mortgage debt financing will implode.

Subprime mortgages were just the large tip of a giant iceberg comprising generic mortgage and other consumer loans, corporate loans, complicated financial derivatives markets with complex counterparty arrangements, and a so-called shadow banking system which accounted for as much as half of all credit extended in advanced economies between 2004 and 2007[4]. Somehow, these debt structures and the enormous expansion of financial obligations had been allowed to proliferate and expand throughout the prior two decades, under the twin banners of financial innovation and market-dominated financial globalisation.

In an editorial on 25 June 2007, entitled 'Why finance will not be unfettered', the *Financial Times* referred to the liberation of finance as one of the most significant transformations brought about by today's era of globalisation, and noted an independent estimate that the ratio of global financial assets to world GDP had surged from 109% in 1980 to 316% in 2005. This three-fold rise in the weight of finance in the global economy over a relatively short period of time should have set alarm bells ringing. The *Financial Times* went on to argue that the survival of unchained financial capitalism could not be taken for granted, and that the full benefits of financial globalisation would only be realised if regulators were on the ball and globally coordinated, central banks understood the modern processes of credit creation, and the rich paid a fair share of the overall tax burden.

But it was already far too late. The warnings were appropriate, but the countdown to the meltdown had already begun, and the response would only resurface after the full scale of the economic carnage had become clear. But who was to blame, and what did emerging markets, which were not referenced in the editorial, have to do with it?

The search for villains

The history of financial crises shows that the perpetrators of financial wrongdoing or incompetence are always sought out and exposed and, occasionally, incarcerated. This crisis has been no exception, and while the search for human scapegoats is a natural reaction, it tends to detract from the far more important systemic causes – that is, those arising from the capitalist and global financial system, itself.

Bankers clearly did engage in reckless and unsafe lending practices. Homeowners were naïve in acquiring imprudent levels of indebtedness. Regulators did not do their job, since the most significant institutions that failed were in the regulated banking sector. Supervisors either did not or could not keep a close enough watch on institutions that were outside the scope of their operations. Credit rating agencies, which collected fees from banks by rating the complex financial products the latter brought to market, stand accused of not offering reliable or trustworthy guidelines and advice, at the very least.

However, these were all agents of the crisis, not the root cause. We could not have had such a permissive financial system, with such runaway debt accumulation without the extensive political deregulation of financial services that was ushered in by the Reagan and Thatcher administrations in the 1980s in the US and UK, respectively, but continued under the Clinton administrations of 1993–2001, and the UK Labour government after 1997. In 1999, for example, after 20 years of pressure from the banking industry and its political protagonists for progressive dilution, the US Congress finally repealed the Glass-Steagall Act of 1933, which had been introduced 60 years earlier amid a banking crisis to prevent bank-holding companies from owning other financial institutions, and in effect drawing a line between commercial and investment banking within the same institution.

The reasons for this Act, and the folly of its repeal, were exposed by the crisis. When the restraints over the functions of financial institutions are abandoned, conflicts of interest and culture are encouraged within increasingly large institutions, and information about risk positions tends to become hidden and buried in corporate silos, which obscure the aggregate risks being run by individual financial entities. Banks and bankers became very powerful in the 1920s, and again in the 1990s and 2000s, and they achieved substantial influence not just in their own sector, but also in political circles and in the broader economy. By 2007, for example, the financial services and real estate sectors were generating about three fifths of the annual expansion in the UK's GDP, and about 55% of that of the US. The financial sector had become big, bloated, and very powerful.

Moreover, we could not have had such a fertile backdrop for a severe financial crisis, had it not been for the atomic cloud of financially footloose funds circulating around the global economy[5]. As an indication, global foreign exchange turnover reached an all-time peak of $3300 billion per day in the first half of 2008, before declining after the crisis by about 25% in the first half of 2009. Half of the turnover was undertaken by banks among themselves – that is, not conducted for an identified customer. These volumes contrast, for example, with world exports which average roughly $40 billion per day. The explosion in financial transactions was attributable partly to global credit creation, and partly to the build-up in global trade imbalances, in which China and many other emerging nations chose to run large external surpluses and acquire vast quantities of foreign exchange reserves, especially after 2002. These reserve assets were duly deposited in Western banks or invested in government securities, and contributed to the credit mania of the time.

The context in which this happened, however, can only be appreciated by considering the succession of financial crises that rocked the global economy over a long period of time, specifically from the 1980s onwards (see Table 3.1). In fact, from 1990 until 2009, in every year there has been at least one banking system in crisis and one property market collapsing[6]. Why didn't anyone in authority spot the connections and warn us that some sort of deep-seated credit event was unravelling?

A short history of busts

There were two crises in the 1980s. The first comprised the US savings and loan associations, which made a series of ill-advised real estate loans and were caught out by the extreme interest rate developments of the decade when tough monetary policies were introduced to combat high inflation, forcing short-term interest rates (at which the savings associations borrowed their funds) to rise significantly above long-term rates (paid by borrowers). The second was the global stock market crash in 1987, which was viewed seriously at the time but had a negligible economic impact and was quickly forgotten. However, the whole of the 1980s witnessed a developing country, and especially Latin American, debt crisis, triggered by the decision by Mexico in 1982 to suspend interest and principal payments on its $80 billion of foreign debt, owed largely to US banks.

The background to the crisis had involved some familiar 'friends', including financial deregulation and innovation, and

Table 3.1 Episodes of widespread financial stress in advanced economies

Year	Event	Key features
1982	US banking sector	Sovereign defaults in Latin America, global recession, Mexico debt service moratorium, US savings and loan crisis
1987	US stock market crash	October 1987 crash, Brazil debt service moratorium, US dollar record decline
1990	Nikkei crash	US junk bond market collapse, Nikkei falls 50%, US investment bank Drexel Burnham Lambert bankrupt, systemic banking crises in Argentina, Brazil, Hungary and Romania
1992	ERM collapse	European exchange rate system breaks, Japan asset bubble punctured, Scandinavian banking crisis, systemic banking crisis in India, debt restructuring in Argentina, Egypt, the Philippines, Poland and S. Africa
1997	Asian crisis	Balance of payments and financing stress in several nations, Thailand devalues and triggers regional currency crisis, capital flight, emergency policy measures, recession, and six years of balance sheet repairs and debt reduction
1998	Long-Term Capital Management	US hedge fund collapses, Russia default, financial stress in Mexico, Brazil
2000	Dot-com crash	Technology sector-led decline in stock markets, debt restructuring in Russia, systemic banking crisis in Turkey

(Continued)

(*Continued*)

Year	Event	Key features
2002	WorldCom, Enron defaults	Scandals generate financial market havoc, starting with the demise of accountancy firm, Arthur Andersen, WorldCom bankrupt, severe stress in emerging markets
2007–09	US sub-prime crisis	Sub-prime housing finance markets freeze and fall, quickly migrates to entire banking system, credit crunch, US investment bank Bear Stearns fails and is acquired by JP Morgan, US Federal housing agencies Fannie Mae and Freddie Mac effectively nationalised, AIG, Northern Rock failure and rescue, Lehman Brothers bankrupt, Royal Bank of Scotland and Lloyds nationalised, systemic western banking crisis, largest global recession since the 1930s, widespread recourse to unprecedented and financial, fiscal and monetary measures

Source: How linkages fuel the fire: the transmission of financial stress from advanced to emerging economies, IMF, *World Economic Outlook*, April 2009, and author

excessive borrowing, particularly of short-term debt. When oil prices soared in 1979–1981, and then the US resolved in the 1980s to quash inflation by raising short-term interest rates substantially, a financial crisis was inevitable. By 1983, 27 countries owing nearly

$250 billion had rescheduled their foreign debt or were in the process of doing so. In Latin America, 16 countries, including Mexico, Brazil, Venezuela and Argentina, accounting for 75% of all developing country debt, had to restructure or reschedule their debts.

The crash of the Japanese stock market proved to be significantly more serious for Japan than it was for the global economy. It was to precipitate a crisis which has lasted for more than two decades. The European Exchange Rate Mechanism (ERM) crisis in 1992 was also a regional problem. The ERM was a long-term practice run for the creation of a single currency, and the crisis originated in the maintenance of fixed exchange rates among participating countries at levels that were not sustainable without punishing high levels of interest rates that were equally unsustainable. The British government was obliged to take the pound out of the ERM, and the British have never since seriously come close to joining Europe's single currency. The crisis delayed, but did not prevent, the creation of the Euro. During the early 1990s, the Scandinavian banking system was rocked by a property price collapse and excessive exposure to the sector. Similar developments occurred in the UK, though without bringing the banking system, as such, into question. During the early part of the 1990s, there were on-going banking problems in Argentina, Brazil and some countries in Eastern Europe.

In 1997–1998, a series of currency shocks began with the devaluation of the Thai Baht; within two months the crisis had spread to Malaysia and South Korea, and then it tore through Asia. By this time, Long Term Capital Management had failed and Russia had defaulted. In 1998, the US Federal Reserve had taken on a more global persona that was to prove as crucial to the mitigation of financial crises as it was to their propagation. In effect, it became a global central bank, changing liquidity conditions in the global economy and the overall levels of world interest rates in response not only to local demand, employment and inflation conditions in the US, but to global financial conditions too. The trouble was that the Federal Reserve only had one *modus operandi*, which was to fight financial fires with loose credit policies, not to prevent them by taking away pre-emptively the proverbial punch bowl.

In fact, the credit cycle from the 1980s onwards could have been arrested or tamed by central bankers at various points. In December 1996, for example, as people were becoming slightly alarmed by the never-ending rise in US and global stock prices, Federal Reserve Chairman Alan Greenspan spoke to the American Enterprise Institute on the subject of 'The Challenge of Central Banking in a Democratic Society'. In the speech, he asked, 'But how do we know when irrational exuberance has unduly escalated asset values, which then become subject to unexpected and prolonged contractions as they have in Japan over the past decade? And how do we factor that assessment into monetary policy?'

These questions were to hound Greenspan for the following decade until his retirement from the Federal Reserve, and even after he had stepped down at the end of his period of office. Greenspan, and his peers in other Western nations, persistently refused to acknowledge that central banks should intervene to puncture credit and asset bubbles. This was understandable up to a point because the use of interest rates in the conduct of monetary policy is a very blunt weapon, and raising interest rates to quell stock market speculation, for example, would also hurt small businesses and many other borrowers who might not be irrationally exuberant at all. However, central banks had other tools they could have deployed, including higher margin requirements on stock transactions, and increased capital, liquidity and reserve requirements for banks. They could have urged governments to use the law to impose tighter controls over lending activities. Given that there were tools available, but that they all called for greater regulation, the refusal to use them was all the more poignant. The culture of financial globalisation and of the primacy of markets had planted deep roots stretching back over a decade, and to the aftermath of the Asia crisis in particular.

On 15 February 1999, *Time Magazine* carried a front page picture of Alan Greenspan, US Treasury Secretary Robert Rubin, and his deputy Larry Summers (now Barack Obama's Chairman of the Council of Economic Advisers) under the banner headline 'The Committee To Save The World', and with the side heading, 'The inside story of how the three marketeers have prevented a global meltdown – for now'. At the time, that was precisely how it felt, but there was a sting in the tail – those last two words were the most important ones in the whole story.

Together, Greenspan, Rubin and Summers epitomised the triumphalism that had been seen a decade earlier when the Berlin Wall came down. They could take credit from having contained the knock-on effects of the Asian crisis, and then the Wall Street and Russia shocks the following year. They believed in a model of global financial integration, which emphasised the wisdom of markets and deregulation. Against a backdrop of economic optimism and success, created by the information and communications technology revolution and what was believed to be a new era of sustained economic growth, the apparently successful response to successive financial crises generated relief and confidence. And a lot of hubris.

In 2005, Greenspan explored in great length the nature of something he called the 'interest rate conundrum'. This was the failure of long-term interest rates to rise as expected, as the Federal Reserve increased short-term rates. The role played by the investment of emerging nation foreign exchange reserves in longer-term government and quasi-government bonds was clearly identified. One of his governors and his eventual successor, Ben Bernanke, also spoke that year in an address to the Virginia Economics Association about the global savings glut, that is the excess savings in emerging markets, and their significance in underpinning global trade imbalances, and low long-term US interest rates[7]. Greenspan, Bernanke and other central bank officials were all clearly cognisant of the financial dislocations arising from global imbalances, and the respective roles of the US on the one hand, and China and other emerging markets on the other. However, they either assumed that this was a long-term problem which would adjust slowly, or that it was more of a curiosity than a potential crisis.

No one in authority thought that the structure of the global financial and trading system was deeply flawed, and it did not occur to many people that the policies being championed by Washington, London, and other European capitals were actually exacerbating those flaws. For what appears certain is that the excesses in the global financial sector and credit system that erupted in 2007–2008 have their origins in a fundamental belief in financial deregulation, and in the aftermath of the crises of 1997–1998. Policymakers were in awe at the power and perceived innovative effectiveness of unfettered global finance, and failed to recognise the significance of the 180-degree turn in the economic development strategies of China and other Asian economies.

The global savings glut

So why and how did China, East Asia, Saudi Arabia, Russia and other major oil producers and emerging markets assume such a pivotal role in the global economy as the sources of lending? After all, the standard economic development model stipulates that poorer countries tend to borrow – that is, they tend to import capital from richer nations to help finance growth. In other words, major developing countries tend to import more than they export, run trade deficits, and borrow capital from the rest of the world to finance the deficits. Richer nations do the opposite. They run trade surpluses, and finance those surpluses, in effect, by exporting capital. This is pretty much how the world worked until 1997. Consider this extract from Bernanke's savings glut speech:

'I will argue that over the past decade a combination of diverse forces has created a significant increase in the global supply of saving – a global saving glut – which helps to explain both the increase in the U.S. current account deficit and the relatively low level of long-term real interest rates in the world today. The prospect of dramatic increases in the ratio of retirees to workers in a number of major industrial economies is one important reason for the high level of global saving. However, as I will discuss, a particularly interesting aspect of the global saving glut has been a remarkable reversal in the flows of credit to developing and emerging-market economies, a shift that has transformed those economies from borrowers on international capital markets to large net lenders.'

The argument that rapid ageing in advanced societies was one reason for high savings rates – that is, as the baby boomers prepared for retirement – was and is theoretically correct, but in practice mistaken. Japan's households, which had a strong reputation for frugality, were high savers until about 1990, but their savings rates fell continuously thereafter. High personal savings were certainly not characteristic of the US or the UK, and while Germany could have been singled out as a high saving economy, the reason had precious little to do with ageing. Rather like Japan, Germany has a long history of relying on export-led growth, and of investing its savings surpluses in ways that perpetuate this.

However, the sea change in emerging and developing country behaviour, to which Bernanke alluded, is critical. And it all started with the Asian crisis.

Thailand's 1997 devaluation triggered Asia's biggest shock since the Second World War. Previously, most Asian economies ran trade deficits with the rest of the world, and imported capital. In order to attract foreign capital, most governments pegged their exchange rates so as to give foreign lenders confidence that they had nothing to fear from exchange rate-induced losses on their investments or the profits or dividends they would repatriate. Thailand, Malaysia, Indonesia and most other countries tried the impossible, and failed.

They pursued fixed exchange rate regimes, but simultaneously allowed capital to flow freely in and out of the country. This was unwise. If you are going to fix your exchange rate, you have to control capital coming in, so that you don't lose monetary control at home, and going out, in case it threatens your currency. If you want to have flexibility in capital transactions, you have to allow the exchange rate to fluctuate. You can do one or the other, but not, as Asian countries were to find out, both.

In fact, they not only maintained open capital accounts, but also chose to attract foreign capital by removing restraints over trade and project finance, and encouraging foreign banks to arrive. As a result, local banking competition intensified, and marginalised local banks were left to concentrate on increasingly less credit-worthy companies and projects[8]. Most of the financial capital coming in to the Asian economies comprised US dollars lent at short maturities, and much went to finance real estate, golf courses, and other economically dubious projects – in much the same way as occurred 10 years later in Eastern Europe.

Once the Thai Baht was devalued, the dam broke and other Asian currencies quickly followed suit. Capital was gone in a moment, the Asian crisis started, and it would take six years for the banking systems in the region to stabilise and be restructured, and before sustainable economic growth could resume. But the Asian crisis wasn't just another crisis that came and went, disappearing anonymously into history. It was a seminal event that changed the way the world worked, with adverse consequences that did not become apparent until the financial crisis erupted.

Fundamentally, the Asian crisis was to alter the way that major emerging markets thought about their role and position in global-isation. Interestingly, China was barely affected by the crisis. It had a pegged exchange rate and tight controls over capital movements, but the crisis convinced Beijing that, in future, it would need a war chest of foreign exchange reserves to defend itself, if needed, from the speculative power of mobile capital. The rest of Asia, and indeed emerging markets in general, followed suit.

This meant a major shift in development strategy. In reality, however, this sea change simply replaced one type of dependency on the West with another. Instead of running trade deficits and depending on foreign capital to finance growth, Asian countries would henceforth run trade surpluses to generate growth, depending on foreign demand, and use the surpluses to become financially stronger and increase foreign lending. The significance wasn't realised at the time, but as Bernanke observed in the above passage, the Asian crisis marked the point at which the emerging world ceased to be reliant on Western capital, and instead became the suppliers of it.

With China and other countries choosing to run large trade surpluses and invest financial capital in advanced capital markets, there were only two choices open to the US and other Western nations. One was to accommodate the emerging market shift, and accept the need to run bigger trade deficits. The other was not to do so, but this could have resulted in greater trade friction. In the absence of internationally agreed codes of financial conduct and economic behaviour, there was a real threat of much weaker levels of global economic activity and growth. We chose to accommodate the emerging market strategy. The US, in particular, experienced a dramatic widening of its current account deficit to almost 7% of GDP, while China's surplus rose to about 10% of GDP. Global imbalances had reached unprecedented proportions, and the capital flows to which they gave rise were highly destabilising.

Today, sadly, nothing much has changed. By 2010, global imbalances had narrowed as the recession and weak growth in final demand brought about an improvement in the current account positions of the US and other advanced nations. Meanwhile, China's surplus fell to about 6% of GDP. Oil producing nations and others that ran surpluses all experienced a decline. But this was purely a cyclical phenomenon, created by the economic crisis. Away from the headlines, the underlying trends in national savings and investment that drive current account positions, that is external surpluses or deficits, were pointing to some all-too-familiar problems.

US and European households might have been saving more, but the sharp rise in governments' financial deficits offset this to a significant extent. And in China, the policies that were adopted to contain the impact of the crisis appear likely to maintain an exceptionally high external surplus in the medium term. China implemented some measures to boost domestic consumption, but the lion's share of the programmes was designed to boost investment, property and industry, with scant attention to the structural changes needed for a more meaningful and sustained increase in the purchasing power of its citizens.

Faced with the same global imbalances that existed before the crisis, the same choices are open to us. If rich countries, especially the US, accommodate sustained, large emerging market surpluses, it will be because their consumers return to their profligate ways and/or because their governments will not correct savings deficiencies by restraining public borrowing and spending. The outcome would almost certainly involve a fiscal and foreign exchange market crisis that would force economic retrenchment, and perhaps another serious recession or depression. During 2010, Greece, Spain and Portugal all succumbed in this way. If we do not accommodate them, the consequences would most probably entail a comprehensive global economic slowdown, in which protectionism and political tensions would flourish.

This debate, therefore, is only partly about the US and Europe. A high level of globalisation means that these two regions, comprising about half of global GDP, cannot break the policy deadlock on their own. They need partners. The other half, led by the BRICs, have a role to play too. If they remain intransigent or reluctant when it comes to structural reforms and exchange rate appreciation, they will compromise their own economic stability and security, and continue to destabilise the global financial system. Although most emerging markets snapped back quickly from the crisis in impressive style, they have yet to confront the real challenges arising from the change in global economic conditions.

Back from Armageddon

While it had been confidently asserted that Asia and other emerging markets would be able to stand aloof from the Western crisis, the shock waves proved to be far stronger than expected. For several months after the collapse of Lehman Brothers in September 2008, you could look out of the windows of any skyscraper in Singapore, the world's largest container port, and see hundreds of ships anchored offshore, mostly with nothing to on- or off-load. The container terminals were empty. Shipping, a vital life-sign of economic activity in Asia, buckled as the impact of the global financial freeze made trade finance more expensive and harder to arrange, and as the sudden lurch into recession in the West led to a collapse in the demand for Asian exports, sometimes by as much as 30–50%. The manufacturing supply chains in the continent, which were the bedrock of the region's economic success during the previous decade, now offered a darker picture, with negative shocks compounded as they spread from country to country and back again.

If world trade had collapsed for any length of time, globalisation would have gone into reverse and the principal victims in the global economy would have been the poorest developing countries, but they would also have included the BRICs, Turkey and Poland in Europe, Malaysia and Indonesia in Asia, Mexico and Chile in South America, and South Africa and Nigeria in Sub Sahara Africa.

Real GDP, which had still grown by 5.6% in all emerging and developing nations in 2008, eked out a 1% rise in 2009, but thanks only to China and India, which managed to grow by about 8.5% and 5.5%, respectively. Without China, Asia's growth rate dropped from 4.2% to 1.2%. In Latin America, growth of 4.2% in 2008 turned into a 2.4% contraction, with Brazilian GDP falling by 0.7%, and Argentine GDP falling by 2.5%. Growth in Russia, central Asia and Eastern Europe turned from 6% in 2008 to −6% in 2009. Countries in the Middle East and Africa, which had expanded by over 5% in 2008, managed only about 1.5% in 2009.

The shocks were felt all over the emerging world, especially by countries in Eastern Europe and central Asia, such as Hungary, Ukraine, Kazakhstan, Latvia, and Lithuania that had incurred large foreign currency borrowing. Countries that depended on oil and other commodity exports were damaged as prices collapsed. Crude oil, for example, which had reached an all-time high of $147 per barrel in July 2008, plunged to $40–50 per barrel over the winter of 2008–2009.

A widespread shortage of US dollars developed as Western banks pulled back on international loans and credit facilities, in turn squeezing the liquidity and lending capacity of banks in emerging markets. In the second half of 2008, loans made by Western banks to emerging markets fell by $800 billion, a drop of 14%. The credit squeeze and heightened fears of economic contraction led to a sharp rise in the value of the US dollar. This meant that any emerging banks or governments with US dollar loans to repay or refinance faced additional costs. Capital markets that channelled equity capital and other non-bank forms of finance, dried up. Bonds issued by emerging markets dropped from over $500 billion in 2007 to about $200 billion by 2009, foreign direct investment into emerging markets fell from $657 billion in 2007 to less than $300 billion in 2009, and portfolio investment (mainly equities and bonds) flows which had amounted to over $230 billion in 2007, flowed out by about the same amount in 2008. Worker remittances, that is, monies sent home by migrants working abroad, and upon which millions of families in developing countries depend, fell by nearly 30% from $232 billion in 2008 to $170 billion in 2009.

This wasn't supposed to happen. Emerging nations were believed to have decoupled from the advanced world, thanks to robust home-made sources of economic growth, and to the fact that they traded so much among themselves. The crisis demonstrated unequivocally the hollowness of the decoupling proposition. It indicated first, that those home-made sources of growth were over-shadowed by the dependence on exports, and second, that the high level of integration of emerging nations into global finance and manufacturing supply chains made them all vulnerable to recurring shocks arising anywhere in the chain.

In a note prepared in advance of the G20 meeting in April 2009, the World Bank warned that only 10% of all emerging and developing nations had a low level of vulnerability to the crisis. It said that the negative impact of the crisis on growth would drive an additional 53 million people into poverty (defined as income of less than $2 per day), on top of the 130–155 million who had suffered from the rise in food and fuel prices in 2008. It also predicted shockingly that if the setback to growth was not reversed quickly, an additional 200,000–400,000 babies might die each year between 2009 and 2015.

In the end, most emerging markets were able to shake off the worst effects of the crisis, and were spared the large-scale political and social turbulence that followed the Asian and other debt crises of the late 1990s and early 2000s. Many, especially China, implemented significant economic and financial stimulus programmes to offset the shocks. Russia committed around $200 billion to the support of its financial services industry, because banks ran short of liquidity and of foreign currency needed to service foreign debts. South Korea offered banks debt guarantees worth $100 billion. Several banks in India, South Korea and Hong Kong received new capital injections from the government, so that their solvency, measured by the ratio of asset to their capital, was strengthened. Moreover, the IMF introduced a new $50 billion standby loan programme for 14 countries, including Hungary, Pakistan and the Ukraine, and introduced flexible credit lines, without conditions, for Colombia, Mexico and Poland.

Gradually the global credit crunch eased thanks to the extraordinary financial and monetary policy measures adopted by the US Federal Reserve and other major central banks. This did not mean, though, that the decoupling proposition had been right all along.

It simply meant that at the time, most emerging nation governments, banks and households were strong enough, financially, to take measures to offset the negative shocks of the crisis. Simply put, emerging market balance sheets – that is the balance between the assets and the liabilities, of governments, banks, companies and households – were strong. By contrast, in Western economies for example, it was sometimes quipped that for banks in particular, there was nothing left on the right side of the balance sheet – that is, the assets – and nothing right on the left side, that is, the liabilities. Many emerging nations were running large balance of payments surpluses, and had accumulated significant foreign exchange reserves, and their budgetary positions were healthy. Brazil and India were able to increase social spending to help the poor and promote employment programmes. China's large stimulus and public infrastructure programmes almost certainly saved the country from even greater social unrest, especially among the 100–120 million pool of rural migrants. In many emerging markets, the response to the crisis by governments and employers was to cut wages, working hours and benefits so as to keep people in work[9].

The financial position of most major emerging markets at the time of the crisis, then, was quite different from the situation in many large Western economies, where the overhang of debt limited the capacity to respond to the crisis and the responsiveness of the economy in the face of countervailing measures. Balance sheets in emerging countries were, for the most part, clean because they had been forced to implement major regulatory and economic reforms after the Asian, Russian and Brazilian financial crises at the end of the 1990s. In future, they might not be so fortunate, because there is no guarantee that clean balance sheets will stay that way. In fact, in response to the crisis, governments increased their borrowing, and banks increased their loans, sometimes frantically, and nowhere more so than in China. If these trends were to continue, balance sheets would certainly become vulnerable again to sudden declines in asset prices or to other debt-related disturbances.

The difference between decoupling and having the wherewithal at the time to take countermeasures is important. The latter is why most emerging nations were able to stage an impressive, but cyclical, bounce back from the depths of the crisis. The former focuses more on the vulnerability of emerging markets to an economic structure, which relies on export-led growth, strong demand conditions in advanced nations, and advanced levels of financial and economic globalisation. Many of these conditions now hang in the balance, or are liable to be much less forceful in the coming years.

Many emerging markets boast large export sectors, with Malaysia, Vietnam, Thailand and Taiwan at 65–90% of GDP, and China, the Philippines and South Korea at 30–45%. But the structure of trade reveals an important weakness that these figures mask. Over 60% of Asian exports shipped within the continent, for example, are so-called intermediate goods – products that feed supply chains that normally end up in China, where goods are assembled and then exported to the West. Moreover, the Asian Development Bank has estimated that just 22% of all Asian exports end up as final demand in Asia. In other words, 78% of Asian exports end up outside Asia – 59% in the US, Europe and Japan, and 19% in other countries, directly or indirectly[10].

The heavy dependence on exports as one of the main drivers of growth and development has been a dynamic agent of change over the last 20 years during the heyday of accelerating globalisation. But the world pretended that widening global trade imbalances were somehow part of a new natural order of things in the global economy. In the end, though, this model proved to be the Achilles' heel of emerging markets when the Western financial and economic crisis erupted. The bounce back in emerging markets from the crisis has been robust – it's just that, in general, it's the wrong sort of bounce back.

What's wrong with it? Quite simply, it is not being accompanied by more radical changes in economic and social policies, which would lessen their dependence on exporting to the West over the medium to longer term. This should be a central feature of economic and political strategy in the largest trade-oriented emerging markets. The Western world is experiencing a protracted workout, in which the basis of the boom of the last 25 years is being consigned to history, and structural changes required for the next one will have to be made and nurtured. The challenge embraces not just banking and financial reforms, but the role and structure of credit and savings, the shift to a low carbon economy, the changes needed to accommodate rapid ageing, and the development, integration and exploitation of new bio-, nano-, and information technologies. In other words, the presumption that the Western economies will return to the status quo ante, with their past growth drivers intact, is a delusion. Consumer demand growth in the West may now be a shadow of what it has been, and it follows, therefore, that emerging markets will be forced to look elsewhere for their growth drivers in the future.

The crisis has taught us about the perils of global interconnectedness, but also about how to take advantage of such mutual dependence to implement a globally coordinated response embracing macroeconomic and regulatory agendas. It has warned us that international institutions should be adequately resourced, and that emerging markets with large surpluses should play a big role in this regard. It has also reminded us that institutions such as the IMF and the World Bank need to be much more than just financial soup kitchens for the least creditworthy nations, and to play an active role in global economic governance. Perhaps we should take a leaf from the book of climate change. Notwithstanding the arguments that have erupted over the accuracy of its data and research methods, the Intergovernmental Panel on Climate Change serves as a model of a global body that doesn't make policy *per se*, but that has served as a catalyst for the evolution of the debate about climate change and about how we should make and coordinate policies to address it. Similarly, we have an opportunity now to demand that the G20 forge a similar institution for global economic governance, where the costs and benefits of international economic cooperation or dissension could be spelled out clearly.

The journey to Armageddon and back has not been completed. If, for political reasons, we cannot resolve the problem of global imbalances, it may simply have been a foretaste of worse to come. The translation of an old Chinese proverb, 'may you live in interesting times', could not be more apt. It was never meant as a salutation or gratuitous comment, but as a curse.

Chapter Four

Atomic Clouds of Footloose Funds

At a meeting of the Board of Governors of the Asian Development Bank in 2006, the Indian Prime Minister, Dr Manmohan Singh, said, 'The present level of global imbalances cannot be sustained forever. It calls for action both from countries having current account surpluses and those having current account deficits.' The call fell on deaf ears.

Many economists in the private and official sectors had drawn attention to the potentially destabilising effects of chronically unbalanced trade and the accompanying expansion of capital flows – the atomic cloud of footloose funds cited in the last chapter. Yet, there was no meaningful response among policy makers. The world economy was booming, and with such a favourable back-drop, policy makers assumed complacently that things would work themselves out in the end. They seemed to take the same sort of view as senior executives in the banking industry; former Citigroup Chief Executive Officer, Chuck Prince, famously said in an interview in July 2007 that 'when the music stops, in terms of liquidity, things will be complicated. But as long as the music is playing, you've got to get up and dance. We're still dancing'. Citibank was to pay a heavy price for such complacency, as indeed did the world economy for the inertia of policy makers.

Global imbalances were an obsession for economists in the IMF, the Bank for International Settlements (the central bankers' central bank, based in Basel, Switzerland), leading economic commentators and private sector economists for much of the 2000s. They made a cameo appearance in the last chapter to put the Armageddon experience into context, but here I will look at the issue in more detail, examining why they have become excessive, how the status quo predisposes China, in particular, to risks, and the continuing dangers we face by leaving them unresolved.

The tentacles of the financial crisis stretch beyond the realm of the economy, encompassing matters as far-reaching as national security. They have demonstrated the vulnerability of America's dependence on China and a few other countries for foreign borrowing, and the risks that China, in particular, poses to itself and to the world economy by accumulating financial power in this way.

One of the many consequences of the crisis has been an unprecedented peacetime expansion in public borrowing and public debt. It was crucial to allow this to happen, because private sector spending and borrowing ground to a halt, and may not resume with any significance for a very long time. In the UK, public borrowing rose to about 13% of GDP in 2009, and in the US it rose to about 11% of GDP. There is no question that the issue of public indebtedness will cast shadows over, and generate serious challenges for, Western economies for a decade or so.

If the US budget deficit remains excessive over the next few years, and the Congress lacks the will or cohesion to address its decline over a period of time, the US could face new and serious financial crises, when it is already weakened by the consequences of the last one. The US current account deficit could rise to over 15% of GDP by 2030, or more than US$5000 billion per year, and its external debt could rise from $3500 billion to around $50,000 billion, at which point it would represent 140% of GDP and seven times the value of its exports[1]. An outcome such as this would cause any emerging market to collapse into crisis, and not even the US could get away with it. The US would have to act to prevent such an outcome voluntarily, or be forced to react to it under extreme duress. Nevertheless, it shows that the world still faces an extremely dangerous threat to the stability of the financial system. US citizens, accustomed to more-or-less steady increases in prosperity and fundamentally optimistic in their outlook, could pay a heavy price in terms of living standards and jobs.

It has become quite evident that major emerging market governments are distinctly uncomfortable about the status quo in global finance. To date, though, their concerns and criticisms have been somewhat superficial and ill founded. For example, the Governor of the Peoples Bank of China, Zhou Xiaochuan, stated in March 2009 that the US dollar should be replaced as the world's reserve currency by the Special Drawing Right (SDR), which is an IMF accounting unit comprising the US dollar, Euro, Japanese Yen and British Pound. He probably had no expectation that this would happen, certainly not any time soon, but he clearly wanted to make a point, namely that a global financial system based around the US dollar is now an anachronism. He may be right.

Others have gone further and criticised America's attempts to spend its way out of recession, to reform healthcare at this time, and to employ large financial stimulus to stabilise the economy. China's chief banking regulator, Liu Mingkang, took aim at the Federal Reserve in November 2009 by saying that a weak US dollar and low US interest rates risked creating a new global asset bubble. These criticisms reflect a frustration about the state of global finance, centred on the US, but they are hardly constructive. They also serve to deflect discussion about any role or responsibility that China and other emerging markets have for the creation of global imbalances.

Let us look more closely at global imbalances, bearing in mind that China and other emerging peer countries were the ones piling up big surpluses, and the US was running large deficits. Never before has a poor country, China, ever lent so much to the richest country on Earth, and never has the US been so reliant on a single creditor with whom it vies for political and strategic influence.

The $11 trillion elephant in the room

Unbalanced global trade is an integral part of capitalism and globalisation. The growth in demand and productive capacity is always going to vary across countries and within economies, and these variations show up as trade surpluses and deficits. Surplus nations have capital to lend to the rest of the world, while deficit countries borrow that capital to finance their shortfalls. Chronically unbalanced trade occurs when these surpluses and deficits become both very large and structurally entrenched, giving rise to unsustainable flows of capital and endangering financial stability. In the run up to the crisis, the state of global imbalances could be discerned from the rise in the US external deficit to 7% of GDP, and in China's surplus to 10% of GDP. Typically, alarm bells are supposed to ring when these surpluses and deficits move beyond 3% of GDP for any length of time.

As global trade imbalances became progressively larger, so did the volume of capital movements. According to the Bank for International Settlements, net capital flows to 23 large emerging market economies amounted to about $1 billion a year in the 1980s, helping their foreign exchange reserves to rise by about $11.5 billion. In the 1990s, capital flows strengthened, and their reserves grew by $62 billion a year. These trends continued in the 2000s, so that in 2007 alone, total capital inflows amounted to $1440 billion, net capital inflows amounted to $439 billion, and reserves grew by nearly $1000 billion[2]. Much of the growth in capital inflows was accounted for by foreign direct investment, but financial capital became increasingly important, and half the growth in foreign exchanges reserves could be traced to the growing surpluses in the current account of the balance of payments.

The strong increase in the foreign exchange reserves of emerging markets has become an important symbol of global imbalances and of the phenomenon of capital flowing around the world, far out of proportion to underlying transactions in world trade and direct investment. This, though, is a very recent phenomenon.

Foreign exchange reserves are mostly denominated in US dollars and are held by national central banks, in the form of bank deposits or short- to medium-term government or other highly rated bonds. Globally, the US dollar component varies from year to year, but is typically around 65%. Some richer nations hold significant amounts of Euros, and more modest amounts of Japanese Yen, Sterling and

Swiss francs. Countries that peg their exchange rates to the US dollar, or that are essentially part of a US dollar-zone, such as many countries in Asia and Latin America, tend to have most of their reserves in US dollars. In Eastern Europe and the Baltic republics, by contrast, Euros figure more prominently.

Central banks hold foreign exchange so that nations can always pay for imports in case something untoward happens. Typically, they are supposed to hold at least three months' worth of imports. For example, the terrible Indian Ocean earthquake, or Asian tsunami, that happened at the end of 2004, devastated the fishing and coastal agricultural industries in many countries, including Sri Lanka. At the time this quite poor country held only two months' worth of imports in its reserves, and was obliged to ask the IMF to freeze repayments on loans for a limited period. Natural disasters, labour unrest, commodity price volatility, and political and economic instability could all figure as bona fide reasons for countries to hold enough foreign exchange reserves to get through tough times. But how much is enough? And how much is too much?

Global foreign exchange reserves increased from $2000 billion in 2000 to just over $8000 billion at the end of 2009. Virtually all of the increase was accounted for by 18 emerging markets: China, Hong Kong, Taiwan, South Korea, Singapore, Indonesia, Malaysia and Thailand, India, Brazil, Argentina and Mexico, Russia, Poland and Turkey, and Algeria, Libya and Nigeria. The 18 countries combined now account for 65% of world reserves, compared with 44% in 2000 (Figure 4.1).

The BRICs' reserves rose from $331 billion to $3300 billion, or from 13% to 41% of world reserves. Of this, China's reserves increased over this period from $168 billion in 2000 to over $2400 billion. Russia's reserves rose from $32 billion to nearly $400

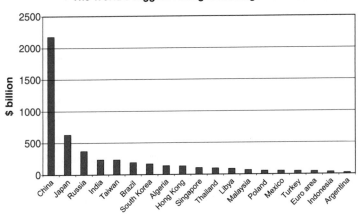

The World's Biggest Foreign Exchange Holders 2009

Figure 4.1 FX reserves in US dollars (billion)
Source: IMF

billion, though they had peaked at $600 billion in 2008 at the height of the oil price boom. Brazil's went from $32 billion to $225 billion, and India's rose from $38 billion to $275 billion. Among advanced economies, only Japan saw a material rise in reserves, from $354 billion to just under $1000 billion.

It simply wasn't in the script, however, for emerging nations to amass reserves on the scale that occurred, and these are not the only manifestation of the massive accumulation of financial capital by emerging markets. Many set up Sovereign Wealth Funds (SWFs), which are separate state agencies created to invest some of the surpluses generated by global trade in a wider range of assets than just bonds. SWFs receive much of their financing from balance of payments surpluses and foreign exchange operations. Some SWFs, notably in oil and commodity-producing nations, invest to provide income streams and capital growth that can be tapped to sustain government and private spending in the event that commodity prices fall. Others, like those in China, Russia, South Korea, Hong Kong and Singapore, have a different purpose, namely to invest today's assets for the benefit of future generations.

In 2009, there were 50 SWFs, with assets of about $3800 billion, but about 11 SWFs accounted for approximately three quarters of the total assets. These large SWFs were headed up by the Abu Dhabi Investment Authority, and followed by Norway's Government Pension Fund-Global, the Saudi Arabian Monetary Agency-Foreign Holdings and China's State Administration of Foreign Exchange Investment Company, and China Investment Corporation. The other major funds included another Chinese agency, two in Singapore, and others in Hong Kong, Russia and Kuwait. These funds hold assets of between $120 billion and $630 billion. The remaining 39 SWFs typically hold much smaller, though still significant, assets and while they include agencies in Australia, Ireland, France, the US and Canada, the bulk is in emerging nations, and quite concentrated in the oil and gas sector. In fact, about $2300 billion of all SWF assets are owned by oil and gas SWFs.

So long as global imbalances persist, SWFs will continue to expand, building large portfolios of financial and physical assets around the world. Leading investment banks think that SWFs could amass total assets of $10–15,000 billion by 2015. This depends on the two vital assumptions, however: first, that global imbalances persist as now and, second, that commodity prices continue to rise. These assumptions are actually quite unlikely to hold. If the world cannot sort out the imbalances problem, it is inevitable that there will be further acute financial turbulence.

The distortions in the global economy and financial markets created by the investment of $11,000 billion of assets accumulated by emerging markets continue. Ultimately, global imbalances can only be reduced in a positive way if the extra saving that richer countries will be obliged to make are offset by lower savings in emerging nations. That means extensive changes in policy. Will China be able to embark on large-scale economic reform without first embracing political reform? Will it have the will and capacity to implement reforms in a timely and positive way? And, if not, what? History offers us some insights.

Twentieth-century imbalances

Global financial crises have different scripts and actors, but they all coalesce around common structural phenomena. These tend to be associated with irresolvable conflicts between domestic and international obligations that emerging or new economic powers face in pursuing monetary and economic policies. A pattern has evolved in which newly important economic powers, which have immature financial systems and governance, emphasise export-led economic growth and suppress the value of their currencies at inflexible levels. This strategy may fulfil specific domestic goals and aspirations, but may be incompatible with domestic stability and global financial order. In the 20th century, the US, Germany and Japan all pursued monetary, economic and trade policies that contributed to global savings and investment imbalances, unstable foreign exchange markets, asset bubbles and, in the end, acute financial and economic distress[3].

The political and institutional failure to manage the imbalances in the 1920s merit particular attention. As the basic contours are sketched out here, you may want to think simultaneously about more contemporary parallels, where modern-day China and the US represent the former US and Europe respectively.

After the suspension of the Gold Standard due to the First World War, the US rejoined in 1919, six years before Britain. It believed, along with the established orthodoxy, that it was essential to the restoration of a normally functioning international economic system. But the global system had been unbalanced by the war. America now owned a rapidly growing proportion of the world's gold bullion reserves, which had allowed its money supply to inflate. In Europe, on the other hand, there was a chronic shortage of gold, but too much money that had been created to finance the mountain of war debts.

European countries needed gold to help service debts and finance economic reconstruction, but the global system, now under strong American influence, didn't allow this to happen. America was in pole position to help put the global system back together again, because the UK, along with France and Germany, emerged from the First World War indebted and weakened economically and politically. Across the Atlantic, the US was none of these. It was the 'new kid on the economic block', and the world's largest owner of monetary gold reserves. It was a rapidly growing and high-saving economic power, riding the tide of the new automobile and other consumer product industries, and pursuing policies that favoured its exports.

The contrast between the old pre-1914 world and the new one was stark and caused a major dilemma for the US in the 1920s – one it never resolved: whether and how to execute a monetary policy that would support the operation of the Gold Standard and the reconstruction in Europe, or whether to prioritise stable inflation at home and control the stock market speculation that accompanied the Roaring Twenties. The latter would have called for tighter credit policies, the former for easier policies. The Federal Reserve leaned firmly towards easier policies but ended up doing both at inappropriate moments.

Note that at the time, the US Federal Reserve System was a very young and inexperienced institution, having been founded by Congress in 1913. The Federal Reserve was split politically. The Act that led to its creation empowered the members of the Federal Reserve Board in Washington, but the Board was in almost continuous conflict with members of the twelve regional Federal Reserve banks over monetary policy and operations.

Benjamin Strong, Governor of the Federal Reserve Bank of New York, favoured greater independence for the regional Federal Reserve banks, and until his untimely death in 1928 supported easier monetary policies. Strong's view was designed, in theory at least, to allow gold inflows to the US to be recycled back to Europe, where they were needed for economic reconstruction.

The jostling for power and control over monetary policy, though, wasn't confined to the internal workings of the infant Federal Reserve. The Secretary of Commerce, one Herbert Hoover, also had a strong interest in how the Federal Reserve conducted its business. Hoover, in fact, was a staunch believer in tight credit policies to keep a lid on inflation and stock market euphoria at home, and he had allies on the Board. When his supporters eventually got their way in 1928–29, after Strong's death, they unleashed a financial firestorm.

But the US still had the problem about the imbalance in gold reserves. In fact, Strong made the situation worse. Gold kept flowing in to the US during the 1920s, and he felt interest rates were low enough already. He didn't want to compromise low US inflation by lowering interest rates still further. Instead, he simply removed the gold from circulation, so that the money supply would remain contained. US interest rates were pinned to levels that were too high for the smooth working of the Gold Standard, and too low to prevent a steady, and eventually excessive, creation of credit.

After 1925, the conflict about what sort of monetary policy to run intensified when Britain, with encouragement from the US, returned to the Gold Standard – at the wrong exchange rate level – one that pressured Britain to deflate and try to lower prices, wages and employment. That stimulated even more credit and asset inflation in the US. The equity market in the US alternated between bubbling and going off the boil until about 1926, before staging a powerful rally, later spurred by a modest half percent cut in interest rates in the middle of 1927. The Federal Reserve did raise interest rates between February and July 2008, and again in early 1929, but to no avail. By the time the Fed decided to try and dampen down the equity market, it was probably too late. Then by acting indecisively and riven by factions, it stood by, as if a bystander, as the equity market reached for the sky and then crashed.

This outcome was the result, in large measure, of America's failed attempts to reconcile its domestic and Gold Standard obligations. Alan Greenspan, reviewing the period, wrote that:

'The excess credit, which the Fed pumped into the economy, spilled over into the stock market – triggering a fantastic speculative boom.

Belatedly, Federal Reserve officials attempted to sop up the excess (bank) reserves and finally succeeded in braking the boom. But it was too late: By 1929, the speculative imbalances had become so overwhelming that the attempt precipitated a sharp retrenching and a consequent demoralizing of business confidence. As a result, the American economy collapsed. Great Britain fared even worse, and rather than absorb the full consequences of her previous folly, she abandoned the gold standard completely in 1931, tearing asunder what remained of the fabric of confidence and inducing a world-wide series of bank failures. The world economies plunged into the Great Depression of the 1930s'[4].

The return to gold represented an attempt to fix exchange rates that were inappropriate, and caused recurring tensions for the US and European nations as they sought to balance or prioritise domestic and external financial goals. The US could have abandoned the Gold Standard earlier, or at the very least pushed for more flexibility and allowed its exchange rate to revalue in terms of gold. Unable or unwilling to act as a leader in global finance, as Britain had done before 1914, and without the kind of agreed rules that characterised the Bretton Woods system from 1946–1971, the US left its footprints on the financial chaos that was to follow, not least on itself.

The second example comes from the 1960s and 1970s, during the last years of the Bretton Woods system. The US was experiencing rising inflation and trade deficits, and its overall economic performance paled next to that of Germany and Japan, which had been expanding at an annual rate of 6% and 10% respectively. When the first oil price shock occurred in 1970–1971, the US economy buckled, and the Federal Reserve reduced interest rates from over 9% to less than 4%. The US dollar should have declined, but to defend the fixed US dollar price of gold at $35 per ounce, the export-hungry nations of Germany and Japan both experienced significant increases in their foreign exchange reserves, which trebled as a share of their GDP between 1968–1971. Eventually, they became wary of the inflationary consequences of accumulating US dollars in their reserves, and wanted to switch some of those US dollars into gold. In the summer of 1971, however, foreign holdings of US dollars were already three times the value of America's gold reserves, held at the US Bullion Depository, located near the US army base of Fort Knox in Kentucky, and known colloquially as Fort Knox.

Fort Knox was simply not up to the task of meeting the demand for gold. In 1970–1971, the US was faced with increasing pressure on the gold reserves, a growing balance of payments deficit, and rising inflation resulting from the failure to fund adequately large-scale expenditures on the Vietnam War and social programmes at home. Eventually, in August 1971, President Nixon closed the gold 'window' – symbolising the US commitment to buy and sell gold at the fixed price of $35 per ounce – and devalued the US dollar. He also announced a temporary freeze on wages and prices and a 10% tax surcharge on all imports. These actions ended the convertibility of US dollars into gold, and effectively killed off the post-Second World War Bretton Woods global system, though it would limp on until the advent of floating exchange rates in 1973.

As in the 1920s, the established power, this time the US, had to manage external financial tensions with Germany and Japan, as a result of structurally unbalanced trade. Germany and Japan were mercantilist and rising economic powers and, like the US in the earlier period, they were unable or unwilling to pursue the kind of reforms that might have allowed them to pursue alternative economic growth strategies, and take more global financial responsibility.

The burden of global rebalancing fell exclusively on the US, and although the 1970s saw two oil price shocks that contributed to a decade of unusually high inflation, there is little question that the financial and credit policies followed by the US, Germany and Japan beforehand exacerbated it.

Japan in the 1980s offers an even stronger example of such conflicted objectives, as it grew in economic stature and rivalled US hegemony. Japan was also a high saving, fast-growing, protectionist competitor. Its banks' assets were the biggest in the world, and its companies, especially in the steel and automobile sectors, were buying up the world. Yet it had no wish to entertain any responsibility for the global financial system, and for many years it maintained an undervalued currency, often necessitating intervention in the foreign exchange market to stop the currency from rising.

For the first part of the 1980s, Japan didn't have to try too hard to keep the Yen weak, because the US dollar became unjustifiably strong as a result of the stern and successful anti-inflationary monetary policies introduced by the then Chairman of the Federal Reserve, Paul Volcker. Ultimately, the Group of 5 countries – the US, Japan, Germany, France and the UK – agreed to meet in New York in September 1985 at the Plaza Hotel, and came up with the so-called Plaza Accord. The US persuaded Japan to loosen its monetary policy and consider structural financial reforms, got a commitment from Germany to cut taxes, and managed to secure a general agreement by all to intervene in the foreign exchange markets to depreciate the value of the US dollar, especially against the Japanese Yen and the German Deutschemark.

By 1987, the US tried to draw a line under the US dollar, which had been falling too far, too fast. At a meeting at the Louvre in

Paris, Japan and Germany were persuaded to play the role of economic 'locomotive' – that is, they agreed to stimulate their economies directly by cutting interest rates and using budgetary policy more actively. These measures were expected to cause their exchange rates to stabilise or even weaken a little, effectively bringing the US dollar depreciation phase to an end.

The idea was to share the burden of stabilising the foreign exchange markets between the US on the one hand, and Japan and Germany on the other. Had the burden fallen solely on the US, the negative economic consequences on economic growth and employment would almost certainly have been greater. However, the right time for action was years earlier. By the summer of 1987, there was still upward pressure on US interest rates, but for reasons that remain unclear to this day, Germany and Japan both increased their interest rates. When the German Bundesbank raised its official interest rate in October 1987, the US responded by threatening to remove the floor under the US dollar. The world went into a stock market meltdown.

The 1987 stock market crash had no lasting consequences for the global economy. Yet it was to prove a way-station to a much bigger crisis that erupted in Japan in 1990, the aftermath of which still haunts this country today. The Japanese Yen kept on getting stronger, partly because its trade surplus proved stubbornly large, trade friction with the US and the EU increased, and Japan chose to pump large sums of money into its banking system and economy in order to stop its exchange rate from rising. This continued for the most part of the 1980s, fuelling an investment and real estate boom that has become legendary. Famously, before the bust, the 7.4 square kilometres of the Imperial Palace in Tokyo were valued at more than the entire stock of real estate in California.

Once again, the emerging power, Japan, was too beholden to its export-driven economic structure, and too eager to take the risk of loose domestic money and credit creation as it attempted to stop its currency from appreciating against the US dollar and other currencies. Rather than embark on structural reforms designed to switch away from exports towards domestic economic growth, Japan tried to reconcile its monetary conflicts the wrong way. The liquidity it created fuelled the mania stage of the credit boom and asset bubble. Towards the end, in 1989, the Bank of Japan, which controlled interest rates, defied the Ministry of Finance, which controlled policy on the Yen, by beginning, belatedly, to increase interest rates. That was the catalyst, and when credit and asset price inflation burst in 1990, the outcome was a crash that we now know to have preceded Japan's lost decade. Realistically, it is more like two lost decades – and still counting.

In each of the three examples – America in the 1920s, Germany and Japan in the 1960s, and Japan in the 1980s – financial tensions centred around the role of exchange rates in the global financial system, but they reflected economic and financial distortions in their own economies, and imbalances with the established economic hegemonies of the time. In each case, although the economic position of the hegemonies was an integral part of the problem, they were never able to resolve the imbalances on their own. The other part of the problem, therefore, was that the emerging powers failed to reconcile domestic and external policy responsibilities. They rejected structural reforms designed to lower their dependence on exports, and did not countenance sufficient or any exchange rate flexibility as a means of changing their growth models. In the cases of the US and Japan, in particular, the outcomes included credit inflation, asset bubbles and financial and economic stress.

The new imbalances

The Asian crisis of 1997–1998 was the starting point for the imbalances of the 21st century. Emerging markets, shocked by their vulnerability to capital flight and the weak protection afforded by low levels of foreign exchange reserves, resolved to build up a war chest of reserves so as to be able to cope better in any future turbulence. To do this, they would have to aim for much stronger trade and current account positions. So, for example, while emerging markets typically achieved small current account deficits or surpluses of between −2% to +1% of GDP between the 1960s and 2000, their aggregate surplus shot up to about 4–5% of GDP, or roughly $700 billion per year, in the years following 2000.

The surge in the surpluses, especially in Asia, reflects exceptionally large increases in savings. This doesn't mean that consumption in emerging countries has been weak. The evidence is firmly that consumer spending and living standards in most major emerging markets have continued to rise. Over the last 40 years, the share of consumption in emerging market GDP has averaged about 60%, much lower than in the US and the UK, but not far off the average for advanced economies.

However, after the Asian crisis, important changes began to happen. GDP growth began to take off after about 2002. Although consumer spending grew, the share of consumption in GDP started and continued to decline. In China, it has fallen from 45% in 2000 to 36%, while in Russia, it has declined from 54% to 45%. In Saudi Arabia, it has fallen from nearly 50% to 25%. These developments mean that non-consumer parts of the economy have been expanding much more rapidly. While the growth acceleration in most countries came from trade or from the impact of rising commodity prices, it arose in China because of the expansion of investment and exports. Before 2002, China's exports amounted to about $250 billion, and its current account surplus was less than $20 billion. By 2008, these had grown to $1300 billion and $400 billion, respectively.

Today, the average annual income in Asia's emerging markets is about $3000. If you drill down a level, however, it is easy to see that popular stories of rising living standards for many urban dwellers contrast with the more difficult lives of poorer workers and slum inhabitants, and most rural citizens. In China and India, there are enough high-income households to support the sales and activities of global luxury brand companies, but nowhere near enough to support broad-based domestic growth. Despite the fact that visitors to emerging market cities can be in awe at the proliferation of luxury shopping malls, high performance automobiles and transportation systems, private consumption in general has not been able to keep up with the much faster growth in production, import substitution and exports championed by large, favoured companies.

The dominance of large industrial export conglomerates in emerging markets is not uncommon. To some extent, this is because of still low levels of economic development, relatively immature financial systems and capital markets, and the advantages of size that accrue as economic development proceeds. Politics and political interests, however, also play a key role, whether the beneficiaries are state-controlled, as in China, or family owned, for example in Hong Kong, India, Malaysia and South Korea. Capital and wealth in many emerging countries tend to be concentrated among political elites, whether directly as part of the government apparatus, or whether they benefit indirectly from political leverage and favour. To a significant degree, therefore, global imbalances to which emerging markets are contributing arise from a strong emphasis on export industries, which, in turn owe their status to political structures and decision-making. It bears repetition, therefore, that it is hard to imagine that global rebalancing in emerging markets can occur – that is, a shift away from exports towards higher levels of domestic demand – without political changes as well.

In the case of many emerging markets, especially smaller ones, this doesn't really matter much. If their economic and political structures remained the same for another 50 years, and if they continued to form important parts of global manufacturing supply chains, the world would be fine. The nub of the problem turns out to be that the lion's share of the accumulated current account surpluses since 2000 have accrued to China and oil-producing countries.

Oil-producing nations are in a different league than China. They received the windfall benefits of the sharp rise in oil prices in the years before the crisis, and still benefit from elevated prices for oil and gas. However, some oil producers, like those in the Gulf, have small populations and little diversity in their economic structures. Others, for example, Saudi Arabia and Nigeria, are more populous, and their young adult populations are expected to rise strongly in the next one to two decades. However, for the most part, their financial systems are relatively undeveloped, their wealth is determined by global energy prices, and their impact on the global economy affects all oil consumers, emerging as well as advanced countries. As relatively small or undiversified economies, they cannot offset their surpluses by boosting aggregate demand at home, except over the very longterm by promoting greater economic reforms to increase employment and economic diversity, as a hedge against the time when oil reserves dwindle or become exhausted.

China is different because of its economic and financial size, its manufacturing exports, and its status as one of the world's biggest lenders. Its exports dropped by 17% in 2009, but started to pick up again in 2010. To fully comprehend China's accomplishments, consider that in 2000 China's share of world exports was only 3%. Today it is about 10%, above the 8% share of the US, and if the last decade's growth rate in exports were sustained, China would account for close to 15% of world exports by 2014, and 25% by 2020. This would eclipse even America's dominance of world trade in the aftermath of the Second World War, and amount to more than double Japan's share in 1986.

In 2000, China had net external debts of around 9% of GDP but, thanks to its trade performance, it now has external assets of over 30% of GDP, with foreign currency reserves being the largest component. This is bizarre for a country with a per capita income of about $3000, or less than 10% of what it is in advanced nations. It is important to appreciate why and how China's savings have increased to create this situation.

The export share of GDP in China rose from 22% in 2002 to 38% before the crisis, and the trade surplus share of GDP trebled to 10%. These shares fell back in 2009, but in the absence of radical changes in China's savings and investment trends, they will almost certainly rebound.

Chinese households save a lot, roughly a quarter of their income compared with about 17% in the mid-1990s. However, given the scale of the rise in overall GDP, the savings rate in terms of GDP has remained relatively stable at around 11–12% of GDP for 20 years. It has never been lower than 10% of GDP, and only exceptionally higher than 12% for a brief period in the late 1990s.

So why do the Chinese save so much? Many of the economic and social reasons are explored in the next chapter, but for now consider just three factors. First, China's population has been enjoying not only rising incomes but also a significant fall in the dependency ratio of younger people on the working age population, from 55% in 1985 to under 40% in 2008. This phenomenon is a classic pointer to higher levels of savings. As the number of children declines relative to the number of workers, there is less demand for parents to spend their incomes on the younger generation. And as those parents move into their 40s and 50s, their incomes rise, and so do their savings. Second, the level and breadth of social service and social security provision by the Government remains quite low, even though the authorities have slowly been extending coverage. Third, the stickiness in high savings rates reflects the rising private burden of spending on housing, education and health care. This reflects the removal of social protection by state companies and institutions in the wake of reforms in the past, but also rising income levels, population ageing, and the development of strictly limited consumer credit mechanisms.

Nevertheless, it isn't actually Chinese household savings that have driven the national savings rate up from 40% to more than 50% of GDP since 2000. Instead, it is the sharp rise in the profits and savings of China's enterprises, especially in the steel, automobile and other heavy industry sectors. The rise in enterprise savings accounts for almost all of the increase in the current account surplus, from 2% to 11% of GDP. This didn't just happen but was the result of deliberate policies to promote heavy industry and exports that emphasised cheap credit, an artificially low cost of capital, and the maintenance of an undervalued exchange rate. Because Chinese companies have weak ownership structures, and cannot or are not allowed to pass on their profits to households in the form of dividends or other claims on their earnings, the only course open to them is to hoard them and to continuously re-invest them in productive and export capacity – under state direction, of course.

China has been experiencing a 'supply shock', in which its industrial base has expanded rapidly. The beginning of over-investment is now developing. Once China was able to satisfy its own demands for steel, cement and so on, excess production found its way to foreign markets in the form of exports, that challenged competitors for global market share. The $600 billion official response to the financial crisis in China was focused on spending and lending programmes, many of which were designed to benefit established sectors and help them stabilise their exports. Less than 4% of the announced programmes were earmarked for spending on education and healthcare. Social spending in these areas could release a lot of discretionary consumer spending by China's households. Property construction, which is the biggest single driver of domestic demand for steel, automobiles and related industrial materials did benefit significantly as the authorities attempted to arrest the 2008 fall in Chinese housing activity. This, however, should not detract from the deeply entrenched structural characteristics of China's high savings, and its export-oriented growth model.

The global economy doesn't have that much time to allow China to change in an incremental fashion. The pressure on China to show visible signs of its willingness to change is growing and much of this pressure revolves around reform of the exchange rate regime, and policy initiatives to change economic tack towards domestic demand. If China were to do these things, the prospects for global rebalancing would doubtless improve considerably. The fact that it is resistant to such change only underscores the largely domestic focus of the Chinese authorities, and the financial stability risks it is running by trying to sustain the status quo.

The end of the renminbi regime

China's foreign exchange reserves stand at $2500 billion, or about 50% of its GDP. If the US dollar assets of state banks and China Investment Corporation are included, total reserves may already be over $3000 billion. No one needs so much in a foreign exchange armoury. To address the surge in reserves, in 2007 China created its SWF – China Investment Corporation – ostensibly to allow some of the reserves at least to be managed more comprehensively and over a longer time frame than if they had remained in the central bank. There is, however, still no coherent policy as yet to address the greatest ever accumulation of foreign exchange reserves in economic history.

China's foreign exchange reserves can be viewed as a symbol of China's financial power, and of the leverage it commands over the US, as its most important creditor. But there's another way to look at this, which is to see China's financial armoury as the product of its dependence on the US economy and on the US consumerism of the last 10 years. If the US economy is now restructuring, China will have to change. Otherwise, it could be on the receiving end of a shock to the value of its reserves at the very least, as the US dollar falls in value. More significantly, if it doesn't change its exchange rate policy, the tendency to even bigger trade surpluses and more unsustainable credit expansion will increase. Worst of all for China, it could end up being the target of much stiffer trade protectionism, which really would go to the heart of the economic growth upon which the legitimacy of its rulers depends.

Before 1994, the RMB was not convertible into other currencies, and there were multiple exchange rates for different kinds of transactions. Sweeping financial reforms were then introduced, the exchange rates were unified at RMB 8.7 to the US dollar, and controls over payments for exports, imports, interest, profits and dividends (otherwise known as current account transactions) were abolished. By July 2005, US pressure on China to 'do something' about what was perceived to be its deliberately undervalued exchange rate resulted in a move towards a crawling peg arrangement (tightly controlled flexibility), and an immediate 2.1% revaluation of the RMB. In 2007, some capital transactions were also relaxed for industrial companies, banks and tourists. Nevertheless, more capital continued to flow in to China than flowed out, and by the time the crisis erupted the exchange had risen to about RMB 6.8 to the US dollar, or about 21% higher than in 2005. Fearful of the global recession and the threat to exports, China then again pegged the exchange rate until June 2010, when the Peoples' Bank of China announced that it would restore immediately the pre-crisis crawling peg arrangement.

The central bank rather than the State Council or a top ranking Communist Party official announced this decision, and so the significance of the move is uncertain. The move came just a week before the G20 summit meeting in Toronto, where the US and a few major emerging markets, including Brazil and India, were expected to put the spotlight on China's intransigence on exchange rate flexibility. Moreover, new pressure had been accumulating in the US Senate for trade sanctions to be imposed. Most likely, therefore, the announcement was timed to spike the guns of the US and a few other critics of its exchange rate policy.

There is a long-running and contentious debate about the extent to which the RMB is undervalued, and about how much of a change might be needed to have a meaningful impact on China's surplus and the US deficit[5]. For some people, the RMB could be as little as 10% undervalued, or even at the correct level. They think a tightly controlled currency, with minor adjustments over time, is appropriate provided that China uses monetary policy in support of this goal, and encourages much greater capital outflows by banks and other financial companies. For others, the RMB may be under-valued by 25–50%, but there is no unanimity as to whether even a 20–30% revaluation of the RMB would play a significant role in reducing global imbalances.

Even though economists argue at great length about their the-ories and models of exchange rate and trade competitiveness, changing the RMB regime is only partly about trade. More impor-tantly, the RMB regime, rather than any specific exchange rate level, represents an important symbol of China's economic devel-opment strategy, and of the risks it is running with regard to its own financial stability.

China's economy over-emphasises exports, and the country over-invests to support profits and jobs in the export sector. By contrast, too little attention is given to ways of supporting a rising share of consumption in total GDP, and greater production of goods and services aimed at realising this goal. A relatively inflexible RMB is, in effect, a tax on consumption and a subsidy to exports. While it is certainly true that this model of development has allowed China to compete effectively in global markets, and serviced her need for rapid economic growth in the past, the crisis has turned this argument upside down. This is predominantly because the US will no longer be willing or able to play an accommodating role by running the deficits that were the other side of China's surpluses. It is quite possible that China is now compromising its hard-won trade status and benefits for the sake of an undervalued exchange rate that may, in any case, be unsustainable. China's vested interests should be to take the sting out of the issue altogether.

In any event, the RMB regime has had two other undesirable effects. First, the surpluses, which the regime has helped to create and consolidate, have kept domestic Chinese and global interest rates artificially low, and distorted the path of Chinese economic development, and of global finance. These issues have become more transparent since the crisis occurred.

Strictly speaking, as China became globalised, its plentiful supplies of labour and relative shortage of capital should have caused real (inflation-adjusted) interest rates to rise, reflecting the relative scarcity of the capital compared to labour. But the pegged exchange rate and the obsession about exports meant that this could not happen. China accumulated financial surpluses instead. These have ended up in the US, where they helped to suppress real US interest rates that should have risen to reflect the steady decline in US national savings. Because real interest rates globally were too low, Western investors and financial institutions pushed the proverbial boat out looking for more and more innovative, geared and dangerous financial products in what was known as 'the search for yield', or the search for income.

Second, the RMB regime has increased the risks of financial instability in China. Since China cannot or will not offset its trade surplus by exporting capital in the form of RMB assets to the rest of the world through normal corporate and financial sector capital transactions, the pegging of the exchange rate means that the balance of payments cannot adjust. As a result, the central banking authorities – the Peoples' Bank of China and the State Administration of Foreign Exchange – have to mop up the US dollars flowing in to the economy. This shows up as a significant expansion in foreign exchange reserves, which are then on-lent by the State, specifically by buying US dollar assets such as Treasury bills and bonds and, until the crisis, mortgage-backed securities.

State ownership of the banking system and attempts to 'sterilise' the expansionary domestic impact of this growth in reserves on the money supply – that is, selling RMB assets to local banks in exchange for US dollars – have allowed China to avoid a resurgence of inflation so far. However, there are technical and practical limitations to the effectiveness of the policy of sterilisation, and inflation started to rise in the latter part of 2009 and the first half of 2010.

A cheap currency, excessively low interest rates, and immature capital markets lead to the under-pricing of capital that encourages excessively rapid growth in capital spending and credit. The Peoples' Bank of China started to respond to this in 2010 by raising bank reserve requirements as a first step in the attempt to rein in excess bank lending. With a pegged currency, however, a tighter monetary policy can only aggravate China's financial stability, because even more capital may be sucked into the country, adding potentially to credit creation.

China is in a quandary of its own making. The RMB is a tightly controlled currency, and financial markets see it as a one-way bet to appreciate in value. As the Chinese state and its banks continue to accumulate a vast stock of US dollar reserves, monetary control is undermined, raising the threat of asset bubbles, and a major risk of financial loss arises from the eventual appreciation of the RMB.

So what is to be done?

China could try and encourage other countries to hold more RMB assets, since it has already replaced the US as the biggest trading nation in a group of countries that now accounts for nearly half of its trade: Japan, Russia, Malaysia, Hong Kong, Singapore, Australia, Taiwan, the Philippines, South Korea, and Indonesia. Moreover, it signed a trade agreement with Brazil in 2009 whereby some, limited, trade would be settled in RMB. Total trade settled in RMB is still small at some RMB 70 billion, but it is 20 times the volume recorded six months ago. But China cannot increase its lending in RMB without changing the rules and regulations applied to capital flows and exchange rate convertibility, which would be tantamount to abandoning the RMB regime. Anyway, China's financial and capital markets are far too narrow in depth and breadth, and it is not at all clear that foreigners want to hold assets denominated in RMB, for reasons ranging from liquidity to the Chinese legal system, and overall financial governance.

It could, in conjunction with other emerging nations, call for governments and international institutions to create more assets denominated in Special Drawing Rights (SDRs), as an alternative to the US dollar[6]. The new 250 billion SDR allocation agreed at the G20 meeting in April 2009, for example, will take the total SDR share of global reserves to about 5%, and further increases are quite likely. However, the IMF is the only issuer of SDRs, and controlling the supply of SDRs would require the granting of significant authority to the IMF. Moreover, there is no capital market infrastructure to support SDR issues on the scale that would be required, and who would want to own large volumes of SDR-denominated bonds? The world's insurance companies and pension funds have to match the duration and currency of their assets and liabilities, and no non-local currency does this better than the US dollar.

The constructive thing for China to do would be to announce a significant revaluation of its currency, coupled with an accelerated programme for the dismantling of remaining controls over capital movements, and new arrangements for increased currency management flexibility, if the authorities are not willing to allow a freely floating currency. This would take the sting out of protectionism, and aid and abet the process of global re-balancing as other nations took advantage of improved opportunities to export to China. It would take pressure away from the EU and Japan whose currencies have appreciated too much against a US dollar that cannot fall against China's pegged currency. Most importantly, it would help the Chinese economy to shift to a different structure, in which it would increase the production of goods and services for home consumption, and become more self-reliant and a stronger global partner.

The trouble is that China's economic strategy seems still to be focused inappropriately on quite a rigid currency regime and the expansion of heavy industrial capacity, and the West is losing patience. Signposts towards greater protectionism are becoming increasingly clear. At the end of 2009, for example, in a significant move, the US International Trade Commission approved new tariffs on imports of Chinese steel pipes following a previous decision to place tariffs on Chinese tyre imports, and EU governments decided to extend anti-dumping duties on shoes imported from China. Trade friction could become increasingly severe in the run up to US mid-term Congressional elections in November 2010, and thereafter. By 2012, the US presidential election campaign will be in full swing, while China will be preoccupied with preparations for the 18th National Communist Party Congress, at which new leaders will be installed.

China is caught in a trap. Within the next five years, and preferably sooner, it is going to have to confront the conflict in its domestic and external monetary policies once and for all. It can no longer expect the economy to grow at 8–10% per year for any length of time without significant changes in either the RMB and/ or domestic interest rates. To keep the RMB under control, in what is tantamount to exchange rate protectionism, the authorities are compromising local monetary and financial stability, and also putting themselves and the US on a collision course that could result in grave outcomes for world trade and its own social stability.

Sooner or later, this trap will be broken. In the best case, China will reform its domestic financial system voluntarily and in a timely way, allow the RMB to become significantly more flexible, and replace gradualism in monetary and financial affairs by a more robust domestic growth strategy embracing rural and social reforms. In the worst case, the global economy could end up as described above, in a repeat of the historical examples illustrated earlier.

China is today where America was in the inter-war period, and where Japan was in the 1980s. It is the dominant holder of global savings and reserves, but with a twist. America and Japan both supplied copious amounts of private capital into the global economy, but in China's case, it is government capital. The network of financial relations across the world is intrinsically more political. Moreover, financial immaturity or, indeed, financial nationalism, threaten to frustrate any real chance that it might act at a global level, from which it would also doubtless gain. Unscrambling domestic and external policy conflict would mean having to work with the US and global institutions, and addressing matters that would most likely be seen as interference and as a threat to national interests as defined by the Communist Party. The US cannot be oblivious to these tensions, and has vested interests in trying to ensure that China does not react, as it has done on many occasions in the last two millennia, by turning inwards and building barriers to the world.

In a nutshell, the world has to make the case that China and other emerging markets should restructure their economies, modernise and deepen financial systems, and allow excessive savings–investment imbalances to diminish. What that means in practice is raising the incomes of the poor and of rural citizens, and improving the provision of and access to education, healthcare and social insurance. It means expanding the collection and investment of people's savings, and strengthening the mechanisms to distribute corporate profits to citizens and investors. The IMF could play an important role in this process, providing confidence in arrangements that would allow emerging markets to focus more on domestic growth and borrowing, and offering financial insurance against the risk of destabilising capital and currency flows under some circumstances.

China protests that it is still a poor country, not a global power. The reality is more complex. It is relatively poor still, but it is far too important nowadays in global trade and finance not to take global responsibility for leadership and change in the global economy. China may feel like an increasingly confident teenager, mature enough to have strong views but not old enough yet to take full responsibility, but it needs to grow up, and quickly. Otherwise, its astounding economic successes to date could be compromised or reversed.

Chapter Five

After the Crisis: Catharsis or Chaos?

There is an old rhyme that some statistics teachers recite to their pupils, and it goes:

A trend is a trend is a trend, but the question is, will it now bend?
Will it alter its course, through some unforeseen force,
And come to a premature end?

It is worth bearing this in mind as we contemplate the predictions and prospects for emerging markets. I have already stated that economic and business extrapolations look more tenuous nowadays. The financial crisis and the journey to and from Armageddon have left us with unresolved global imbalances, and an unprecedented peacetime explosion in public debt and borrowing in Western nations and Japan. It has pushed the world's economies and nations into more adversarial, populist, even nationalistic relationships. Emerging markets can claim they were not the trigger for the crisis, as such, but their fingerprints – in particular those of China – are at the scene, so to speak. Globalisation and interconnectedness between advanced and emerging markets and financial systems are a bit like your home plumbing, when you can't fix a major problem without setting off unstable reactions somewhere else. So as Western countries attempt to restructure and reform, emerging markets will have to follow suit, especially those, like China, which are major creditor nations.

This chapter, therefore, looks to the future, first by noting that economic euphoria and financial instability are strange, but persistent, bed-fellows. And when it comes to China in the world economy today, it is important to consider its situation compared with another large Asian economy, Japan, some 30 years ago. I will show that just as Japan was feted as the new superpower in the 1980s and came to a stickier end than anyone could then imagine, so there are some troublesome parallels with China today. In fact, the way things are going, China may be creating a comparable type of bubble in its economy and asset markets. Puncturing the bubble quickly may be distressing, and compromise the exchange rate system, but it would be more manageable and consistent with longer-term stability than doing so too late. Or to quote Macbeth, 'If it *were* done when 'tis done, then '*twere* well it *were done quickly*'.

Later, I will broaden the focus to emerging market economies as they look to catch up, and consider why their prospects are not about forward looking numbers on spreadsheets, but about their ability to implement structural reforms, designed to sustain long-term expansion. India and China warrant particular attention. In India's case, it is because its labour markets and employment constitute the Achilles' heel, while in China, it is the unbalanced economy.

Euphoria in context

There exists today an almost unbridled optimism that China, and to a significant extent India, is bound to realise the greatest economic potential of all, and a confidence that several emerging nations – including Brazil, Mexico, Indonesia, Poland, and Turkey – will continue to expand, modernise and offer exciting opportunities. How can we know if, at a time of great financial and economic angst, such euphoria is warranted?

Financial crises are often unpredictable, but the legacy they leave is even more uncertain. Sometimes they are the catalyst for much needed reforms that improve the functioning of the financial system and the economy for a generation. Sometimes they leave lasting scars and unfinished business that return as crisis in the near future.

In the developed world, the US and Japan throw up two contrasting examples. America's financial crisis in the 1930s led to extensive changes in economic governance, and reform of the banking sector that constituted the bedrock of six decades of economic success after the Second World War. However, Japan's financial crisis in the 1990s never really resulted in radical restructuring of the banking sector, or structural reform, as the authorities were never prepared to risk the over-arching commitment to social consensus and cohesion. The 1990s are often called Japan's 'lost decade', because the failure to restructure and reform led to a long period of economic stagnation, soaring public debt and the cumbersome challenge of price deflation. But 2010 marks the start of a third lost decade.

Emerging nations have also experienced mixed fortunes in the wake of financial crises. In an extensive and acclaimed study of financial crises, Carmen Reinhart and Kenneth Rogoff laid out a long history of 'events' going back to 14th-century England, and found that serial debt default is a nearly universal phenomenon as countries struggle to transform themselves from emerging to more advanced structures[1]. Sometimes, crises are sufficiently far apart as to create the illusion among policy makers and investors that, when the second or third crisis occurs, they say 'this time is different'. This is rarely, if ever the case.

Argentina is a case in point. It has lived through a long history of cycles of expansion and optimism followed by default and despair. It entered the 20th century as one of the world's richest countries, and left it as one of the most troubled – a position that has not changed. Argentina defaulted on $100 billion of foreign debt in 2001, a fifth of which remains unpaid and unserviced. The country managed to achieve economic growth of close to 4% in 2010, and it has a balance of payments surplus of about 2% of GDP. It remains, though, a financial pariah in global credit markets, and still hasn't really sorted out the weaknesses in its public finance system.

An institutional and constitutional conflict erupted in 2010, when a presidential decree ordered the transfer of $6500 billion from the central bank's foreign exchange reserves so that the government could repay some private creditors, and allocate funds to the Treasury so as to help service debt payments to multilateral creditors. When the central bank Governor, Martin Redrado, refused to transfer the money, another decree was issued to oust him. Inflation, another familiar Argentine problem, is accelerating again, and though the official reports indicate inflation in a range of 7–9%, economists think that it is running at more than twice that speed.

The key issue from the standpoint of this book is that it demonstrates the significance of good institutions and good governance. The use of presidential decrees to over-ride congressional debate and decision-making flies in the face of both. It doesn't detract from the fact that Argentina's income per head is similar to Brazil, and more than twice that of China. And it doesn't mean that the Argentinian economy isn't important. It is a major producer and exporter of agricultural products such as soy beans, honey and corn, it has oil and gas, and it has a manufacturing sector that accounts for over a fifth of GDP. These economic strengths, however, are overshadowed by political and institutional short-comings, which render the economy unstable, and undermine its credibility. As we shall see, stable and effective government that has popular backing matters.

Brazil, by contrast, has been a model for successful change and governance, but only in the last several years. It too experienced a succession of economic crises, defaults, excessive inflation and currency panics from the early 1960s until 2002. In 1983, it defaulted on its external debt. In 1990, it experienced inflation of over 2900%, the sixth hyperinflation since it gained political independence in the 19th century. From the mid-1990s onwards, though, Brazil tried to break away from its political and economic past, and introduced a succession of reforms that have restored stable and low inflation, fiscal discipline, a credible and sometimes strong currency, and better all-round economic performance.

Notwithstanding having to go to the IMF for a loan in 2002 to stave off another financial crisis in the wake of Argentina's crisis, Brazil stuck to its guns. It continued to improve economic and budgetary governance, and persisted with structural reforms to the tax, pension and bankruptcy systems. Brazil was one of the last countries into the recent global financial crisis, one of the least affected, and the first one out. In this case, good politics, good governance and effective democratic institutions made a big difference to the way that the economy functioned and, importantly, to the way the country was perceived by foreign creditors.

Reinhart and Rogoff show how little we often learn from others' mistakes, and how much the phrase 'this time it's different' must make the gods smile wryly. They argue that the ability of governments – and investors – to delude themselves in times of economic optimism always gives rise to periodic bouts of euphoria, or mania, that often end up in tears. Today's euphoria about emerging markets, and predictions of enduring success are quite understandable, but when considering their prospects, we should be especially careful not to ignore the political soft spots or disadvantages which can compromise economic potential all too easily. Think only about the predicament of Greece, a former Western European emerging market, whose debt crisis threatens much more than its capacity to survive as a member of the Euro Area. Greece has spent half of its 181 years of political independence in a state of default or debt restructuring. Should we have been so surprised about the crisis that erupted in 2010?

Euphoria and delusion were also on display in Russia and central and Eastern European countries, and not only because they suffered a trade shock when trade finance dried up and when Western demand for imports slumped. International investors had been very enthusiastic about these countries, and local banks and real estate markets, in prior years. I remember attending a few Eastern European real estate conferences as a speaker in 2004–2006 in, for example, Moscow, Prague and Warsaw, where the macroeconomics speech was like the national anthem: obligatory but of little relevance to those gathered together to network and make deals. Some countries, such as Russia, had 'cleaned up' the mess from the 1998 default, and were enjoying the windfall gains from rising energy prices. Some others were considered as 'hot' as they aligned their economies and policies ever more closely to the EU, or as they prepared to join the single currency.

When the crisis occurred, however, they were exposed as having borrowed far too much, especially in foreign currencies. That meant that as local currencies devalued, the value of debt, denominated in, say, Euros or Swiss francs climbed even further, which in turn compromised the solvency of banks and other borrowers. Hungary and the Ukraine had to go to the IMF for help, while several countries experienced sharp devaluations and had to implement harsh austerity programmes.

Still on the subject of euphoria, it is worth noting that for all the plaudits heaped on China for its strong and successful response to the crisis, the country's credit policies bear close monitoring. The amount of credit as a share of GDP was about 160% before the crisis, far higher than in Brazil, India, Russia and several other Asian emerging markets. By the end of 2010, it may reach 200%. That would be close to Japan's level in 1991, and not too far away from the US in 2007. Sino-euphoria is having its day, but the combination of a credit and an investment boom is obscuring the causes of possible instability which lurk on the horizon.

Will the Sun also set on China?

In 1989, at the height of Japan's post-1945 expansion and the peak of its credit boom, the former editor of *The Economist* published a prescient book, *The Sun Also Sets*². This is how Bill Emmott began:

> 'Four decades ago Japan was written off as a contender for political and economic power; two decades ago it was no more than a voice offstage; now it is a leading player in virtually every arena of international endeavour. Its companies are impossible to ignore, at home or abroad; so, still, are its exports; so, increasingly, is the capital it is sending overseas in truckloads; and so, at last, are beginning to be its politicians and diplomats. The Japanese are no longer coming. They have arrived.'

Emmott wasn't fooled. He understood well that the US had even then been pigeon-holed as a declining power, and that successive shocks – the Vietnam War, the Iranian crisis, Ronald Reagan's economic and budgetary policies, the trade deficit and the weak US dollar – had compromised American power. However, he denied that a Japanese century was likely because it would involve heroic assumptions, including a major economic shock in the US, an increasingly sclerotic Europe, and growing cooperation between China and Japan's Asian neighbours to open up their economies and markets.

Twenty years on, Emmott's heroic assumptions have been realised more than he or anyone else could have anticipated, but Japan's century never happened, and the idea disappears further and further from view. He said China was in the process of eclipsing Japan, and that the latter might simply become an Asian

Switzerland – rich and comfortable but of low geopolitical and economic importance.

He was sceptical that Japan would always be a nation of savers and producers, and that the country's lead in semiconductors, cars, consumer electronics, automation and financial services would be the ticket to an even mightier economic empire. He concluded that the sun would set on an ageing Japan as personal sector savings declined, and as higher government and company borrowing turned its legendary trade surpluses into deficit. To revert to the global imbalances parlance of the last chapter, the eventual decline in national savings, and rise in borrowing in Japan would change its savings and investment imbalance, and thereby lead to a fall, or even a deficit in the current account balance.

The household savings rate has declined from about 15% of income in 1990 to about 3% today, and the government has certainly ended up borrowing more over a protracted period. In 1990, Japanese government debt stood at 60% of GDP, and today it stands at almost 230%. The current account surplus did decline but still registers a surplus of about 2% of GDP, thanks to high levels of corporate savings, which, together with household savings, just about offset the level of government borrowing.

With hindsight, we can see that Emmott's then controversial view was not only correct, but also rather understated. The book came out at a time of momentous events, including Japan's passage from boom to bust, the fall of the Berlin Wall, and the dawn of an accelerating globalisation. The world economy, apart from Japan, went into overdrive in the 1990s and early 2000s for reasons that have been outlined earlier. However, it also became unstable in ways that could not have been anticipated in 1989.

The notion of American decline seemed rather fanciful in the 1990s, during the two presidential terms of Bill Clinton, and while Silicon Valley was propelling information and communications technology to the top of everyone's agenda. George W. Bush's subsequent two presidential terms, however, unquestionably accelerated and aggravated America's decline. Foreign policy and international relations developments between 2000 and 2008 need no additional mention here, but economic, financial and fiscal mismanagement was also rampant, weakening America's global economic and political status even then, and especially during 2007–2008.

It was during the 2000s, for example that the excesses of finance evolved into a dangerous mania, unfinanced tax cuts drove the government's fiscal position into structural decay, and the US current account deficit widened to an unprecedented degree. President Obama is trying to pick up the pieces, but the fate of his controversial programme for comprehensive healthcare reform underscored that the US will be fully preoccupied with a quite different agenda, namely to stabilise the economy, lower unemployment, restructure the financial sector, and fix its bloated public sector deficit. This agenda only confirms that the notion of decline, at least in some relative economic sense, will continue to command attention.

However, if America's position now is worse than it may have appeared in 1989, will China be able to capitalise in ways that eluded Japan 20 years ago? Japan remains an important economic power, accounting for about 8% of world GDP, but it has become increasingly irrelevant as an economic force in the world. Over the last 20 years, it has grown at an average rate of 1.1% per year, all of which can be accounted for by limited productivity growth, which has offset a persistent decline in the workforce. The underlying rate of growth remains on a declining trend, and Japan's still advanced and rich economy is certainly declining in a relative context. In time, it could decline in an absolute sense too.

The parallels between Japan and China today might seem far-fetched. China is not an advanced economic nation with an already sophisticated infrastructure and financial system and a high level of income per head. When Japan built its infamous 'bridges to nowhere' in the 1990s as a way of cushioning the slump in the economy, the charge was that the expenditures used taxpayers' money to finance noncommercial and pointless public projects. Even if there is waste and inefficiency in China's public works programmes, it should be able to get far more 'bang for the buck' in building modern infrastructure to support an economy of 1.3 billion people.

In the wake of the crisis, for example, China accelerated its high-speed rail development, vowing to increase the passenger network by a third to 16,000 kilometres (9944 miles) over the next 10 years. The core of this project is the country's most expensive ever engineering project, namely to build a tunnel to cut in half to five hours the train time from Beijing to Shanghai. On paper, this type of capital investment, including also airports, highways, dams and so on, should boost local economies, add to workers' incomes and generate lasting improvements in productivity. It may take much longer than generally expected for the payback from such infrastructure projects, but it's hard to argue that such investment is money wasted.

But it would be wrong to dismiss the parallels out of hand. Like Japan, China's strength in the global economy is not measured as well by GDP as it is by its enormous exports and, as already explained, by the accompanying explosion in its capital exports and foreign assets. Like Japan, China's massive net creditor status gives it the opportunity to extend its influence through foreign and commercial policies, and to use its loans and aid as a bargaining chip with countries and global institutions. In China's case, moreover, it also allows a build-up in military and naval capabilities.

Like Japan, China has a large excess of savings over investment that can be traced to high levels of household savings and rising levels of corporate savings. The resulting external surpluses in China are larger than Japan's ever were. Tinkering with policies doesn't help to address the circularity of a structural problem. A controlled and undervalued exchange rate exacerbates the imbalance between (relatively backward) domestic and (high profile) external demand. It sustains trade competitiveness and export growth, and enriches large export companies, which channel their profits into higher investment to enhance export capacity. The outcome assures persistent high levels of domestic savings, high external surpluses, and the export of financial capital.

There was no consensus in Japan to allow the Yen to increase in value, and to use the stronger currency as an agent to turn the economy's focus away from an over-reliance on exports and the corporate and investment structures that supported them. The lack of such consensus meant that Japan could not cooperate adequately with the US in addressing the causes of economic and trade disputes, and contributed in no small measure to the financial polices that were to prove its undoing. The worry is that China is heading the same way.

I shall conclude on this topic later, but it is appropriate now to move the focus away from financial instability towards the underlying trends in and constraints surrounding the economic development of emerging markets as they look to catch up. I will draw attention in particular to the necessity for major emerging markets to adapt, for India to create jobs, and for China to rebalance its economy.

Catch-up constraints

Thirty years ago, income per head in China and India was a mere 2–3% of what it was in the US. Leaving aside oil-producing countries and small states and principalities with low populations, the highest ranking emerging market, in 36th position, was Hong Kong, where income per head was closing in on half the US level.

Today, China's per capita income is about 9% of the US, India's is about 4%, and Singapore is the highest ranked of the emerging countries at 74%. While the catch-up process may have flattened out for some of the earlier emerging countries such as Singapore, Hong Kong, South Korea and Taiwan, it should continue in China, for example, until its per capita income is at least 50% of the US. Such a five-fold relative improvement would be a startling achievement, but it is most unlikely to occur before 2050, if at all.

In a recent study, the G20 countries' GDP was predicted to grow from about $38,000 billion in 2009 to $161,500 billion in 2050, with as much as 60% of this increase accounted for by the BRICs plus Mexico[3]. We can go further to underscore the significance of this shift. The BRIC plus Mexico share of G20 GDP is forecast to rise from just under 19% to nearly 50%, while that of the former G7 industrial nations is expected to fall from over 72% to 40%. And when looking at China and India alone, these two countries' GDP is expected to rise by $60,000 billion, and that is the equivalent of the whole of world GDP in 2008. It is probably safe to assume that unless emerging market governments make profound policy errors, or succumb to inertia in the face of pressing demands for reform, the process of catch-up will endure[4].

However, according to this study, the GDP success of emerging nations only tells a part of the story, because when allowing for population, per capita income levels remain quite low and are expected to increase much more slowly. China's eye-popping catch-up since 1990 saw per capita income treble to about $1000 in the decade to 2000, and treble again to $3000 in the following years to 2008. The current prediction is that per capita income will reach $9000 by 2020, $20,000 by 2030, and $33,000 by 2050.

This is more or less where Singapore, Spain and Hong Kong were in 2008 and, assuming the US manages to keep growing at about 2.5% per year, then China's per capita income in 2050 would still only be a third of the US. India's per capita income in 2050 is expected to be about $10,000, ten times its level in 2008, but still only 10% of the US.

The focus on GDP is a convenient way of portraying super-ficially the shifting structure of global growth. But projections and extrapolations based on the wizardry of numbers in spreadsheets isn't what catch-up is about. What really matters is whether, in the process of economic development, governments can derive legiti-macy and support by ensuring that the rewards of economic growth are distributed equitably, and that human effort, savings and capital are channelled into productive activity and wealth creation without risking financial stability. Looking at the last 20 years or so of catch-up by emerging markets, Andy Cates at UBS has identified four particular economic trends[5].

First, although emerging countries have clearly performed extremely strongly in recent years, the excitement is relatively new, with the acceleration in globalisation since 1989 marking the turning point. In fact, we could argue that the real significance of emerging markets in the global economy only gathered more significant momentum after 2000, when they started, as a group, to capture a rising share of global GDP. Much of this change has been attributable to China.

This is not to minimise the successes of emerging nations in lifting millions of people out of poverty, modernising their economies and improving economic governance. But there is little question that global macroeconomic conditions since 1990 could hardly have been more conducive to their success. The rising tide of globalisation did indeed lift most economic boats, and it is hard to argue that emerging markets, as a whole, were punching significantly above their weight.

The *actual* growth rates shown (Figure 5.1) for advanced economies and for emerging and developing countries since 1970 show broadly similar cyclical changes, indicating that, at one level, decoupling of richer and poorer countries from one another hasn't really happened. But if we remove the cyclical variations or noise, we can see that the *trend* growth rates of the two groups show a more interesting path, converging steadily until the late 1990s, and only thereafter, diverging towards a historically wide gap.

This emerging market phenomenon, though, can largely be accounted for by China and India. Excluding these two nations, the growth trend in emerging and developing countries was somewhat lower than in rich countries until about 2007, so that their share of global GDP actually slipped. The principal reason was the series of financial crises that rolled through Asia, Russia and parts of Latin

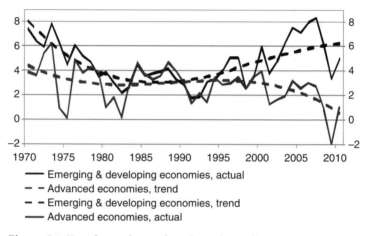

Figure 5.1 Trend growth rates have been decoupling
Source: DSG Asia

America from 1997 until about 2001, with aftershocks that lasted
several more years.

Second, the strongest region within the emerging country group
has unquestionably been Asia, with or without the inclusion of
China and India. Between 1998 and 2008, the global GDP shares
of Russia and Brazil both fell, and that of all other developing
economies rose by a mere 1%, thanks only to the 12% gain
made by China, India, the original Tigers (Hong Kong, Singapore,
South Korea and Taiwan), and also by Malaysia, Indonesia and
Thailand.

The significance of China and India can be seen by considering Asia with and without them (Figure 5.2). Actual growth rates
in China and India were more volatile than in the rest of Asia
from the 1980s until the Asian crisis. Subsequently, though, roles

were reversed. The growth performance of China and India became more solid and stable while the rest of Asia experienced extreme volatility. The Asia crisis in the late 1990s caused enormous economic suffering before a V-shaped recovery followed in 2001-02. Subsequently, Asian countries growth performance was more subdued than it had been in previous decades. With or without China and India, Asia's trend growth rates were fairly similar until 2000. Since then, though, the gap has continued to widen, emphasising the significance of the continent's two largest nations.

The third trend concerns the better politics and demographics that have allowed Asia to stand tall, compared with other emerging markets. Politically, you could argue that Asia had advantages that eluded other countries. They relied on centralised authorities, which commanded legitimacy and were able to direct resources to

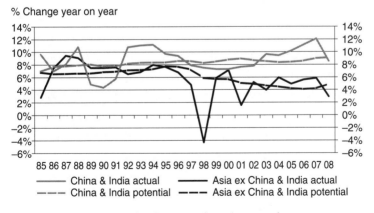

Figure 5.2 China and India dominate the Asian growth story
Source: DSG Asia

strategically important parts of the economy, such as education, infrastructure and labour markets. Asian countries were encouraged and chose to develop institutions that engaged with and benefited from globalisation. A long list of favourable factors included openness, high educational attainment standards, political stability, good macroeconomic governance, robust property, labour and other laws, and a culture of entrepreneurship. They also got a helping hand from the Cold War. Against a background of armed conflicts and covert political activities in Asia for several decades after the Second World War, America provided assistance and access to trade for Japan, and also for the Asian Tigers. More generally, the US, a Pacific as well as an Atlantic power, has always defined its national interests in terms of a pacified and prosperous Asia, in which leading competitors are, of course, politically friendly.

Good politics and good demographics work well in tandem. How else could we explain the sharp difference in economic performance between Asia and Latin America over the last 40 years, despite the fact that the age structure of the two regions was and remains comparable? In the last 20 years, the working age population in some countries, such as Brazil, Mexico, Turkey and South Africa, grew about as fast as in Asia, but they couldn't match Asia's economic performance. In China and South Korea, on the other hand, the working age population grew no faster than in the US, Canada and New Zealand, but their GDP growth rates were many times as fast, at nearly 10% and 6% per year, respectively. In other words, good demographics form the principal component of catch-up, but only if the structure of political institutions is designed to capitalise continuously on social and economic development at home, and economic integration abroad.

I shall explore the demographic theme in more detail in the next chapter.

Emerging countries with growing working age populations are likely to save a lot.

Taking average savings as a share of GDP over the last 20 years, the highest savers (30–50%) have been China and Malaysia by a mile, followed by Singapore, South Korea, Thailand, Indonesia, and Hong Kong. Brazil, South Africa, Turkey, Argentina and Mexico had the lowest savings rates at 20–25% of GDP, but these were still elevated. Having a large savings pool is important because this finances the investment that leads to future growth and prosperity.

China's household savings as a share of disposable income rose from 15% in 1990 to just over 25% in 2008, but India's has risen even further, from 20% to 32%. In fact, India has the highest household savings rate in Asia. In South Korea, on the other hand, a richer, more developed and much more rapidly ageing economy than either India or China, the household savings rate has fallen from 25% to 7% in the last 20 years. Household, corporate and government savings finance the investment that is the rocket fuel of future economic growth. China's average investment rate as a share of GDP over the last 20 years was almost 40%, and is currently estimated in the region of 50%. No one else comes even close, though Malaysia, South Korea, Thailand and Singapore average around 30–35% of GDP.

As savings grow, it is also important to develop financial institutions that can collect, administer, and invest those savings wisely, and financial structures that allow the savings of companies, in effect a part of their profits, to be distributed to households in some form. This, if anything, has been a significant shortcoming in

China's economic development, and in several other countries too. Balanced economic development requires broader and deeper financial markets to allow households and companies to borrow, thereby lessening the dependence on high levels of savings. They help to foster a more productive use of capital, entrepreneurial activity, and a vibrant small- and medium-size enterprise sector, which is important for employment creation. Moreover, they are essential if the vast majority of the population, especially in rural areas, is to gain access to financial services, including banking, insurance and securities markets.

Emerging markets' participation in globalisation and the integration of trade has proceeded far more quickly than the development of financial institutions and markets. The result of this phenomenon is that the accumulation of savings in China, oil producers and other surplus countries has been difficult to arrest, and has ended up either as government lending to the US and other deficit countries, or as a one-way stream of capital into more and more enterprise investment. Over-investment is a classic cause of economic boom and bust, even in poorer countries with a structural demand for higher levels of investment over time. Consequently, weak and underdeveloped institutions will inhibit important solutions to structural imbalances at home and abroad.

Fourth, according to UBS, about three-fifths of the variations in emerging country growth rates over the last 20 years can be put down to demographics, the quantity and quality of its workers and skilled professionals, the initial level of per capita income, and savings and investment rates. The remainder is largely explained by measuring capital and labour inputs directly, and captured by total factor productivity (TFP). In Chapter 2, I pointed out the high growth rates that many emerging markets have achieved, especially when set against those of richer countries. Much of the superior growth comes from total factor productivity, and that is precisely what should happen, except when political and institutional barriers, or natural phenomena, contrive to arrest or slow down the process.

Better economic efficiency and governance, rising educational attainment, openness to new ideas, the exploitation of technology and deployment of internet technology in particular, the use of best-practice global production and management techniques, and the improvement in the quality of institutions all figure prominently in explaining higher levels of TFP. These are all about politics and institutions, and it is important to remember that, from this standpoint, the past may not always be a good guide to the future.

Moreover, it is undoubtedly true that during the last 20 years particularly rapid advances in the pace of globalisation had strong positive effects on many of the factors cited above. Open trade and finance, constructive engagement with global companies and institutions, and the diffusion of education, information and technology all contributed to the spark in economic growth, captured by TFP. If the pace of globalisation has reached a plateau, or slows down, there will be some impact on the performance of emerging markets. The underlying pace of economic growth could slip to 6–8% per year in China and India, and to 3–5% for many other emerging markets, before longer-term deceleration sets in. This would represent a moderate, but not substantial, setback, though there might be important implications also for important emerging market financial centres such as Singapore and Hong Kong, and possibly

Shanghai, which China wants to have up and running as a financial centre by 2020.

The general economic impact of slowing or stable globalisation is not especially threatening, but a faltering or reversal would be much more damaging. Trade barriers, taxes and levies would impede exports, while the possibility of capital and currency controls would restrain credit and finance. Open economies, or those with a high dependence on trade, such as China and much of the rest of Asia, would be badly affected as global demand weakened, transportation and shipment costs rose, and supply chains fractured. Commodity producers, such as Russia, Mexico, and Indonesia, Chile and Brazil would suffer too.

Emerging markets, then, have much at stake when it comes to globalisation, and to the international relations and institutions that allow it to work efficiently and fairly. It follows, therefore, that they have strong vested interests in how the Western economies come to terms with their challenges and problems in the next decade, and what the implications might mean for them. Among the major emerging markets, India might be able to stand up to a more volatile and restrained global economy relatively well, but nowhere are these questions more important than in China.

India's opportunity

Although India experienced its first post-colonial catch up in the first 10 years of independence, it wasn't sustained. By the 1960s, India faced food supply crises and was growing at 3.5% per year, a meagre rate for a developing economy in which the labour force was growing by 2.5% per year. The Green Revolution in the 1960s and early 1970s, embracing higher yielding crops and large inputs of fertilisers and water, boosted agricultural production and efficiency, but broader measures of economic development were held back by centralised and inward-looking policies pursued by the Indian authorities. Although economic growth picked up in the 1980s, India laboured under rising public debt, minimal foreign exchange reserves, high inflation and public borrowing, and the occasional 'dash for growth' that was terminated by financial turbulence. New reforms from the 1990s onwards, which improved the supply side of India's economy and facilitated its integration into the global system, lifted exports, currency reserves, capital inflows and productivity. The increase in economic growth, from 6.6% in the 1990s to 8% in the last several years, augurs much better for India's future, despite the slippage during the global economic downturn in 2008–2009. A disappointing summer monsoon in 2009, with rainfall about 28% below the long-term average and 40% lower in northwestern India, didn't help – certainly not the 600 million people dependent on agriculture and for whom irrigation and pumped water do not substitute for rainwater. Food price inflation soared to nearly 20% in early 2010, raising general inflation from zero to about 10%.

Notwithstanding temporary and short-term business cycle interruptions, some economists think that India is already the next Asian Tiger. In other words, India could now be on the cusp of a phase in which its growth rate might resemble that recorded by the original Tigers in the 1970s and 1980s, and by China more recently. In a different context, I have suggested that India almost resembles an Asian America, when considering its demographic structure and potential and its penchant for services and advanced technologies[6]. This is not to compare and contrast in contemporary terms, but to view India as having similar characteristics to the United States in recent decades. It's democratic, entrepreneurial and, above all, young.

India's population is expected to rise by 270 million by 2030, not far short of the entire population of the US today, and another 130 million by 2050. Even more significantly, the rise in India's population of working age by 2030 will be almost as large as today's tally of the working age population in all of Western Europe. India's prospective labour resources, coupled with high levels of personal savings and an aptitude for high technology, should stand the country in good stead.

India is strong in service-producing industries, technology, steel, automobiles and automobile components. It saves about 35% of its GDP, up 15% since 2000, and so it is not surprising that India's investment spending and economic growth should have also strengthened since that time. Unlike China, it is not heavily trade dependent. Exports of goods and services account for just 22% of GDP and, since 2005, it has been running modest current account deficits, currently around 2.5% of GDP. So India, also unlike China, has to borrow overseas to finance its deficits.

Provided that foreign borrowing remains manageable, India is well situated to move its growth rate up a gear or two. With a national savings rate of 35% of GDP, capital inflows from overseas amounting to about 5% of GDP, and a rough estimate that each 4% of GDP adds about 1% to sustainable GDP growth, India could lift its growth rate to about 10% per annum in the next several years.

If India could sustain a 10% growth rate over the next 20–30 years, there's no question that it would become an increasingly significant economic power, finally lifting its share of world output that has barely changed in the last 20 years. It won't get close to China or the US, but it could be as big as Japan by the time it celebrates 80 years of independence in 2027. Although the Indian state is sometimes criticised as having been a drag on economic development because of its susceptibility to populism, the last years of reforms and shifts in the boundaries between the private and public sectors have encouraged private companies and citizens to step forward. Private providers of goods and services have increased in importance where the State has failed to provide basic services in several areas, including education and health care, irrigation and water, and power in urban areas[7].

But there are also important constraints over India's future development, including the current tide of rising inflation, a consolidated public sector borrowing requirement of almost 10% of GDP, poor infrastructure development, fragmented regional markets, and the protracted nature of decision making. Bureaucratic restrictions and regulations, weak governance, and low political accountability to voters, especially in the provision of public services, represent obstacles to economic development, and there probably isn't a major sector where structural reforms are not required. In fact, while India's relatively more closed economy, compared to China, might help it to keep global economic shocks at bay, it also makes those reforms all the more important.

India's Achilles' heel, though, is job creation, a task in which it has a poor record, and at which service-producing industries in poor countries do not excel. Service industries are generally less labour intensive than large-scale manufacturing, but in India's case legal and planning restrictions applied to the retail and financial services sectors are also important. It could do a lot better by freeing up the flow of labour into service industries, where at least they won't be automated out of work by capital and robots in a few years. Although India's measured unemployment rate is just 7%, the real rate is probably far higher. Too many people classified in full time work are poor or living below the poverty line, and most people either work in the public sector or in the non-organised sectors of the economy, where wage and employment conditions are poor and people are only loosely integrated into the labour force.

In the next 15 years, India will have to find 375 million jobs for the population now aged 0–14 years, who comprise about 31% of the entire population. Employment creation on this scale would be unprecedented without a major expansion in labour-intensive manufacturing production, and India is advancing only slowly on this front.

Moreover, though stories abound about India's education system and its skilled labour force of engineers, technology specialists and scientists, the country's literacy rate is still only 61%, and only 7% of 18–24 year olds are educated to university level. There are large gaps in the national education system, with 20% of 6–14 year olds not attending school and a very high dropout rate, even though the vast majority of rural dwellers, for example, live within a couple of kilometres of primary and upper primary schools.

To graduate in the economic power league, India will need to improve the functionality of government and of institutions, especially regarding the delivery of public goods and services, including infrastructure and education. It will need to attend to poverty. Officially about 200 million people live below the poverty line, but unofficial estimates put the real number as high as 350 million. Three quarters live in rural areas, where the poverty rate is over 20%. India's poor, according to one expert, are making a 'modestly plodding climb out of considerable income deprivation'[8]. It will need a second Green Revolution to help boost agricultural productivity. It will have to ensure long-run stability of low inflation and good fiscal behaviour, and work to strengthen the structure of financial markets and services, trade with regional neighbours and, above all, create environmentally-friendly manufacturing activity and employment rates, especially for the young. The hors d'oeuvre of accomplishment since 2000 has been promising, but the challenge of turning this into a recipe for lasting success rests on political and economic reforms and resolve, based on some attributes that China lacks, including a political institutional framework that offers some guarantee on individual and commercial rights, and a long-standing commercial culture. Maybe India's biggest risk is shooting itself in the foot with a dysfunctional political system that is apt to lapse periodically into inertia and ineffectiveness.

The rebalancing of China

China has rebalanced before. It did so when introducing radical reforms in 1978 in order to move towards a socialist market economy, and again after 1993 when control over policy, previously ceded to more conservative factions after Tiananmen, returned to the reformers. Today China's elite and intellectuals have again embarked on an as yet inconclusive series of significant debates about whether and how to reform.

The debates embrace China's policies in relation to US arms sales to and support of Taiwan, Iran's nuclear ambitions, trade relations and the foreign exchange regime, economic development strategy, the environment and climate change, and Internet and information access. China's increasingly assertive and confrontational approach could reflect the confidence that comes with economic power, and be amenable to negotiation and dialogue. But the new tougher stance might also mask a fundamental weakness in the leadership. On the one hand, it may be insecure in the face of hard-line factions in the Communist Party, already gearing up for the leadership change in 2012. On the other, it may be concerned by popular resentment about income inequality, human rights, and the effects of globalisation, environmental degradation, corruption, and inadequate social services. There is an implicit danger that China could end up overplaying its hand, especially with the US, and mistaking its weaknesses for strength.

Consequently, the most important issue for China-watchers is not what its GDP might be in 2030. It is whether or not the social, political and economic thinking that gained traction from the 1990s onwards can bend and adapt in the 2010s in a constructive way to address China's new challenges at home and in its international relations.

From both a domestic and also an international perspective, the main economic challenge concerns 'imbalances'. I have already addressed in some detail global imbalances, the role played by China's external surpluses, and the significance of China's savings and investment imbalance in generating those surpluses. The latter, though, go to the heart of how China grows, how the economy works, and what role public policy plays.

It bears repeating that while exports and capital investment have generated the lion's share of economic growth, Chinese consumers have been anything but frugal. In 2009, Chinese consumption rose faster than GDP for the first time in a decade, thanks to the government's attempts to offset the impact of the crisis. It created a lot of construction jobs, raised social transfer payments, and lowered taxes to stimulate automobile purchases. The fact remains, though, that the share of consumption in GDP remains very low. In the early 1980s, it was about 50%, but as China prioritised the export and capital investment sectors of the economy, it has fallen to about 36%.

China's economic expansion since the financial crisis was heavily reliant on fixed investment, and accounted for almost all the growth in the economy in the first half of 2009, and grew twice as fast as household consumption in the whole of 2009.

This is a mark of an unbalanced economy, and the big policy challenge is to rebalance it by redirecting jobs and capital permanently towards the consumer and domestic goods and services sectors, and by taming the investment boom before it goes bust on its own.

Taming the investment boom

Fixed investment, especially in heavy industries, such as steel, cement and aluminium, has accounted regularly for 60–80% of economic growth, and the investment cycle is in its 12th year of a boom. The Chinese authorities must act to moderate the investment boom and the flow of excessive credit, not least because the latter could easily end up in a growing bad debt problem in the banking system. To avert this, China has recourse to credit and interest rate policies, but to rebalance the economy, it has to pursue structural reforms and use industrial policy.

The emphasis could swing away from investment in heavy industry output, which doesn't create a lot of jobs anyway, to investment in service-producing industries, which is more labour intensive. Heavy industry also contributes in a major way to rapid energy consumption growth, which is environmentally and financially costly. China uses almost as much energy as the US, but it is far less efficient, using three times as much energy per unit of GDP.

The other side of the over-investment, or under-consumption, to which China's economic indicators point, is an unusually high level of savings. Picking up on a point made before in the book, the accumulation of savings that has built up since 2000 can be traced to Chinese heavy industry enterprises, for example, in steel, automobiles, machinery, materials and chemicals. These are well represented in the 10 largest listed companies in the 'A' share market, which account for over three-fifths of the earnings of all participating companies, and all of which are state-owned enterprises. In general, Chinese enterprises have weak ownership structures. They have no way of dealing with residual claims on their earnings (for example, by paying dividends to citizen shareholders), and have an almost limitless capacity to borrow money from banks, which are only too willing to lend aggressively. Consequently, additional measures to rebalance would provide for reforms to allow companies to distribute their profits rather than to recycle them back into more investment, and for more commercially-based lending and borrowing criteria.

Investment was also the principal focus of the extraordinary economic and financial stimulus measures that China announced at the peak of the financial crisis in late 2008. As a result, about a third of new bank loans made in 2009 went to finance new infrastructure, such as railways, airports, roads, new towns and so on. Another third was earmarked for water conservation, the environment, transport systems and energy and electrical supply utilities. Only 13% of new loans financed new consumption. In the first half of 2010, the rate of credit expansion was the third highest in the last 30 years. On the two previous occasions of rapid credit expansion, in the late 1980s and in 1993, inflation rose to 20% and 25%, respectively.

Too much industrial capacity has been accumulating for some years and, if current trends continued, could become a serious problem. In some sectors, notably steel, it already is. In 2004, when the government last tried to tame the investment boom, steel capacity was 400 million tonnes. In 2009, capacity surpassed 700 million tonnes, with 58 million tonnes of capacity under construction. Domestic demand is running at 200 million tonnes a year. Over-capacity is also recognised in an array of other activities, including aluminium, where production capacity is almost twice as big as demand, and in cement, coal, shipbuilding, glass plate, solar panels, wind turbines and soybean crushing.

Infrastructure spending is often deemed a self-evident 'good', but in the context of China's investment boom, it is a double-edged sword. It generates strong demand growth in the short term. But the construction of trophy towns and projects, or at least excessively rapid construction, also creates a lot of extra, and possibly excessive, capacity. Until the capacity can be taken up and become economic, the economy could then face a growing risk of bad loans for the banks that financed the infrastructure as too much supply, of commercial buildings for example, caused real estate prices to decline. One leading Chinese academic and former member of the monetary policy committee of the Chinese central bank has argued that even large-scale infrastructure spending may not be as 'good' as it appears on paper. He said that hasty and under-supervised implementation contributes to ubiquitous waste, and that the prospective economic and social returns are less than promising[9].

These failings are not unique to China, but they are the inevitable consequence of institutional shortcomings. These include the lack of independent scrutiny over costs and benefits, the lack of public accountability as regards corporate activities and social needs, and the environmental consequences of breakneck economic growth. The problem, of course, is that independent scrutiny and public accountability mean that power has to be diffused to non-state entities, which is not possible in China. As Will Hutton has put it, there are no custodians of justice, such as watchdogs, whistleblowers and independent judges – who also, incidentally, fulfil important functions in subjecting public spending and projects to intellectual rigour and efficiency tests[10].

It is true, of course, that China is a poor country, and it follows that it has an almost insatiable demand to build capital in the form of more roads, bridges, railways, airports, social facilities, and industrial plant and equipment. China's physical capital (buildings, equipment and infrastructure, for example) per head of population is estimated at about $9000, which equates to about 8% of the level in Japan, and 5% of that in the US[11]. Consequently, it makes no sense to assert that China is anywhere close to 'over-investment' in this comparative sense. As one asset management firm has argued, population density in China is quite high, and much unlike the US. About 96% of the population lives in about 46% of the country, mostly in southern and eastern provinces, and the arguments for ever more prestigious national infrastructure projects hold much less weight than in, for example, the US. The authors point out that there is too much capacity building up in the railway network, that China is already the leading builder of 'bridges to nowhere' and that most of the airports built since 2005 have been built in sparsely populated areas[12]. I think the point here is not to say that China doesn't need more and better infrastructure, but that it needs to have a robust commercial or social reason, and that it needs to be targeted better at consumer and social needs.

Even before the massive public spending and bank lending stimulus programme was announced at the end of 2008, China was already building boom towns that are, at least for now, ghost towns. Ordos in Inner Mongolia in northern China is a major coal mining region with a population of 1.5 million. A new development has been built in about five years, designed to house another 1 million residents. Its newly built roads, wide avenues and high rise apartment blocks, architectural creations and sculptured gardens testify to the boast that it has the second highest income per head in China, after Shanghai. The reason is because it is virtually empty. Traffic policemen stop and wave on traffic lines that would embarrass any modern city, and the apartment blocks have been sold, but not to owners in residence.

Or consider the town of Chenggong, a part of Kunming in southwest China, which was also completed in the space of five to six years, complete with high rise buildings, marble-tiled municipal offices, a show case high school, university campuses, banks, estate agents, and a modern road system. There were about 160,000 inhabitants when the original announcement was made in 2003 regarding the development of the city, and its plan to be home to 1 million people. Eventually this will probably happen, not least because the broader area of Kunming has 7 million people, but perhaps not without some sort of financial accident along the way, arising from bad loans, over-building and over-capacity.

The township of Huazi in the Yangzi River Delta was once an agricultural community, populated by bamboo huts and ox carts, that has become a significant industrial and commercial location. It claims to have the highest per capita income of any village for its 30,000 inhabitants ($11,700). It is already the site of a 328-metre (1076 feet) tower, housing a revolving restaurant, and is aiming to build a new skyscraper that would be the second tallest building in the world after Dubai's Burj Khalifa[13]. One can only wonder why?

The mega-stimulus programme announcement in November 2008 was followed by the creation of thousands of so-called 'investment platforms', or what we have come to know in the Western financial crisis as special investment vehicles – entities that borrow to invest, but which do not report their assets and liabilities transparently, or at all. Officially, there were 8221 such platforms as at mid-2009, over half of which existed at local government level, with the bulk of the remainder at municipal and provincial level. These platforms are locally controlled, state-sponsored companies that package government funds collected from land auctions and other fees, and borrow from banks to finance infrastructure spending on water projects, roads, commercial construction, housing and so on. Remember, these local authorities have significant responsibilities for delivering the 8% annual economic growth that China requires as diktat.

According to the China Banking Regulatory Commission, local governments are estimated to have taken out 6000 billion yuan in loans in 2009 ($880 billion) – or 17% of GDP – and it is estimated by independent observers that local government debt could reach about 11,000 billion yuan ($1610 billion) in 2010. This number excludes additional committed credit lines – that is, credit lines from banks that haven't yet been drawn – of a further 7500 billion yuan ($1100 billion). All of this matters, because the amount of general public sector debt in China is not transparent or well understood, the focus being principally on central government debt, which amounts to a lowly 22% of GDP.

There are two main reasons why these rather esoteric and opaque 'platform' entities are important. First, their debts are not reported as part of the overall consolidated accounts of local governments. In other words, they are 'off budget'. The land they own, purchase or requisition, sometimes in desolate and commercially questionable areas, is used as collateral to acquire loans to finance infrastructure development. If we were to add their liabilities to official figures, China's public debt would not be the lowly 22% of GDP as suggested above, but closer to 60% of GDP. That figure includes officially reported debt, the debts of state-owned enterprises and municipal and provincial debt, including the so-called platform entities. But it excludes other national platform debts and contingent liabilities, such as non-performing loans in the banking system, which would raise the national debt to nearer 70% of GDP.

Second, the investment platforms, which have weak cash flows and controls and are often staffed on the basis of political rather than commercial qualifications, get significant revenues from land sales. No one knows for certain how large these land sales have been since 2008, with estimates ranging between 20–40% of revenues. Land sales are important because land prices are closely associated with property prices, creating close ties between the interests of local governments, land developers and banks. Over the next few years, many of the loans incurred to finance infrastructure projects will doubtless go bad. Some 2500–3000 billion yuan of 2009–2010 loans could end up this way[14].

The key issue is what happens to those debts, and implicitly to the lending banks and the government's financial position when land values drop significantly, most likely in the wake of an economic slowdown and more emphatic restraint over bank lending and liquidity. It's never possible to anticipate precisely when property and land price cycles run out of momentum or what the catalyst might be. We know, however, that they always do end, and often abruptly. There is no reason to suspect that in China things might be different. It is only a question of how far land prices rise and when more aggressive credit tightening is implemented.

In 2010, Chinese property markets captured the attention of many economists and investors, as well as the authorities in Beijing. Property investment has boomed to account for about 13% of GDP, and 22% of all urban fixed asset investment. By the spring, property prices in 70 large- and medium-size cities were rising at close to 12% per year, slightly higher than in the period before the financial crisis, and were 10% above pre-crisis levels. This marks a long cycle starting in roughly 2000–2001, so that in many places prices have risen by two to three times. Well-known investors and hedge fund managers, and some independent economists, have argued that Chinese property is a massive bubble that will burst soon with far reaching consequences. They point to globally high ratios of house prices to incomes and to rents, and to anecdotal signs, such as overbuilding and industrial companies opening up real estate divisions.

The contrary argument is that it is largely high-end properties that are too expensive, that rapid urbanisation, not speculation is the main driver, and that restrictive mortgage lending practices limit the potential for speculative and irresponsible financing. In fact, the authorities tightened property market conditions significantly in 2010. In April, the State Council began placing restrictions on property loans, land auctions and new construction, and in May, it outlined a proposal to gradually introduce property taxes. The minimum deposit on the purchase of a home was increased by 10% to 30% on a first property, and to 50% on a second property and, in Beijing, purchases of a third property were banned altogether.

Beijing is worried about speculative conditions in the property market but is committed to an expansion in the stock of housing. In May 2010, the Ministry of Housing and Urban-Rural Development agreed with provincial and city governments to add about 7 million affordable housing units this year alone, including just over a million refurbishments.

Nevertheless, during 2011–2012, China will almost certainly experience a significant rise in the non-performing loans of banks. This does not necessarily portend a banking crisis, such as the West experienced in 2008–2009, because China's banks are state-owned and the authorities could recapitalise them quite easily out of assets held in its foreign exchange reserves, as it did about a decade ago. Beijing is in a good position to stop a potential banking crisis from erupting. However, there is no such thing as a costless or painless resolution of a banking crisis, whether that crisis is overt or not. Someone has to pay, and the 'someone' is invariably the taxpayer or consumer. But if Chinese households eventually have to bear the cost of cleaning up the banking system again, that means that the much sought-after rebalancing of the Chinese economy will be even further delayed.

Investment booms never last. Eventually, the returns to investment decline, the debts incurred to finance them become more burdensome, and capital spending retrenches to allow demand to catch up with capacity. Over the next several years, China will either manage capital investment and the property cycle down gently, or it will experience a more abrupt slump, most probably accompanied by some form of banking crisis, in which the consumer will have to pick up the tab. The chances of the former are normally quite slim, and so if China does not seize the opportunity to rebalance the economy towards more consumption and domestically focused production soon, the latter is more likely.

The consumer and the countryside

Turning to consumption, the low consumption share of GDP, and per head of population, is also a matter that merits attention before it, too, gets out of hand. If things stay the same and China's GDP grows at 9% per year, and savings and investment are still 50% of GDP in 2020, China's external surplus in RMB or US dollar terms can only expand, aggravating global imbalances. Even if this international dimension were considered unimportant in Beijing, there are equally pressing domestic reasons to pay attention. Weak consumption per head could exacerbate social tensions, especially because income distribution in China already favours urban workers and coastal regions. Moreover, China's rural work force and rising middle class are liable to become increasingly restive politically if their rising economic aspirations and demand for social spending continue to play second fiddle to the investment and exports of state-owned enterprises.

China's consumption and savings issues are deep-seated structural phenomena. They revolve around the subdued performance of rural incomes and employment, the inability to distribute enterprise savings, weak and immature financial institutions and markets, low levels of social security and health care coverage, and the obligations to pay for education and pass on assets to children.

These phenomena are widely recognised. The key, though, is to do something about them. China has implemented some measures to address them. Since 2005, the authorities have sought to boost consumer spending by increasing the disposable income of peasants and rural workers by abolishing some agricultural taxes and raising government procurement prices for agricultural products. In June 2009, the State Council announced a transfer of 10% of state-owned enterprise shares that had been issued in recent initial public offerings to the Social Security Fund. Later in the year, permission was granted for workers to transfer pension accounts across provinces. About RMB 850 billion, or nearly 3% of GDP, was allocated to health care programmes for the period 2009–2011, comprising lower charges and new rural cooperative medical care services, and to higher education and housing subsidies. The proposed pension system for rural employees to be enacted in 2010 will initially cover 10% of rural areas but spread to the whole country by 2020.

However welcome these measures are, they do not really tackle the root causes of China's under-developed consumer sector. At little more than a third of GDP, this is not simply an illusion caused by the more vigorous expansion of investment. It is fundamentally about weak and low incomes, especially among the 700 million people who live in the countryside, and about additional institutional shortcomings, such as limited property rights, a limited welfare system, and the absence of organised labour unions, which would normally constitute an important pressure group, not least for higher incomes.

Chinese workers may have started to take things into their own hands. In 2010, after a spate of strikes at several factories in the manufacturing belt in Guangdong Province in the south of the country at the end of May and beginning of June, workers were given substantial pay rises. In one macabre case, 10 employees committed suicide, drawing attention to the poor conditions, including social alienation, constant overtime, assembly line tedium, and relentless overnight work that exist in many factory towns. This happened at Foxconn, the company that employs 300,000 people to make the iPod and other high technology products, and which ended up raising wages initially by 30%, but after two more initiatives, by 70% in most cases. Honda, the Japanese car manufacturer, had to suspend production when workers at a component factory in which it is a majority owner, went on strike for higher wages, which were eventually raised by 24–33%. But this just encouraged workers to strike for and get higher pay at another of its component companies. And workers at the Toyota Motor Corporation affiliate, Toyoda Gosei Company in Tianjin, and some of its component factories, went on strike for and won higher wages.

These wage increases are bound to have a 'demonstration' effect, encouraging other workers to demand higher pay, and other companies to concede them. If, even in the absence of organised labour union pressure, China's workers were able to secure steadily higher incomes, the knock-on effects on consumption would be mostly positive. Households would have more to spend while not necessarily having to run down their savings a lot.

Yet these developments may be more like gentle foothills, en route to the mountain of higher consumption. The authorities may fear the inflationary impact of higher wages and neutralise it by raising interest rates and tightening monetary policy further. They may balk if rising labour costs cause too many Chinese export companies, that operate with slim profit margins, to go bust, and foreign firms to quit China in search of lower labour costs elsewhere. But the most significant issue for Chinese companies and the government is whether China has arrived at the so-called Lewis turning point. This is named after the economist Sir Arthur Lewis who, in 1954, explained how, with particular reference to Asia, economic development eventually saps the unlimited supply of labour in the countryside, leading to a more sustained advance in the wages of industrial workers. In modern China, this merits close attention for, as I shall explain later, China is already starting to run out of cheap workers and the rapid change in China's age structure in the next 25 years is bound to exacerbate this trend. For the moment though, there is still a large enough pool of migrant workers coming to the cities to work, and remember that Chinese and foreign companies can themselves migrate inland to towns and rural areas where labour is more fluid and wages are lower.

There are also several policies that the government could take to encourage Chinese households to contribute more to the economy. The authorities could cut personal taxes, raise government consumption and minimum wages, and tax the dividends of state-owned enterprises and distribute the proceeds. They could boost household income by offering higher deposit rates to savers, and allowing the RMB to appreciate. Further, they could liberalise prices for land, energy and utilities, so that they reflect better scarcity and environmental concerns, and spur a shift in spending away from manufacturing to the services sector. Such measures would have to be part of sweeping changes in the rural economy.

When Mao Zedong died in 1976, the rural sector of the economy accounted for two-thirds of GDP. Today it is a mere 11%. Then the rural population accounted for 83% of the total population. Today it is 55%. However, the rural share of total employment has fallen only slightly, from 75% to around 67%. Assessing China's prospects depends crucially on what happens to the countryside because, if Tiananmen Square represented the limit of urban social unrest, the next few years could easily witness a similar test for the rural sector.

Chinese leaders often refer to 'harmonious development', which is essentially about balanced and well-ordered economic and social structures, and nowadays it is used to emphasise the elimination of rural poverty and the reversal of environmental degradation. However, China's basic problem, according to one of the leading experts on Chinese agriculture, Professor Robert Ash, is that there are too many people in the countryside, with too little arable land. Ash has found strong evidence of increasing land shrinkage as a result of economic policy, such as urbanisation and infrastructure construction, as well as changes in farm practices and natural disasters. The area of arable land is now below what it was in 1998. He has also shown that too many farms are too small to be efficient[15].

Notwithstanding the radical decision by the Communist Party Central Committee in October 2008 to give explicit encouragement to land transfers that would create larger, more efficient farms, the social and economic problems brewing in the rural sector may be gathering momentum. The 2008 initiative may not be the leading edge of land privatisation, as some domestic critics fear, but it will most likely lead to the additional displacement of rural workers, and a threat to employment from more capital-intensive farming techniques. At a time of rising unemployment and under-employment, this would surely have negative repercussions for rural inhabitants and for urban migrants wishing to return home.

Whether or not China is prepared to embark on a much stronger pro-rural and pro-consumption shift in policies is most unlikely to be resolved in the near future, not least because the National Peoples' Congress in 2012 will rubberstamp a change in the China's leadership structure. Even then, it is not possible to know if and how structural reforms will be taken up. One commentator has argued that the challenge cannot be taken up without breaking the grip on power that is held by the elite factions of the Communist Party, which come mainly from coastal and urban areas, and which therefore have strong vested interests[16]. The urban–industrial elite dominates the upper echelons of the Communist Party, and Hu Jintao's chosen successor, Xi Jinping, head of the coastal provinces of Fujian and Zhejiang, comes from a similar background. Like Robert Ash, the author claims that behind the banner headlines surrounding exports, manufacturing strength, and social and political achievements, lies an agrarian crisis.

In other Asian countries, such as Japan, South Korea and Taiwan, large gaps between rural and urban wages closed up or narrowed significantly during their catch-up phases. As that happened, the excess of rural labour declined, manufacturing wages rose, and this then spurred capital investment and innovation. China, on the other hand, has allowed the countryside to languish, with income per head in rural areas never exceeding 40% of that in urban areas. From the 1990s onwards, agricultural incomes, in particular, suffered from the demise of collective rural industries, which had created substantial employment. Substantial rural–urban migration followed, resulting in downward pressure on urban incomes too.

Although wage rates have risen in Chinese cities in the last 2–3 years, they have not changed enough to alter the general picture of wage stagnation in China. In 1995, wages were about 50% of GDP, and enterprise profits were about 20%. In 2008, these shares had shifted to 40%, and 32%, respectively. Since urban wages are so much higher than in the countryside, it follows that rural citizens will have fared relatively, and absolutely, badly.

Neglect of agriculture has become one of the main reasons for the lowly consumption share of the economy, and therefore a source of China's large trade surplus and growing financial power in the world. That was almost certainly not what was intended, but it is how things have turned out. China's commitment to the economic development model that has succeeded so well in the last 20 years needs a re-boot. If global exports are not going to come bouncing back with a pre-2007 gusto, and the underlying export-heavy industry-investment structure of the economy remains intact, there is little hope for a resolution of global imbalances. That may be the least of China's worries, though the possible consequences of reactions by other countries, including the US and Europe, are not trivial.

In the last months of 2010, the Communist Party is expected to meet to agree a general policy platform for the 12th Five Year Plan (2011–2015). Its main goals are expected to include more equitable income distribution, improvements in the urbanisation of rural migrants, moves to a low carbon economy, and a shift in economic structure from investment and exports towards domestic consumption.

But experience of the prior Five Year Plan reveals where China is strong and where it is weak. The Plan's goals, as they pertained to economic growth, per capita income, public services, population and labour, and energy efficiency were largely met. Those that were associated with or needed more extensive economic and social reforms, for example the promotion of service-producing industries, research and development spending, the management of rural–urban migration and income distribution, were not realised.

Planning for the next five years

It is not just the post-crisis status quo in a global context that will matter to China. At home, it has to convince vested interests in the Party, local governments in urban areas that have prospered from the economic and social status quo, that they must now be willing to back new and sometimes radical reforms, including to the exchange rate regime that may not be in their interests. In the longer run, these reforms may avert the possibility of growing social and political unrest. In the short term, they may avert the looming risks of a bubble, and a subsequent economic downturn some time in the next few years.

The nature of the RMB regime means that local interest rates are lower than they otherwise should be. If total GDP is growing by 13% per year (9% real growth and 4% inflation, for example), interest rates should be comparable – perhaps a bit lower or higher depending on the overall goals of economic and inflation policies. However, the US dollar link means that local interest rates are roughly the same as, or much closer to, those in the US. Consequently, banks and other entities have strong incentives to borrow from the central bank at low official rates, and lend money in to the economy, where the promise of high returns and rising asset prices invite capital, and the risk of over-investment in companies, industries, and assets including property.

And that's how bubbles start. Credit in China is controlled not through markets and interest rates but by diktat, and by an oligopoly of powerful bankers, many with strong political connections or aspirations, that run the major commercial banks. Even though the 2007–2009 financial crisis demonstrated that unfettered financial markets were instrumental in causing mayhem and were ineffectual in controlling it, lasting confidence in one of the top committees in the Chinese political system as the final arbiter of major credit and finance decisions can hardly be any greater.

No one knows how far an asset bubble in China will inflate. But we do know that an unstable bubble process is under way. China could nip it in the bud, raise interest rates, raise new property taxes, and force the banks to raise more capital, and take the consequences of weaker growth for a while. Or it could let it run, and risk rising inflation, which might then require even stronger economic medicine. In the event of a 'hard landing', land prices could fall by over 50% and property prices follow suit, and while lower prices would still be higher than they were several years ago, the consequences of a property bust for the Chinese banking system, the economy and social cohesion would be alarming.

There is no doubt that China will continue to respond, reinforcing measures already taken to regain control over runaway bank lending and increase the reserve requirements Chinese banks must hold at the central bank. And following the abandonment of the US dollar peg in 2010, it is possible, but by no means inevitable, that China will increase the use and flexibility of official interest rates to contain credit creation. But the likelihood is that all of these responses will be too little, too late, and that bubble risks will roll on into 2011 and 2012. Global financial markets can only hope that the bubble in Chinese asset prices and the early signs of rising inflation remain relatively subdued, and the authorities must hope that broad economic stability will endure until the National Peoples' Congress in 2012.

China doesn't need to slow its rate of growth necessarily, other than to accommodate the longer-term decline that comes with an ageing population and, eventually, with economic maturity. China's challenge is to re-focus the production of domestic companies away from overseas towards domestic demand, and make sure that domestic consumption rises steadily as a share of GDP. This requires explicit policies to ensure an appropriate distribution of income, and a shift of resources into commercially-viable local companies, as well as the reduction of red tape and corruption, and the elimination of currency distortions, subsidised credit, and the drawbacks of an underdeveloped financial system.

For the time being, though, China remains wedded to the essence of the economic development model of the last 20 years. Gradualism is seen as good, and the existing currency regime is viewed as the key to economic stability, and the delivery of a stable and high rate of growth. However reasoned and fitting this position may have been before 2007, the crisis has undermined it.

China needs to change tack. Historically, the Confucian state has demonstrated its effectiveness in making things happen, but equally it has sometimes been resistant to change, chauvinist and suspicious of outsiders, and autarkic. In more modern times, sweeping reforms were introduced in the late 1970s, and again in the early 1990s. Another 20 years have elapsed, and the time has come again to influence future economic trends through political reforms. Only political reform and institutional flexibility can keep China on course.

Chapter Six

Older and Wiser: Demographic and Technological Challenges

Even though, as we have seen, the financial crisis has shocked the global economic system and presented new challenges and risks for emerging markets, good politics and economic management, and sound institutions give countries layers of protection against occasional financial storms. While the long-run reasons for fast economic growth in emerging markets remain sound, the fortunes and failures of these countries over the next decades will be determined by two phenomena, which they can control and manage: demographics and technology[1]. Put another way, it's going to be about how people and societies adapt as they become more populous and older, and about how they manage to harvest the knowledge, embodied by people, to generate innovation and higher productivity.

If the world of finance, which I have explored at some length, is fickle, then demographics are destiny. Demographics are about people: their numbers, attitudes, behaviour and skills. People determine the rate and nature of economic and social progress. No one disputes this. Technology and the race for technological leadership, on the other hand, are not just about being clever, but about the quality of social and political organisations and institutions.

Demographics matter to most people nowadays for two reasons. Many people see demographics in terms of 'who's going to look after grandma?' In other words, how will society be able to look after and care for its increasingly numerous older citizens? Some focus on more commercial matters, including how consumer products and consumption patterns will change as societies become 'greyer', and how companies will have to change their branding and advertising strategies. Demographics matter, though, for even bigger reasons. They define a country's capacity to deliver economic and social progress, and they enable countries to project power and, if they are able, to set and implement an agenda for others to follow.

Demographic change, which nowadays means rapid population ageing, is occurring throughout the Western world, and arises from the unique combination of falling or weak fertility and rising longevity, or life expectancy. Normally when the birth rate is roughly 2.07 children per woman of childbearing age, the population tends to replace itself. Most Western nations, except for the US, have fertility rates significantly lower than this. Their populations, therefore, are likely to stagnate or decline, unless there is a sufficiently large rise in immigration to compensate. In most countries, other than the US, Canada and Australia, the amount of extra immigration needed to offset fully the expected demographic shift is politically unmanageable, at least as things stand today. In Europe, other than the UK, and in Japan, immigration would have to rise between 5–20 times in order to keep the population of working age stable over the next 40 years.

Western populations will get progressively older, because the bulge of the baby boomers in the work force is like a snake digesting its prey, gradually moving through the age structure towards retirement and economic inactivity. The boomers are leaving the work force to spend perhaps another 20–30 years in retirement, but their smaller numbers of offspring will not replace them fully, or at all. The dependency ratio (of older citizens on people of working age), therefore, is starting to rise quickly. Put another way, each person over the age of 65 in rich countries today is supported by roughly four workers, though no more than three in Japan, Germany and Italy. By 2050, just two workers will support each older citizen, and only 1.4–1.6 workers in the three countries mentioned.

The main economic effects of rapid ageing will comprise a slowdown in the sustainable rate of economic growth, and a significant rise in the financial burden on individuals and governments for providing pensions, healthcare and old age residential care. If this agenda does not sound demanding enough, remember that the financial crisis has left many Western governments facing unprecedented peacetime increases in public borrowing and public debt. Since the largest and fastest growing components of public expenditure are ageing-related, governments have to find ways of offsetting the impact of rapid ageing on the economy, for example by looking for new sources of economic growth and productivity, and changing labour market and pension systems. They also have to restructure taxation and public spending arrangements to ensure we can pay for ageing societies without imposing an intolerable tax burden on working people.

Do not imagine that this is only a Western problem. Emerging countries face precisely the same challenges but, for the most part, they are about 25–30 years behind the rich world. The factors that have driven down fertility rates and increased longevity are universal. Fertility rates have been falling because of improved literacy and education, especially among females, cheap and readily available methods of birth control, and rising living and health care standards. In Eastern European emerging markets, the fertility rate is the lowest at 1.4 children. It is 1.8 in East Asia, and about 2.4 in other developing countries, except Sub Sahara Africa where it is 4.8. According to the United Nations Human Development Report, the fertility rate in 39 developing countries in 2005–2010 remained relatively high at between 4–7 children per woman. These include most African nations, Pakistan, Bangladesh, Afghanistan and Yemen. Some 32 of these countries were classified as 'low human development'.

Life expectancy is rising because of improvements in health care and disease control, and in dietary and exercise regimes. Some of the poorest countries in the world are outliers. About 59 countries, also including all the poorest, have the lowest life expectancy at birth at between 36–56 years.

Nearly all developing countries are a lot younger than their richer peers. Fertility rates are higher but, with a few exceptions, falling nevertheless. The working age population is still growing rapidly, and the rise in the number of older citizens is occurring but very slowly by comparison. As time passes, though, emerging nations will age, so that by 2030–2035, the age structure and dependency ratios in many major emerging markets will look similar to most advanced nations today. They too will then be anticipating rapid ageing.

There are some notable exceptions to this basic demographic pattern in emerging countries, notably China, but also Singapore, Hong Kong, and South Korea. All are relatively old by emerging market standards, and in many respects compare more readily with many rich nations. China is much younger than the West, but it is the fastest ageing country in the world. China's young people, say, up to 24 years old, will decline in absolute terms over the next 20 years, and the working age population will start falling from as early as 2010–2011, slowly at first, but gathering momentum over the next two to three decades. By 2050, China will be very old. It will have more people aged over 65 than the entire US population predicted at that time, and more people aged over 80 than any other country.

It is important to highlight the economic advantages enjoyed by countries with young and dynamic populations. But we must also be aware that these advantages do not guarantee economic success. Young populations that have poor employment opportunities may just as easily be agents of social and political unrest. Moreover, as young populations in emerging markets age, it is a moot point as to whether emerging governments will be any more prepared for rapid ageing than Western ones are today. The tendency to defer ageing issues to future governments is well established. It matters, especially in emerging markets, because they are ageing with lower per capita income levels than Western countries had at a similar stage in the ageing process two to three decades ago. This is the 'getting old before you get rich' cliché, which conveys both the seriousness and the urgency of the problem.

Turning to technology and productivity, the knowledge that we instil into citizens and workers is the basis for progress. The productivity obtained from applying knowledge and from innovation will become increasingly important as a result of the consequences of rapid ageing. Emerging markets already realise considerable productivity gains as rural workers leave low productivity, low-income jobs for more rewarding and more productive work in factories, offices and on construction sites. Productivity growth is also boosted by the diffusion of knowledge through trade, foreign direct investment, and greater engagement in the global economy, for example when foreign companies set up or 'outsource' production or service facilities in emerging economies. The race to realise the newest technologies and to spur innovation is going to become increasingly important, as emerging demographics become less favourable over time.

Whether out of desire, necessity, pride or, eventually, because of the pressure of rapid ageing, emerging countries will become users and copiers of advanced technologies, and a few, including China and India, will try to out-innovate Western nations in global technology. And yet, for the time being, emerging nations (other than South Korea perhaps), look most unlikely to challenge the lead that developed nations have in terms of the sheer number of knowledge workers, knowledge-based industries and research activities, and the infrastructure required to stimulate innovation. Americans and Europeans fret nowadays that Chinese and Indian universities are churning out more scientists and engineers than theirs do, and this feeds the many fears about the 'irreversible' shift in economic and technological power. But more isn't always better in terms of exploiting technology and innovation. In the US, there are three times as many scientists and engineers per head of population as there are in China, and the infrastructure that supports innovation is unquestionably superior.

Nevertheless, the overwhelming consensus in the economic and business media is that China, and to a lesser extent India, are on course to become the great innovators and technology leaders of tomorrow. While this is a popular prediction, it is also over-simplistic and an exaggeration.

Why demographics matter

Let us look at some of the world's key demographic trends to start. According to the United Nations, world population is predicted to grow from 6.9 billion in 2010 to about 9.1 billion in 2050. Although that equates to a 33% rise, making many environmental and green groups shudder, the growth in the world's population is slowing down continuously. By the middle of the century, the growth rate will have halved to about 0.7% per year. The good news here is that any rate of economic growth above this level would mean that, in the aggregate, people are becoming better off.

But raw population change is far too narrow a lens through which to see the significance of demographics. The broader picture embraces first, existing tensions in the world between population size and distribution, on the one hand, and the scramble for access to food, energy, water and resources on the other; and second, the significance of the change in population age structure.

All but 100 million of the 2.2 billion increase in the world's population will be living in developing countries. Of the 10 most populous countries in the world by 2050, only the US will represent the rich world. Half the growth in world population will occur in India, Pakistan, Nigeria, China, the US, Ethiopia, United

Republic of Tanzania and Bangladesh. Roughly 70% of the growth in global population will occur in 24 of the poorest developing countries. India will overtake China as the world's most populous country in about 2028.

The median age in richer nations is 40 years, that is, half the population is older, and half younger. By 2050, it will have risen to almost 46. In developing countries, the median age is 27 years, and will rise to 37 by 2050. There are some notable exceptions to the current profile. Singapore has a median age of 41, which makes it a little older than Germany. Hong Kong's median age of 42 makes it only a little younger than Italy. South Korea's median age is 38, but it will be as old as Japan in the next 20 years, and China is the fastest ageing country in the world. Its median age of 34 is predicted to rise to 45, at which point it will be older than the US.

The proportion of over 60s in the world will double to 22% by 2050, or from 759 million to 2 billion. In richer nations, the proportion will rise from 22% to 33%, while in developing countries, it will increase from a mere 9% to just over 20%. The number of children aged under 15 is projected to fall from 1.86 billion to 1.8 billion, or from 27% to 20% of the world's population, but 90% of them will live in developing countries, much the same as now. The large shifts in older and younger age groups have profound implications for the working age population, and therefore for the economy.

In Western nations, the 15–59 age cohort is predicted to fall from 62% to 52% of the population. In developing countries, the working age population is expected to rise by about 1 billion, but as a share of total population, it is expected to drift down from 62% from about 2025 onwards. This, though, is heavily influenced by China, without which the decline starts later, in 2035. In the very poorest countries, the working age population is expected to rise by 700 million, and from 55% to 62% of the population. This group includes countries such as Niger, Afghanistan, Somalia, Uganda, Chad and Zambia.

Malthusian flashpoints

The contrast between the demographics of richer and poorer nations could not be starker. Richer nations will account for a mere 14% of world population by mid-century, down 4% from 2010, and a sharply rising proportion will be aged over 60. Most of the world's population growth will occur in younger, developing nations, and most will face the challenge of providing jobs and economic security for their burgeoning numbers of working age people.

These important demographic differences are already dividing rich and poor nations, and are liable to spark tensions and flashpoints in the future. A high level of cooperation and good global and national institutions are essential in addressing current neo-Malthusian issues over energy and resources. Thomas Malthus, remember, was concerned about the effects of over-population on food supply, predicting at the end of the 18th century that food supply wouldn't be able to keep up with population, and there would be a natural tendency for recurring bouts of famine, war and poverty.

But Malthus was wrong. Human ingenuity, scientific progress and, later, the advent of public welfare put paid to his concerns. And when Malthusians worried again in the 1960s and 1970s, significant enhancements in crop yields and farming techniques, and subsequent advances in irrigation and technology, again denied them their moment[2]. Modern Malthusian concerns matter, because the pressures of population growth and longevity on food and natural resource supplies have again become problematic, and because the principal negative consequences will affect emerging and developing nations most, and the poorest among them in particular.

Food and energy prices rose sharply in 2005–2007, and after a global recession-induced decline, started to rise again in 2010. They remind us that the handmaiden of rapid economic and population growth in emerging countries, especially as people migrate to towns and cities, is growing demand for food, protein, water, fertilisers, chemicals and non-renewable sources of energy. Double-digit economic growth in China, for example, has contributed to its voracious appetite for imported oil, but also industrial materials, such as iron ore and copper. This has given added impetus to contemporary Malthusian concerns about sustainability of resources and the environment and, ultimately, about potential geopolitical tensions and even conflict. If you want a really dark view about this, the 1973 American science-fiction film, 'Soylent Green' envisages a world suffering from overpopulation, poverty, pollution and the adverse effects of climate change where survivors depend on processed food rations. Fantasy it may be, but the growth in demand for food and other resources, based on demographics, is currently outstripping the world's capacity to provide them over the longer term.

Food supply growth has slowed down with the stabilisation of crop yields since about 1990, and with weaker agricultural research and development spending. Stocks of key commodities, such as grains and oilseeds have fallen to record low levels, partly because of the increasing use of these products for animal husbandry and bio-fuels. Moreover, much of the success in developing agriculture in the past has come at the expense of a deterioration in soil quality through the use of fertilisers, and in the quantity and quality of water through irrigation.

Some agricultural prices have retreated due to the financial crisis and the global recession, but they remain high, and concerns about oil, food and water supplies are enduring. Oil powers everything from transportation and construction to manufacturing and food production. Experts disagree about how long existing conventional oil reserves can be tapped at the current rate, but there is widespread acknowledgement that this point could arise within the next decade. Oil production outside the OPEC group of countries is already past its peak, and much uncertainty resides in the size and rate of extraction of oil reserves in OPEC, but principally Saudi Arabia[3]. In any event, if global demand keeps rising, largely due to economic growth in emerging countries, the ability of OPEC countries to determine prices will strengthen, and global supplies will remain tight for as long as it takes to wean the global economy away from crude oil, and to develop alternative energy supplies and more sophisticated energy storage systems.

High food and fish prices reflect the accumulation of years of declining stocks and rising demand, not least due to the growth in world population and life expectancy, and as countries become richer. In China, for example, meat consumption per head has more than doubled in the last 25 years. Rising meat consumption has shifted the balance of land and water use away from growing grains. The adequacy of grain production in the world depends increasingly on good harvests and the avoidance of natural disasters. The World Bank and the United Nations estimate that demand for food will rise 50% by 2030, implying that if supply can't keep up for whatever reason, food prices will continue to rise sharply and contribute to further increases in poverty and disease.

Water availability and declining water tables have also become a source of growing concern, partly because of economic and population growth, but also because of the effects of climate change on glaciers and weather patterns. Agriculture uses about three quarters of the world's usable fresh water, and demographic change points clearly to growing demand for water by farmers. The addition of another 1 billion emerging country urban residents by 2035 and the growth of towns and cities guarantee that the number of countries in which cropland and fresh water are scarce will rise. The United Nations reckons that there are 21 such countries today, and that the number will rise to 48 by 2025, and 54 by 2050, with the number of people affected rising to 4 billion by mid-decade. Most of the countries are in the Middle East and Africa, while 19 Indian cities also face severe water stress. Although China just misses being labelled water-scarce today, its water resources are deemed capable of supporting only half the population in the long term. Already hundreds of millions of people in northern China face water shortages, and such is Beijing's water consumption that its underground water tables are falling steadily, making it all the more reliant on fresh rainwater, which has become increasingly hostage to drought.

Another Malthusian flashpoint is exemplified by the on-going war in Afghanistan, which typifies the demographic contrast between rich and poor countries, and the limitations of conventional military thinking. Afghanistan's median age is 17, women have 6.3 children on average, 46% of the population is aged under 15, and 50% are aged 15–59. In simple military terms, there won't ever be a shortage of potential Taliban fighters. In the US and other rich nations, by contrast, where the demographics are radically different, the willingness of often single-child parents to support extended conflicts where the demographic odds are stacked heavily against them cannot be taken for granted.

How can we address the tensions likely to arise from these Malthusian problems? Environmental and other political lobbies advocate the urgent implementation of population control measures and a deliberate slowing of economic, and especially consumption, growth in order to bring population and resources into better and more sustainable balance. But what they mean, knowingly or not, is that emerging countries, where the fastest growth in population and consumption is occurring, should deny themselves the opportunity to catch up economically and improve their living standards. That just can't be right.

Instead, it is more constructive to ask why these population and resource constraints have arisen, and what to do about them. In so doing, we might also wonder how it is that measures of pollution, congestion, power consumption, and the use of pesticides, are growing around 5–6 times as fast as global population growth. There is no question that the Malthusians have a point: we are using up finite resources rapidly, often wastefully, and in ways that threaten our ecology. And rising global population growth and life expectancy comprise essential parts of the backdrop. The main reason these things are happening, however, is because market systems are not up to the task of ensuring sustainability. Rather than preach population reduction and consumer abstinence to poorer countries, we have to try and augment and improve the working of market systems to resolve four key issues for mankind.

First, whether for anthropological reasons or not, climate change is messing with our eco-systems. I shall discuss this more in the next chapter with particular reference to emerging nations, but it is clear that market systems alone will not help reverse the consequences of global warming.

Second, markets have not succeeded in helping countries and cities in developing countries to overcome poverty, which, along with poor education and literacy levels, is widely believed to be one of the root causes of high population growth. The World Bank has revised its estimates of global poverty, estimating that 1.4 billion people, or a quarter of the world's population, live in poverty compared with a prior estimate of 985 million[4]. The decline in the numbers living in poverty, now defined as less than \$1.25 a day, over the last 20–30 years remains at about 500 million, but it is clear from the numbers that poverty remains a more diffuse and larger problem than thought previously. For people living in such conditions, rapid population growth is not so much a potential boost to economic growth as a response to premature illness and death, and the result of poor education.

Third, while consumerism, or excessive consumption, is generally a charge levied at indulgent Western societies, the consumer culture has spread to large swathes of the emerging world. Urbanisation and the drive towards modernity are typically what rapid economic development is all about and inevitably encourage people to aspire to a higher standard of living. But as citizens become better off, they have been quick to adopt modern consumption patterns, driven not so much by need as by commercialisation, advertising, marketing, and the sprouting of luxury shopping malls and designer stores. Consumer culture in developing countries is growing, not always because people have more leisure time and disposable income, but often because of the concerted actions of an institutional network of retail stores, manufacturers, marketing and display specialists that is supported or tolerated by government policies. Travellers cannot fail to note the contrast between modern city centres in, say, Mumbai, Rio de Janeiro, Johannesburg, Nairobi or Manila and surrounding large slum populations, which are part of the estimated 1 billion people living in such conditions.

Fourth, markets have not been able to give more countries more access to the kinds of technology that would help local economic development, especially in rural areas, or support global programmes involving such initiatives as carbon capture, solar and alternative energy, crop enhancement, and resource efficiency.

The argument about the failure of markets to address environmental degradation, inefficient use of resources, poverty, überconsumerism, and access to technology takes us a long way from the more naïve view of overpopulation. Malthusian concerns would diminish considerably over time if the world's major powers in the G20 would agree to empower and adequately resource global institutions to tackle these significant challenges, similar to the efforts to address global health issues, including the campaign to combat HIV/AIDS.

The goals of economic development and security, therefore, seem destined to generate flashpoints between richer older countries and poorer younger ones. The only way to manage these is for them all to recognise their mutual interdependence, and to support and defer to well-respected multilateral institutions to develop shared strategies. But even if global institutions can develop broader economic and social strategies to address demographic- and resource-related issues, governments of nation states still have to agree and implement them. As the US National Intelligence

Council has pointed out, 'whether global institutions adapt and survive is a function of leadership. Current trends suggest a dispersion of power and authority will create a global governance deficit. Reversing those trends lines would require strong leadership in the international community by a number of powers, including the emerging ones'[5]. I shall return to this theme in the concluding chapter.

Getting old before getting rich

Imagine towns and villages that are dying of old age. What would you expect to see? You would find a large majority of the population aged over 60, depopulated schools, and a plethora of 'for sale' notices outside properties and in estate agents' offices. Local hospitals would no longer offer maternity services, the old would look after the very old, and there would be few jobs and no social opportunities. This is no fiction, for this picture describes what you can see in a growing number of Japanese villages today. Visitors to Italian hilltop villages, or travellers passing through towns in central and Eastern Europe can testify to the same observations. Even in the US, where population ageing is the slowest of all the rich nations, and where immigration rates are high, the retirement community town of Laguna Woods in California boasts an average age of 78, according to the 2000 Census, the highest of any location with more than 10,000 residents.

Economically, emerging market demographics are the same as they are in richer nations. The major differences are where they are in the ageing cycle, and that when their age structures rise more rapidly, their per capita incomes will compare unfavourably with richer economies at the same ageing stage 20–30 years ago. Rapid ageing carries forebodings about slowing economic growth, dying villages, and economic hardship for a rapidly growing number of older citizens, but it is also about the social consequences of low fertility and small family size in countries where filial, rather than state-supplied, care is the accepted custom in old age.

The majority of emerging markets should continue to enjoy what demographers call their 'demographic dividend' for many years. This is the phase during which the age structure rises, not because of expanding cohorts of older citizens, but because of a slowdown in births and a rise in the population of working age. People are living longer in emerging nations, as elsewhere, but the number of old and very old people is not yet rising as fast as the number of people in work. The so-called dividend captures the benefits that come as more and more people become pro-ducers, and their obligations to support children financially and otherwise diminish. Over time, though, as working age people move into their 50s and 60s and then into retirement, the demo-graphic dividend will diminish and then vanish.

In older developed countries, fertility rates are already below the replacement rate of 2.07 children, except in the US. As the proportion of people aged over 65 doubles over the next two to three decades, Western countries will need to raise spending on pensions, healthcare and old age care provision by an additional 7% of GDP. If they had to write a cheque for these age-related costs on the basis of today's money, they would amount to between 150–600% of GDP[6].

Emerging markets should take note, because they are liable to face the onset of rapid ageing with lower levels of income than Western countries have today. Most emerging markets fall in to what the World Bank calls 'middle income' countries, where the average 2008 per capita income was $3260. In the 1950s, when the US and Europe had a median age of 29, slightly older than emerging markets today, per capita income was roughly $10,000 and $5000, respectively. But this was soon after the Second World War, and by the 1970s, when the median age was the same as it is in China today, per capita income had risen to $14,000, and $12,000 respectively. By 2030, China and the US will have a comparable median age of about 40 years. If China's per capita income were to grow by a generous 8% per year, it would still only reach American per capita income in 1970. The consequences for emerging nations, therefore, of ignoring ageing or leaving it to a future government to sort out, are serious. For older emerging nations, such as China, that time has already arrived.

China and Russia represent very different examples of ageing from India and Brazil. China is already a rapidly ageing country, and will experience a dwindling in its cohorts of children and working age people, commencing in the next few years. Russia's population is declining, and may sink from 142 million to about 80–90 million by 2050. Russia, along with countries in Eastern Europe, is also ageing very quickly. India and Brazil offer brighter examples of demographic potential. Both have much younger populations and will continue to experience rising numbers of working age people in the next 20–30 years in absolute terms and in relation to other age cohorts. This is especially the case in India, where a third of the population is under 15. Emerging countries such as Malaysia, Indonesia, Mexico and Chile fall into line behind India and Brazil.

In passing, much of Sub Sahara Africa, and the Middle East and North Africa have favourable demographic trends on paper that are overshadowed by more sinister trends in practice: HIV/AIDS in the case of the former, and potential or actual social and political instability in the case of the latter.

Ageing in China

China has a triple-whammy of ageing. The youth population is projected to decline, the labour force is set to fall, and the number of the nation's over 60s will nearly triple. Between 2010 and 2050, the number of children aged 0–14 will fall by 53 million, and young adults aged 15–24 will fall by 80 million. The work force, aged 15–64, will decline by about 100 million, or from 72% of the population to 61%. Meanwhile the over 60s will rise by 234 million, or from 12% to 31% of the population. Living to a ripe old age is a common characteristic of Asian countries, but the scale of the change in China is unprecedented. The old age dependency ratio is about 11% today, but it is expected to rise to 24% by 2030, by which point there will be more over 60s than under 15s, and to 40% by 2050. In other words, the 10 workers that support each older citizen today will have dwindled to 2.5.

China's demographics are notorious because of the one-child policy introduced in 1980 by Deng Xiaoping at a time when the Communist Party's main concern was classically Malthusian – that is, impoverishment through overpopulation. Because of the historical and cultural preference for male children, Mao Zedong's dictum that 'women hold up half the sky' suddenly rang hollow. At the time, China's fertility rate was about three children per woman, half of what it had been in the 1950s. Nevertheless, this was the first – and only time in modern times – that any government has intervened forcibly into the reproductive decision of citizens. It is hard to distinguish exactly the effects of the one-child policy on China's demographics, as opposed to other more common factors that have tended to lower fertility, such as higher female literacy rates, better education, and free and widely available methods of birth control. Regardless, China's fertility rate is now 1.7 children, considerably lower than it is in the US, and in some of the largest cities, such as Beijing, Shanghai and Tianjin, it has fallen to 1.0, and possibly below.

The policy was reconfirmed as recently as 2006, but while some rural authorities still use a system of rewards and punishments to enforce the policy, it is no longer harshly enforced, and sex detection via ultrasound has been officially banned since 1995. In urban areas, couples are usually allowed to have only one child, though some are encouraged to have a second child if both parents grew up as single children. In rural areas, there are different rules. Some couples are allowed a second child if the first was a girl. Some are allowed a second child if their parents suffered hardship, according to local officials' interpretations. And in the far west of China and in Inner Mongolia, the policy is barely applied at all.

In Shanghai, the local government announced in 2009 that it would offer counselling services to encourage couples to have a second child. You can see why. With a low fertility rate, and 3 million people – or 21.6% of registered residents – aged over 60, Shanghai's age structure is increasing rapidly. By 2020, the over 60s are expected to account for a third of the registered population. This will be the same as for Japan at that time.

The consequences of low fertility, the one-child social experiment, and rapid ageing in China are going to have consequences that fall into two broad categories. The first covers the social repercussions of significant gender imbalance and threats to the Chinese family structure. The second comprises the economic implications, such as lower sustainable economic growth and the lack of adequate social security, especially for rural citizens.

The one-child policy may not have been the only factor contributing to a large gender imbalance, because other Asian countries, and the north of India, where a preference for sons, low fertility and the widespread use of ultrasound are common, are also renowned for large gender discrepancies. But in China, it has certainly contributed to an imbalance of about 120 males per 100 females. In some rural and hinterland areas, it may be as much as 130. But these are average numbers. The gender imbalance rate is typically lower, say 108, for first births, but for second and subsequent births, it can be as high as 140 to 150. This portends growing social problems.

In 2010 the Chinese Academy of Social Sciences reported that, by 2020, about 20% of young men would never be able to marry because of the dearth of young women, and that at age 29 and above, there would be 30–40 million more men than women[7]. According to one demographer, about 5% of men in their late 30s don't marry nowadays, but this proportion could rise to 15% by 2020 and 40% by 2040[8]. As single young men grow older and eventually retire, they will generate additional demands on China's welfare system. Even before then, China will have to pay increasing attention to common-or-garden social problems associated with 'man excess', namely violence, prostitution and crime, including the kidnapping of and trafficking in young girls.

According to a website sponsored by the Academy for Educational Development, a non-profit charitable organisation (www.humantrafficking.org), these problems are already widespread.

Many Chinese women are recruited by groups making false promises of employment, and are later coerced into prostitution or forced labour. Parents are promised that their children will send money home, which never arrives. In some rural areas, women are sold as wives to older and disabled unmarried men, while in cities and towns, they are sold to commercial sex businesses, hair salons, massage parlours and bathhouses. China is a destination country for women and children who are trafficked from Mongolia, Burma, North Korea, Russia, Vietnam, Ukraine and Laos, and internal trafficking of children for sexual and labour exploitation is widespread. Estimates of the number of victims range from 10,000 to 20,000 each year, though there are unconfirmed estimates of close to three times as many. Almost all of the victims are women and children, many of the latter being sold for adoption.

Low fertility, ageing and gender imbalance will also change Chinese family structures. Nicholas Eberstadt, whose observations about marriage appear above, argues that about a quarter of adults, aged 25–49, living in towns and cities, grew up as single children. By 2020, this proportion is predicted to rise to 42%, and by 2030, to about 58%. If these singles also have just one child, or no children, which is what is tending to happen, China's celebrated reputation for large families and familial and filial old age care will slowly atrophy.

Apart from the social implications for millions of children who will grow up with few or no siblings and cousins, there are commerial and business implications too. Business is traditionally done within and between families in networks known as *guanxi*, literally translated as connections, but implying obligations of goodwill and personal affection. Whereas Western family businesses see wealth creation and profit as their prime motivation, Chinese family businesses tend to see the family as their main responsibility. They have enjoyed a revival since China turned its back on Marxism. Data on family businesses are never especially timely, but in 2006, China's family enterprises accounted for about three-fifths of GDP, four-fifths of jobs and nearly three-quarters of local government tax revenues[9]. But because of the preponderance of single children, the emergence of family structures that will be 'top heavy' with parents, grandparents and great-grandparents, and because of urbanisation, it is estimated that just 30% of family enterprises will survive into the next generation, and only 14% into the one after that.

The economic implications of ageing in China will soon start to become more transparent. China's labour force which expanded by 2.6 times between 1950 and 2010, is about to start declining, and is predicted to fall by 10% over the next 40 years. That will still leave 870 million aged 15–64, but the effect of the decline, bearing in mind also the fall in the youth population and the substantial rise in the over 60s, will be keenly felt.

At the very least, the decline in the labour force and the significant rise in old age dependency could knock 2% off the country's current long-term growth rate of about 7–8%. This more or less negates the contribution that a rising labour force and falling child dependency made to the growth rate in the last several decades. In addition, high productivity growth rates are likely to be scaled back over the longer term as a result of the ageing process, a rise in official welfare spending, and the eventual decline in high levels of savings and investment. By the 2020s, in the absence of any untoward financial or other shocks, China's underlying growth rate will become rather more pedestrian at around 5% per annum or so. This will still outstrip anything the West is able to achieve, but it serves to underline the meaninglessness of economic growth projections that don't allow for the consequences of rapid ageing.

For the time being, though, China's 80–100 million pool of young rural migrants should continue to offset the effects of ageing on the productive labour force, even though a large proportion go home in their late 20s or early 30s to tend to parents and grandparents or family businesses, especially if they are single children. The chance to receive lifetime gifts and inheritance bequests offers further incentives. But this pool of migrants will decline in the next decade, in keeping with the demographic decline in the numbers of children and young adults.

In the interim, the main issue that China faces is not so much running out of workers, but running out of cheap workers, especially female migrant workers who tend to gravitate to factory and office jobs. Chinese companies have to compete increasingly on wages, so as to be able to attract and retain workers. Annual wage increases in manufacturing were 10–12% between 2005–2007, even higher in 2009, and in the first quarter of 2010, it was reported that wages for urban employees had risen by almost 13% over the year before. In Eastern Jiangsu province, which exports more than Brazil and South Africa combined, the minimum monthly wage, which was last changed in 2008, went up by 13% (to RMB 960, or $140). And, as I pointed out earlier, widespread labour unrest in southern China in May and June 2010 resulted in some massive pay increases for large groups of factory workers, and an even higher increase in minimum wages in Beijing and other major cities. These trends are indicative of a growing phenomenon in China, namely rising wages resulting from growing tightness in the labour market. And while the problem of general labour shortages may lie several years away, China will not be able to turn a blind eye to the effects that rising wages may even now be having on inflation, especially in the light of the bubble risks discussed earlier in the book.

The economic consequences of ageing in China also go to the heart of the social security system, and to the reasons why many people save so much. The iron rice bowl was an idiom capturing a system, introduced under Mao Zedong, whereby party cadres were empowered to control employment in state enterprises, job security, wages, and the allocation of everything from housing, to grain, edible oil, and cotton rations, to permits for travel, marriage and children. In return, citizens were provided with cradle-to-grave benefits. This system collapsed with the reforms introduced from the 1980s, but it left huge gaps in the social security enjoyed by urban workers in particular. Rural workers suffered too, but their benefits had always been lower and less widely distributed.

Although the authorities have taken steps since 2000 to broaden social security coverage and increase payments, China still lacks national programmes on healthcare, housing subsidy schemes, retirement, and social welfare. Pension assets, for example, account for a mere 2–3% of GDP, compared with 60% in Singapore and 50% in Malaysia. State pensions replace about half of average wages, which is relatively high for Asia, but only 20% of urban workers are covered, and less than 10% of rural workers have any coverage at all. Health insurance can't be transferred between jobs and work locations and is, in any case, expensive. More than half of China's over 60s have to pay their own medical bills, and most of the rest tends to be family-financed.

Moreover, the so-called *hukou* system of household residence permits, first introduced in 1958 to try and control internal migration, represents a continuing weakness as far as the living standards of urban migrants are concerned, and is an important reason why they are compelled to save, and why the gap between urban and rural incomes remains so wide. The system effectively divides urban dwellers into officially registered residents and second-class rural migrants. If you are not registered, you do not qualify for access to jobs, income support, subsidised housing, healthcare or public education. There may be as many as 200 million in the latter category. In Bejing, according to one report, half the 460,000 children born in the city since 2007 cannot be registered officially[10]. *Hukou* in China is about as big an issue as healthcare is in the US. People tend to recognise there's a problem, but quite what to do about it is a source of major contention. If *hukou* is abandoned precipitously, it could spark uncontrollable urban migration and instability. If it isn't changed sufficiently or soon enough, it could generate greater rural instability.

Because *hukou* has created two classes of urban citizens, it is hotly debated in China as a lingering injustice. In March 2010, just before the annual National Peoples' Congress, an unusual editorial appeal to the government was made by 13 big city newspapers in 11 provinces to abandon *hukou* in the interests of free migration and social fairness. Within hours of publication, the website version was withdrawn, and a few days later, one newspaper's editor was sacked. At the Congress, Premier Wen Jibao did acknowledge that *hukou* would be relaxed gradually, starting in small towns and cities. It remains to be seen how far these experiments will succeed. Part of the problem is that it's the larger towns and cities with the bulk of the jobs that have the most significant problems.

Some prominent Chinese academics have seized upon these small *hukou* reforms to urge the Communist Party to be bolder still.

They use the phrase '*guojin mintui*', translated as the state advances as the private sector retreats, in discussions about China's future development. They argue that the government should get out of the way of migration control as one step in a more extensive programme to continue with market reforms, privatise state-owned enterprises, and reduce government regulations. What everyone fears is the potential of the status quo to fuel rising popular discontent over human rights and corruption. The director of the China Centre for Economic Research in Beijing, Yang Yao, has argued that popular resistance and economic imbalances are moving China toward a major crisis, and that strong and privileged interest groups, along with local governments, need to pay more attention to greater equality of incomes and social benefits[11].

To address China's unbalanced economy, I referred earlier in the book to various reforms which could hasten the advent of an economy that would rely more on domestic sources of income and production growth. These should focus on scrapping the existing exchange rate system, raising rural incomes and minimum wages, widening and deepening the social security system, and allowing company profits to be distributed more widely as dividends. Reforms would ideally compress the wide gap between urban and rural incomes and living standards, tilt China's economic centre of gravity away from the coastal provinces and, as a result, tend to lower migrant flows to the cities. On the other hand, if China continues to march into the future with a weak social security system, gaping urban–rural income inequality, and growing numbers of disaffected second-class urban residents, the social and economic pressures arising from demographic changes are liable to do much more than simply dent its growth rate.

Ageing in India

It has become an emerging markets mantra that India is one of the youngest countries in the world. India will overtake China in terms of population size by 2028–2030, and is in a prime position to reap its demographic dividend. In other words, India's birth rate – currently about three children – is dropping gradually, its 15–64-year-old population is going to surge in the next 20 years, and rapid ageing won't set in until the 2030s. This is the heart of the argument for why India's growth rate could rise to a sustainable 10% per year in the next several years. Like China, India is renowned for son preference and has regions where gender imbalance is high but in most other demographic respects, it is quite different.

India's population grew by over 2% per year from independence in 1947 until the mid 1990s. Now it is has slowed to about 1.3%, and by mid-century it will be barely growing at all. But because of the demographic dividend, what makes the next 20–30 years special is that the opportunity for higher growth and rising prosperity has never been brighter. From an economic standpoint, India's overall performance has improved significantly in the last 10–15 years, not least because the Indian authorities have opened the country up to more trade and investment, and embarked on important economic reforms at home. Assuming these trends continue, demographics could then underpin an already promising recent track record.

It is worth underscoring the scale of India's demographic change. The population is predicted to grow by 400 million to 1.6 billion. The working age population is expected to rise from 780 million to 1.1 billion. The growth in the working age population between 2010 and 2020 alone will be the equivalent of the existing working age population in Western Europe, defined in United Nations demographic nomenclature as Germany, France, the Netherlands, Belgium and Switzerland. Between 2010 and 2040, more people will join India's working age population than the entire current working age population of the whole of Western Europe.

The child dependency ratio – that is, those aged under 15 as a proportion of the working age population – has been declining since it peaked at 76% in 1965, but it only slipped below 50% in 2008–2010. By 2050, the dependency ratio will halve. Consequently, India is in that 'sweet spot' where child dependency is falling but rising old age dependency is still many years away.

The optimism deriving from India's demographics, however, comes with an important qualification. India's demographic dividend could turn into a demographic disaster if existing widespread poverty and underemployment are allowed to fester, and as a further 200 or so million people enter the labour force over the next 3–4 decades. There is time to devise and implement more robust strategies to tackle poverty, raise educational standards and change India's economic structure to make it more employment-friendly. But if appropriate strategies are not pursued, or do not succeed, a dysfunctional and severely unbalanced labour market could easily threaten to provoke a backlash against needed economic and social reforms and, possibly social and political instability.

By 2050, India will look like the US does today, demographically speaking. India's median age will be about 38 years, compared with 36 in the US in 2010, and its fertility rate is predicted to decline to about 1.9 children per woman, compared to the current rate of just over 2 in the US. India's dependency ratio will be roughly 47%, comprising a child ratio of 27% and an old age ratio of 20%. In the

US, the total dependency ratio stands at 49%, comprising child and old age ratios of 30% and 19%, respectively. The main dissimilarity, perhaps, will be life expectancy at birth. In India, this is expected to rise by about 10 years to just over 73 years, but this will still fall 10 years short of US longevity today.

The 0–14 year old age group will be around 18% of the population, compared to America's 20%, while the working age and over 60s population proportions will be around 68% and 19%, respectively, the same as in the US in 2010. India's advantage, as suggested earlier, is that the demographic change anticipated over the next decades is unequivocally supportive of a long period of high savings, investment and economic growth, whereas in the US, as in other rapidly ageing countries, it is the opposite, unless it can be offset by higher employment rates and productivity growth.

One noteworthy signal of the onset of rapid ageing in India will become more evident as we get to the middle of the century. Around that time, India's 315 million over 60s will for the first time outnumber the 293 million children aged under 15. In fact, the size of the latter group is peaking roughly now at about 374 million, or roughly 31% of the population, whereas the over 60s group numbers less than 100 million.

India's demographics in 40 years, then, may look like the US today, and the change in India's age structure and dependency ratios in the interim are not unlike those that have occurred in the US since 1970. And in one other respect, moreover, there is a noteworthy parallel. Service-producing industries have been the backbone of India's economic ascendancy, rising from 38% of GDP in 1980 to about 54% in 2009. In 1970, US service-producing industries accounted for a similar proportion of GDP.

The analogies to the US, however, cease at this point, for while US service industries have since expanded to account for nearly 70% of GDP, this occurred in the context of de-industrialisation, rising manufacturing productivity growth, and generally high levels of overall employment. India's situation could not be more different, and the next four decades are not a long time for the economy to resemble the US as it exists today. In effect, India seems to be trying to jump from a low-income agrarian to a prosperous service-based economy, skipping a vital development phase marked by the development of labour-intensive manufacturing, rising educational attainment and labour market reforms.

Because service-producing industries don't create nearly as many jobs as manufacturing, India's reliance on the former is a core weakness as well as a core strength. Service industries account for just 25% of employment, or half as much as their share of GDP, while manufacturing industries employ just 19% of the labour force compared with a 17% share of GDP that hasn't changed much for 40 years. Although employment in manufacturing has been growing at about 3–3.5% per year since 1980, this is about half the rate recorded by South Korea and, more recently, China. Moreover, India remains dominated by agriculture and rural activities, even though their significance in GDP has declined from about 40% to 20% of GDP in the last 25 years. The rural sector remains home to 70% of India's population, and still accounts for 56% of total employment. Unlike China, there is a much weaker tendency to leave the rural sector for urban work and life. India's rural population share is falling but at one-third of the rate in China, while its urban population share is growing half as quickly.

Notwithstanding its high reputation for modern economy professionals, such as doctors, chemists, scientists, engineers and computer programmers, India lags behind other Asian economies in educational achievement. Secondary school enrolments, for example, are lower than in China, and the growth in enrolments in higher education is half China's rate. The illiteracy level for rural inhabitants is about 50% at primary school level, and 70% at the secondary level. China's aggregate illiteracy level is thought to be less than 10%. Illiteracy is intimately related to poverty, and to ill health among children, in particular. Roughly half of Indian children under 5 years are moderately or severely underweight for their age, compared to 7% in China, and this phenomenon is associated with learning difficulties. More broadly, in India 75% of the population live on less than \$2 a day, 42% live on less than \$1.25 a day, and 29% are undernourished and below the official national poverty line. By contrast, Chinese proportions are far lower, at 36%, 16%, and 3%, respectively. The impact of low educational attainment means that far too many people are ill equipped for productivity-enhancing work.

About 60% of India's landmass is classified as agriculture. The land is still home to 800 million people, and provides work for just over a quarter of them. Although India is self-sufficient in food, and is one of the world's top producers of milk, wheat and cotton, the surge in productivity and output growth that were boosted by the agricultural Green Revolution from 1965 until the 1980s has long since slowed down. Allied to India's natural vulnerability to monsoons – India experienced its heaviest rainfall for 37 years in 2009, which reduced output by nearly 3% – is a series of more man-made shortcomings. These include a lack of agricultural investment, low levels of mechanisation and poor storage facilities, and significant bureaucracy and over-regulation. These have accentuated the failure of the authorities to build a more robust agricultural base on which to graft a flourishing manufacturing sector, as China did after 1978.

The result of poor educational attainment, poverty, and the neglect of agriculture can be seen quite clearly in India's chronic unemployment. Although the recorded unemployment rate is a relatively low 7%, underemployment is widespread, especially for females and in rural areas. Reliable data are not available, but the high incidence of poverty among people who are employed in some capacity, roughly 27%, suggests that the true measure of unemployment may be at least 30–35%, or roughly 250 million people[12]. It is probably even higher, taking into account people who are employed on a seasonal or temporary basis, and those who want to work full time but are unable so to do.

The highest unemployment and underemployment rates are among people in the age group from 15–29 years, an age cohort that is on track to grow by about 30 million, or 10% between 2010 and 2025. For these, and indeed many of their elder peers, employment opportunities are compromised further by rigid labour laws, which have tended to cause companies to limit jobs in the so-called 'organised' sector – that is, where employment is regular and contractual – and to expand them in the 'unorganised' sector where wages are lower, benefits are non-existent, and working conditions are inferior.

To succeed in alleviating current unemployment and in employing new entrants to the labour force, India will have to make significant strides in improving its education and urban and rural infrastructure systems, removing unnecessary regulations that suppress employment, and facilitating a more robust manufacturing industry, which, alone, will be able to absorb India's labour. India's successes in some industries, such as textiles, electrical machinery and automobile parts, are widely recognised, as are its aspirations to become a hub in the global technology production. Whether this can substitute for the job creation associated with more familiar mass production manufacturing on a scale commensurate with India's demographics will define India's economic future.

Top dogs in technology

Emerging markets are no longer content to be seen as just the world's reservoir of cheap labour and low-cost brains. They want more advanced technology to speed up economic development and because it brings economic power. The appearance of $3000 cars, $300 computers and $30 mobile phones testifies certainly to their ability to introduce cheap and disruptive technologies into the global economy[13]. The BRICs, in particular, have large markets and big populations, the financial muscle to acquire companies rather than grow organically, and the confidence to look to their own business models, products and processes, and management systems.

Western countries need technology to preserve their existing comparative advantage and prosperity, and to offset the negative economic effects associated with rapid ageing. But what can anyone say in 2010 about what technology will look like in a decade, let alone the next 20–30 years, bearing in mind that previous technological revolutions were impossible to predict?

The information revolution is widely viewed with awe for its speed and the radical ways in which it is changing society. But it isn't unique in either respect. The first industrial revolution, from the development of the steam engine in the late 18th century to the full intensity of the railroads, postal services and the telegraph 50 years later, spawned new theories of organisation, and significant changes in institutions, including factories, banks, intellectual property, limited liability, trade unions, technical universities and daily newspapers. The ideological consequences were enormous as well. Recall that Karl Marx and Friedrich Engels wrote the Communist Manifesto in 1848, at a time of depression and wide-spread revolution in Europe. The second industrial revolution, from the railroads through to the Second World War, was associated with no less significant changes in institutions and attitudes, for example, the development of the welfare state, modern corporations and forms of civil administration, sophisticated financial institutions, and the early development of women becoming involved in work away from home[14].

The current revolution, as we might call it, based on the development of the computer in the 1940s, has given birth to another revolution in information, propagated by the spread of the Internet. Some of the consequences can be seen already, but for the future, they can barely be anticipated. We can certainly testify already to the changes that have occurred in the organisation and functions of companies and the home, and to those that have led to the development of supra-national organisations and large trans-national companies and banks that straddle the line between national and global interests. In the next decades, the information revolution will continue to keep the global economy in a state of flux, since the drive to innovate and change is relentless; and it will support innovation in two relatively new technologies: biotechnology (the use of living organisms in science, engineering, medicine) and nanotechnology (the creation of matter from particles or atoms). Eventually, the fusion of these technologies could revolutionise manufacturing yet again. The economic prize will be glittering indeed and, as with prior industrial revolutions, we can say with certainty that in reaching for it, we will encounter and have to integrate new theories and institutions, and even changes in political values and ideologies. The key to the prize is the quality of institutions and the degree to which they tolerate and encourage dissent and change.

Top dogs in technology, then, have to aspire not only to being able to import and use modern technology, but also to develop a strong and dynamic capacity to innovate. South Korea, Malaysia and Singapore are the main emerging market examples showing the critical role played by innovation and the exploitation of knowledge. They tapped in to the global knowledge economy, developed the quality of education from schools through universities and into lifelong learning, and promoted innovation. They did this by attracting foreign investment, providing constructive administrative and tax regimes for businesses, supporting entrepreneurship, and by exploiting big investments in information technology and the Internet. But none of these things could have been mobilised without high levels of trust between citizens, businesses, public servants and the government, and without the capacity to implement structural reforms in a timely and relevant fashion, supported by all the stakeholders.

It follows that resistance to reform and to the social processes that allow it to happen constitute a fundamental weakness. Because the organisation of political and economic institutions is an important agent of change, I will argue that even though China will become more sophisticated, it will continue to lag behind the US. It is even possible that, in the long run, India might have the stronger potential for technological leadership among emerging markets, because it's already good at technology, and its institutions seem well suited to innovation and creativity.

Technical progress versus technical prowess

In general, developing countries lack the ability that comes with economic maturity, rising wealth and robust institutions to generate technological innovation. Technology has been at the heart of economic growth and advances in social welfare over the last 20–30 years, which are not captured by traditional measures of GDP. And it will be key to addressing climate change and new drivers of economic growth in the future. As I explore this further, remember that you can define innovation in two ways. One involves incremental changes in existing technologies that allow you to do things faster, cheaper and better than before. Japan proved to be a master of this form of innovation, and China and Taiwan, for example, are proving to be worthy successors. The other emphasises new products and processes, often across a broad range of economic and scientific activities that fuse together, creating new rounds of innovation. This form of innovation is associated much more with the type in which the US and some European companies excel.

Many developing countries have incorporated some new technologies very quickly. The penetration of mobile phones, for example, in developing countries has reached the same level as rich countries reached just 15 years ago. For the most part, however, most countries experience technological progress by adopting and adapting existing technologies, usually acquired from the companies headquartered in rich nations. Even in the higher income

BRICs, where most of the advances in modern technology in emerging markets are concentrated, the spread of technology is uneven. In Beijing, Mumbai or other cities, you can find world-class technology at work in a handful of companies, but you would be hard pushed to find much evidence in most companies or in rural areas.

In India, for example, there are cities, such as Bangalore, that are now renowned for their high tech, software, computer, biotech, pharmaceutical and automobile industries, their skilled labour, and research universities. India is renowned for its services technologies, including the processing of tax returns, medical X-rays, and more recently for its 'medical tourism' hospitals, where procedures are carried out at a fraction of the cost in North America, Japan or Europe. But on many measures of technological success, India as a nation is mid-rank among developing countries, and is no higher than many African countries in terms of the spread of technology. In 2007, for example, the number of subscribers to both wired and wireless services per 100 individuals, was 52.3% for urban dwellers, and 6.5% for rural inhabitants[15].

Some measures of technological prowess, such as the numbers of patents and scientific journal articles, are strongly correlated with per capita income, and so it is hardly surprising that developing countries lag so far behind industrial countries. It isn't that they are not capable of progress. China's share of world patent applications, for example, rose from 1.5% in the late 1980s to about 10% in 2004, and about 2.5 million of America's 22 million scientists and engineers were born in developing countries[16]. So, when considering the top dogs in technology and future technological leadership, it is important to note that we are talking about whether a spectrum of structural, pro-technology characteristics are or are likely to be present in emerging countries and, ultimately, whether or not they can catch up with their Western rivals.

We are not talking specifically about the diffusion of technological products and processes, either through trade or as a result of high-tech Western companies setting up manufacturing or service-producing companies in lower wage economies in Asia, Eastern Europe or Latin America. A number of technological achievement criteria, such as patents and journal articles, power consumption, telephone lines, hi-tech exports, Internet users, computer users and so on are all attributes of a modernising economy. On this basis, changes in the last 15 years in the BRICs, Indonesia, Thailand, Turkey and Malaysia have been running twice as fast as in developed economies, but in a world of accelerating globalisation, we shouldn't have expected anything less.

But these achievements do not equate to technological prowess: it's one thing to produce and distribute the iPhone or the iPod in modern factories with sophisticated equipment, it's quite another to imagine, design, brand and commercialise it. Apple outsources most of the manufacturing of iPods to a Taiwanese company, Hon Hai, that assembles them at the Foxconn Technology Group factory in Shenzhen, in Guangdong Province. Here, Sony PlayStations and Nokia cell phones are also produced by a production line of over 300,000 people. It's good economics for China, but not necessarily good business. According to researchers at the University of California at Irvine, only about 5% of the value of the iPOD is retained within China, the bulk accruing to Apple, retailers and component suppliers.

Similarly, many emerging markets have experienced high productivity growth, but most has come from the rise in labour productivity, derived from providing more capital to large working age populations. Over the period from 1988–2008, the highest labour productivity increases in emerging countries were recorded in South Korea (8% per year), Taiwan (6%), and China (5%), followed by Hong Kong, Singapore, Turkey and Chile (3–4.5%). On some measures, Russia and India have fared well too, but not Brazil. For the most part, high labour productivity growth has been associated closely with increases in the stock of capital investment, arising from high savings and investment rates[17].

But the productivity you get from the application of knowledge and from innovation, similar to the total factor productivity (TFP) discussed earlier in this book, depends on different kinds of structural and enduring inputs. Insofar as TFP is a residual, that is, the part of GDP growth we can't really measure from looking at labour and capital inputs alone, the largest beneficiaries in emerging nations since 1998 have all been in Asia, paced by annual growth of 2–4% per year in China, India and Singapore, and with Brazil and Russia a long way back registering barely 0.5% per year.

The kind of productivity growth you get from innovation and the deployment of knowledge depends on openness to trade, foreign investment, and new ideas, and also on investment in education and skill formation, economic and legal governance systems. Other critical success factors include the ability of small firms to raise finance, the level of technological literacy, and the culture of risk taking, in which debate and dissent are encouraged. The top dogs in technology have all of these attributes. They are distinguished further by having the capacity to generate a continuing flow of innovation across a wide range of activities that blend into and reinforce one another, creating true innovative momentum and enhancing welfare over time.

Although not at the frontier of the most advanced levels of technical progress, the World Bank cites two particular examples of success in emerging economies that have run into man-made obstacles. Chile has established a salmon farming industry, second only to Norway, by progressing along several fronts, including domestic fish tank and fish egg production, salmon feeding and processing techniques, and new vaccines. Yet, in 2009, production is estimated to have dropped by over 80% due to the spread of a condition known as infectious salmon anaemia that was attributed to the man-made institutional failures to prevent unsanitary conditions and overcrowding in industrial salmon cages. Technical leadership, therefore, depends on much more than technical know-how. Or consider Indonesia, the world's leading producer of palm oil, the highest yielding commercial oilseed, which has a market share of about 45% thanks to the development in recent years of new varieties of palms, and new crude and processed palm oil refining techniques. But success has been bought at the expense of considerable environmental damage in the form of deforestation, threats to wildlife, and increasing greenhouse gas emissions. It is by no means inconceivable that Indonesian suppliers will come under increasing pressure from large food companies to mend their ways or lose their contracts.

Twenty-first century technologies, and the contemporary challenges of climate change and rapid ageing make the welfare aspects of technological progress especially important. Surging industrial expansion in China increases GDP but no one adjusts this for the costs of putting right the environmental degradation of the air, rivers and countryside. India's economic expansion is catching everyone's eye, but no one really focuses on whether economic and social progress might be better served by strategies to strengthen existing technologies, as opposed to acquiring the most up-to-date ones.

In India and other poor countries, for example, the economic obsession with GDP and the race to modernity have relegated the long-run benefits that accrue from pursuing elementary improvements in basic living standards, agricultural efficiency, water supply, sanitation and disease prevention. These are less status-enhancing than nuclear and missile technology, and less spectacular than high-speed trains and revolving restaurants on top of skyscrapers, but the contrast speaks to a host of contradictions between the pursuit of industrial technologies and the structural shortcomings in agricultural and rural technologies, and to inadequate focus on the attributes that give rise to technological leadership.

Much has been made of the proliferation of mobile phones, Internet usage and computers in emerging countries, and no one can deny the role these have played in helping to strengthen the fabric of economic growth. They have contributed directly to employment creation, for example in India, and to overall productivity growth by helping small businesses, job searches, and entrepreneurial start-ups. Mobile telephone banking, especially in Africa and the poorer parts of South Asia, for example, has become a godsend for hundreds of millions of people and small businesses in vast tracts of the developing world where transportation, conventional telephone systems and business infrastructure are expensive, difficult, or even non-existent. Farmers and fishermen can check prices and weather and market conditions in various locations without leaving their fields or boats. Vodafone, the telecommunications giant, has reported that in India, states with a 10%

higher penetration ratio of mobile phones have roughly 1.2% per annum higher annual economic growth rates[18]. It could, of course, be that higher growth states tend to have more mobile phone density, but the suggested causality seems quite plausible.

Again, these trappings of modern economies do not substitute for technological expertise. In fact, many countries still have considerable weaknesses in the production of 'simple' things, such as electrical power, transportation infrastructure, and the construction of roads and irrigation systems. These shortcomings abound in the poorest countries in Africa, but even in higher income Asia electrical power losses, or brownouts, amount to about a third of total power produced. Moreover, given the low levels of agricultural productivity growth in much of South Asia and Sub Sahara Africa, higher food price inflation and food imports loom in the next few years as their populations increase and age, as suggested earlier.

The race for technological leadership

We can all see the US and Europe competing with the BRICs and a few other emerging nations for leadership in science and technology. Most people would argue that money spent on research and development, the production of scientists and engineers, patent registrations, professional journal articles, and high-tech exports are key indicators of technological progress. On this basis, there is no question that the US and some European countries are still out in front, but also that China is making significant progress in the technology stakes. China will continue to direct large resources and expenditures into these areas, while Western nations are stuck with low growth and remain strapped for cash over the next few years. All that said, technological beauty is often in the eye of the beholder.

The Chinese Internet search engine Baidu with nearly 800 million subscribers, Alibaba, the privately-owned e-commerce, online retail and cloud computing service company, and Huawei Technologies, China's largest network and telecommunications equipment supplier, are just a handful of examples of China's graduation into the high-tech club. But they don't do much that is new and that wasn't previously pioneered in the West, and in the case of Huawei, which has been very successful selling into Europe, it has been able to supply customers with high levels of software customisation thanks to relatively low paid and voluminous numbers of engineers at home.

The only major indicator where China is currently ahead of the US and the EU is its trade surplus in high-tech exports. But this is mostly about goods made *in* China, as a result of foreign technology companies' production in China, rather than *by* China. In terms of the quantity of scientific papers produced, measures of their relative impact, inventions patented in the US, Europe and Japan, science and engineering Ph.Ds, and Nobel prizes, China lags a long way behind. According to the US Patent and Trademark Office, the US (classification according to residence of the first-named inventor) accounted for 50% of the 157,772 patents registered in 2008. Japan accounted for 33,682, South Korea and Taiwan for 15,000, and China for 1225. The state of California alone registered 19,181 patents.

You could point to China's superior growth rates in many indicators of technological achievement (except Nobel prizes) to argue that it is on course to compete with and rival the US and the EU over the next one to two decades. One technological challenge in which China already excels concerns clean energy technologies, comprising solar energy, wind, nuclear power, carbon capture and storage, advanced vehicles and batteries, and high speed rail.

According to a recent report, Asia's clean energy 'tigers' – China, Japan and South Korea – have already surpassed the US in the production of most clean air technologies and are expected to invest three times as much in the next few years[19]. The significance can be realised from what is happening already. The US is expected to import wind turbines from China for the first time in 2010. It has no high-speed rail manufacturing, lags in nuclear power plant deployment, produces less than 10% of the world's solar cells, and is starting late to compete with Japan or South Korea in the production of hybrid and electric vehicles.

These observations are valuable since they suggest that as things stand, the US and EU governments are not investing nearly enough in secondary education, energy and water or infrastructure and have become distracted from implementing large, well-directed programmes to preserve their technology lead. Looking back, it was, after all, the targeted policies of the US government that created its lead in radio technology, aerospace, telecommunications, microelectronics, and the Internet. It has never picked winners in the sense of supporting specific national champion companies, but it has consistently earmarked support for particular sectors deemed to define the future.

Looking forward, if the lack of financial and human investment in new technologies is allowed to fester, the West may become increasingly dependent on foreign high-tech imports, and on imported technologies from emerging markets. This would undermine economic growth and flexibility and, most importantly, their economic security. If for no other reason, it is likely that countries such as the United States, Germany and Japan will presumably try to heed the call to remedy this deficiency.

Alternatively, you could argue that it is just as meaningless to extrapolate innovative capacity and the inputs that propel it, as I have argued it is to extrapolate GDP in the post-crisis world. Linear predictions of technological success based on volumes of patents, scientists and engineers and so on, represent only a mechanical view about how nations may fare in the future. You also have to consider quality and context. For example, just because you are rising up the league table of published scientific articles says nothing about the quality, possible duplication and practical relevance of what gets published.

Cong Cao, author of *China's Scientific Elite* and other works on technology, has highlighted what he calls 'misconduct in science' as a reason why China's ambition to become an innovation leader by 2020 will be impeded. Misconduct, including fabrication and fraud in scientific research papers, has increased because the campaign for international profile and prominence has emphasised quantity over quality as the basis for reward and promotion. Without an autonomous institutional watchdog, it is extremely difficult to expose and prevent such misconduct[20]. A culture that pushes too hard for this type of success and for mere volumes of scientific professionals won't necessarily master the skills of nurturing talent and a creative culture, based on entrepreneurship and social innovation. And it can't, therefore, ensure world-class achievement in a broad sense.

Japan, for example, has unquestionably taken a prominent position in automobile and consumer electronics technologies. It also has about 40% of the world's installed robot manufacturing capacity. It uses robots extensively in factories, where they are sometimes welcomed upon inauguration with Shinto religious ceremonies. It uses them in the production of sushi, in agriculture, as receptionists, and as care devices for the elderly in the home and in hospitals. Impressive as these exploits may be, many robotic devices lack commercial viability or remain firmly in the land of science fiction. Despite its technological and robotic prowess, Japan nevertheless may be held back by the impact of rapid ageing, the future burden of its public debt, which stands at 230% of GDP, and its reluctance to embrace structural economic and political reforms that are essential to drive industrial change and future prosperity.

If it's quality and reputation in emerging markets that you're after, you shouldn't only look to the obvious titans of China and India. Consider Israel, an emerging market in the context of the investor universe. With a population of just 7.5 million, it has twice as many scientists and engineers per head of population than the US, and its high technology output accounts for a third of GDP and three-quarters of industrial exports. It is ranked in the World Economic Forum's *Global Competitiveness Report 2009–2010* as third in terms of the quality of its scientific institutions, compared with China which ranks 35th. It was ranked fourth in terms of patents for invention (China 50th), eighth for innovative capacity (China 22nd), 15th for availability of latest technologies (China 87th) and 16th for availability of scientists and engineers (China 36th). India actually ranked third in this last category after Finland, Japan and Sweden, and just ahead of the US.

It is easy to point to the sheer volume of scientists and engineers produced by China's higher education establishments, but size alone in this context only matters if it is accompanied by the spread of innovative capacity. This involves the application of new ideas and methods to the production of goods and services across a wide range of applications, supported by sound and supportive institutions. These institutions, and particularly research universities, are typically characterised by high levels of academic freedom, free enquiry, no barriers to ideas generated anywhere in the world, meritocratic organisational structures, and the full acceptance of scepticism about what is fact and what is theory. According to the QS Top Universities survey 2009, China had 13 universities in the world's top 600, with Tsinghua University and Peking University the top ranked at 49th and 52nd, respectively, compared to the United States, which had 13 of the world's top 20.

Gordon Chang, author of the 2001 book, *The Coming Collapse of China*, certainly wasn't shy of overstating his case that China was headed to the 'scrap heap of history'. But he has drawn attention, subsequently, to several phenomena in China's education system that repress its ability to produce world-class historians, economists and political thinkers, and complicate the quest for world-class scientists and innovators. These include the demand for obedience, the stifling of free enquiry, and a growing incidence of plagiarism and corruption in schools and universities[21].

China Daily, for example, reported in August 2009 the allegation that Zhou Zude, the President of Wuhan University of Technology, had copied the work of a fellow scientist in a thesis submitted to, but then disqualified from, an international conference. *Shanghai Daily* carried a story in January 2010 about a Tongi University Associate Professor, Wang Hongtao, who was punished (and later resigned), for copying a colleague's online test paper for his own students. And *Chengdu Evening News* reported in July 2010 that Huang Qing, Vice President of Southwest Jiaotong University, was found guilty of plagiarism and stripped of his doctoral degree for lifting work, without citation, from a Nobel-nominated economist's book.

The central issue here is not misconduct, per se, but the fact that it is endogenous to the idea of community, which is prevalent in China, compared to the idea of the individual, as we know it in the West. The emphasis on stability and harmony in the community leads to the view that any member of the community can use any part of the community, including ideas, to further the collective interest. Individual interest and advance are subjugated to the community. There is nothing philosophically wrong with this, but it is different from a system in which competitive innovation by individuals is encouraged.

The different attributes, therefore, of the educational and scientific establishment in the US, and in its world-beating universities, suggest there should be every reason to expect it to maintain its technological leadership for the foreseeable future. The fault line running through this argument, perhaps, is that the financial strangulation of higher education there and in other Western countries as a result of the sovereign debt crisis is an exceptionally serious threat, of which China seems well positioned to take advantage. The financial crisis and the implications of an unsustainable rise in the burden of public debt have already caused universities in many Western economies to raise their tuition fees and or cut back public funding of higher education.

The race for technological leadership, therefore, is now on. The US has an unquestioned lead in most important areas of technology and in innovative capacity but faces major financial constraints in coming years. China is catching up, and faces no financial constraints, at least for now. Yet some technological applications of growing significance may be beyond the reach of China and other BRICs for the foreseeable future.

A few years ago, the Rand Corporation issued a report on the outlook for global technology, examining 56 new technologies that were expected to be commercially available by 2020[22]. It also assessed the capacity of different countries and regions to exploit what it regarded as the most important 16 technological applications, which fell into three broad categories: healthcare services, access to information, and environmental sustainability of goods and services. The BRICs were deemed to be in a class apart from most other developing countries. Thus, while the latter were expected to enjoy the benefits of basic new technologies, such as solar panels and mobile phones, they were not expected to overcome key constraints, such as the lack of technological infrastructure (research universities, business and science parks, and research and development facilities), low levels of technical literacy, and a lack of scientists and engineers.

The BRICs, and countries in Eastern Europe, on the other hand, are viewed as far less constrained in these areas. They are expected to stand out, matching the technological achievements of industrial countries in most, but not all, of the newest technologies. In some of the most sophisticated and complex technologies, however, such as tissue engineering, genetics and genomics (the study of genes, and of the complete genetic information of an organism, respectively), and those incorporating the fusion of information, bio- and nanotechnologies, they are not expected to overcome barriers to the most sophisticated forms of innovation in the next 10–20 years.

The 16 applications included five that all countries were expected to incorporate, comprising cheap solar energy, rural wireless communications, genetically modified crops, filters and catalysts (water purification and decontamination), and cheap autonomous housing (self-sufficient and affordable housing, adaptable to local conditions). The next five applications that would probably elude developing countries in the Middle East and Africa were rapid bioassays (the biological testing of matter or substances), green manufacturing, ubiquitous RFID (radio frequency identification) tagging of products, and hybrid motor vehicles. The next most sophisticated applications, thought likely to be exclusive to the BRICs, Eastern Europe and advanced nations were targeted drug delivery (for example, cancer treatment), improved diagnostic and surgical techniques and quantum cryptography (encoding of data, and secure communications). And the last four, which only advanced nations – including South Korea – were expected to develop, were ubiquitous information access (anywhere, anytime information access), tissue engineering, pervasive sensors (public area sensors that can be networked for surveillance purposes) and wearable computers.

The top group of countries is distinguishable by virtue of having the strongest capacity not just to acquire modern technologies, but also to implement and exploit them. To do this, you have to have strong and supportive institutions, adequate financial resources, and a political and cultural environment that can minimise barriers to innovation and sustain the widespread use of technological applications. The group of countries that follows the advanced group in terms of sophistication and technological capacity include India, Brazil, Poland and Russia, with Chile, Mexico and Turkey aspiring to join. Pride of place, of course, goes to China.

Will China eat our technological lunch?

China's main claim to 21st century dominance is based, above all, on its 1.3 billion people, not on its wealth, measured as per capita income, nor on its overall technological and innovative prowess, notwithstanding its obvious successes in some areas. It is undoubtedly true that China represents an alternative business model along with much greater regulation of complex markets and society. The next generations of non-Chinese speaking peoples will become increasingly conscious of China as a global power and technological competitor, not least because of the proliferation of university degrees in Western nations with Mandarin as an option, and the teaching of basic Mandarin and China studies in secondary schools. But we shall see if Chinese brands, fashions, music, sports and entertainment will 'catch on' and set new global trends.

Google's threat to pull out of China, focused attention on rather different ways in which people now view China, and on its capacity to become a global leader in technology. US trade lobbies, which represent several major US companies such as Microsoft, Boeing and Intel, gave solid backing to China's application for membership of the World Trade Organisation, and have consistently lobbied against legislation aimed at imports from China. Since the crisis, and particularly since the Google announcement, they have become more restive. Foreign companies operating in China are enthusiastic about growth in sales and profits but, with the possible exception of financial services and retailing companies, are increasingly anxious about an unpredictable business environment, and a sort of official protectionism that contravenes the spirit, at least, of the basic principles of membership of the World Trade Organisation. Western governments are also uncomfortable about lopsided rules. For example, the Chinese motor company Geely bought Volvo in 2010 for nearly $2 billion, but foreign motor companies, such as Honda and Toyota, can only manufacture cars in China under a joint venture agreement with local companies.

Foreign companies complain about what they regard as non-legal forms of preferential treatment for local companies. Under the banner of a new government procurement programme, known as 'indigenous innovation', China is moving to give a competitive lift to domestic companies, especially state-owned enterprises. Measures include the application of strict product standards for everything from cell phones to cars, which favour local companies; a revision to patent legislation that could force foreign companies to hand over key technologies to local governments, and anti-monopoly rules designed to limit foreign access to sectors that include construction, machinery, telecommunications and energy[23]. And while US companies and their lobby representatives might previously have been unhappy about China's RMB and other export-friendly policies, they are becoming more vocal in their opposition. It remains to be seen if major US and other foreign companies are prepared to turn their backs on China's mass market. But it will be interesting to see if Western companies at least start to redirect some of their foreign investment programmes elsewhere in Asia, or even back home again.

China will have to tread carefully. Apart from a handful of large local companies that include Huawei Technologies, Lenovo Group (notebooks), Haier Group (appliances), TCL Corporation (consumer electronics) and Zhejiang Geely Holdings and Chery Automobile (automobiles), it doesn't have many domestic corporate champions, and certainly not any global brands. It aspires to being a leading player in the production and export of high-tech consumer goods, such as DVD players and laptops, and in developing electric car prototypes and technologies, and clean energy technologies, including solar panels and wind turbines. While rules designed to create both more local champions and global brands are clearly not unique to China, rules alone will not generate a durable competitive edge in advanced technology. Moreover, China needs access to foreign know-how as it seeks to move up the value chain and strengthen its position as the world's premier manufacturing hub, and will presumably want to buy, where and when possible, stakes in global technology and brands, as shown, for example, by Geely's purchase of Volvo from Ford in 2010.

Recognising the significance of the above, China's Ministry of Science and Technology amended the country's position by announcing in April 2010 that under its indigenous innovation rules, it would consider offering contracts to companies that conformed with Chinese laws, regulations and technology policies, provided they held legal rights to related intellectual property. US and European corporate lobbies welcomed the change in stance, which they hoped would allow technologically-advanced goods and services to be accredited for government procurement without restricting the intellectual property rights. The proof of the pudding, though, will be in the eating.

In spite of its scientific and technological achievements to date, China will continue to confront significant institutional barriers as it eyes a global leadership position. But no one argues that China isn't moving forward, or that the State cannot organise efficiently to realise goals laid down by Communist Party politicians, scientists and intellectuals. Ancient and more recent history testifies to China's ability to do both. But the role of institutions in creating and sustaining a competitive edge matters, as highlighted in Chapter 1 when considering the reasons for the English, rather than Chinese, Industrial Revolution, and in subsequent chapters assessing the institutional stumbling blocks that lie on China's economic and political path.

China's ability to become a leader in global technology and eradicate America's clear edge should be judged not so much on what scientists extrapolate mechanically as its technical capability, but on a rather more mundane and easy-to-formulate criterion. This is whether China's current inferior institutional capacity to adapt and stimulate broad-based and sustained innovation is likely to undergo the kind of radical change that will allow it to chip away steadily at America's advantage, and overtake it. Put simply, what goes in to being a world leader in the production of screen-based goods and green energy products isn't the same thing as what goes in to the design, organisation, knowledge and innovation that drive, for example, the aerospace and bio- and information technology industries. Here the US and parts of Europe are likely to retain pole position for a long time.

They support adversarial but constructive conflict in the process of innovation, and give due weight to the need for proprietary ownership of processes, patents and copyrights in modern technologies. Non-hierarchical and non-political organisational structures are encouraged. Criticism, free thinking, transparency, trust and the rule of law are essential ingredients in an innovative culture.

The management guru, Peter Drucker, argued a few years before his death in 2005 that there would no single dominant world economic power in the 21st century. He asserted that demographics in the developed countries would no longer be able to support such a role, and that neither money nor technology would, for any length of time, be able to offset the growing imbalance in labour resources between them and the major developing countries. The latter would benefit from the availability of training and education methodologies, developed over decades in the

US, which turn unskilled labour into high productivity employees rapidly.

Yet, if the West is succumbing to a qualitative loss in comparative advantage as a result, it nevertheless retains a quantitative edge, based on the supply and skills of knowledge workers, and the institutions in and with which they work. In the aftermath of the crisis, this edge seems threatened by the financial squeeze and by a growing conviction of relative, if not absolute, economic decline. But why should we assume that the US will stand still for the next 20–30 years? It seems distinctly improbable that the strong base on which its technological leadership has been built will be allowed to decay. America, unlike China, already has top quality institutions. If it can succeed over the next one to two decades in revitalising the push towards new technologies and innovation, China may well take a more prominent seat at the table, but there is no reason why it will eat too much of our technological lunch.

Chapter Seven

The Climate Change Catch–22

In a relatively short space of time, climate change has become the most widely recognised environmental issue of the 21st century, thanks to better scientific understanding, increased political engagement, and heightened consumer awareness. While there are a few, mostly cold and often inaccessible parts of the world that could benefit from a rise in average temperatures, most of us will suffer the adverse consequences of unchecked global warming. The biggest risks to life, property, economies and ecosystems lie in emerging and developing countries, partly because of their geography and often because they are relatively poor.

I have already examined how population ageing and the race to acquire new technologies form two big long-term challenges for emerging markets, but climate change is totally different because governments cannot control the consequences on their own. All countries contribute to climate change and environmental degradation as they pursue economic growth, but no country on its own will be spared the adverse consequences of climate change even if it pursues the greenest of growth strategies. The only way that climate change can be addressed is through the highest levels of international cooperation, and something is working to bring nations together. But the stresses and strains in the relationships between rich and emerging nations over climate change run deep.

Rich countries discovered the environmental consequences of the greater exploitation of the world's resources only with hindsight, and having already attained historically high levels of income. Caring about the environment is now *de rigueur.* Emerging countries, though, view the problem from a different perspective, and with foresight. For them, the issue is also about fairness, history, and economic growth. Since rich countries account for about two-thirds of the carbon put into the atmosphere since the middle of the 19th century, emerging countries insist that the costs of averting climate catastrophes should not be shared equally. They assert their right to pursue economic growth, for how else can they improve the living standards of their citizens? As the chaotic December 2009 Copenhagen climate change talks demonstrated, coordinating a large number of interest groups spanning richer and poorer nations, energy and commodity producers and consumers, and green technology hares and tortoises, is inordinately challenging. We have to hope that future climate negotiations will be carried out in a better spirit.

It is for scientists to establish, according to their hypotheses and tests, the extent to which climate change, leading to global warming, is natural or anthropogenic – that is, manmade. But the rest of us can only acknowledge that, on current trends, climate change will intensify environmental damage and pollution, and undermine economic progress. It is easy to understand why this is a particularly sensitive issue in emerging markets.

Climate change is going to be a thorny issue for them for three reasons. First, many of them will be especially affected by the adverse consequences of global warming, partly because they tend to be situated in low-lying and/or hot areas where they are vulnerable to flooding and/or drought, and partly because relatively poor countries generally can't or don't spend enough money to protect themselves against such consequences. Some of the fundamental attributes of life, including survival itself, but also basic living conditions, homes, health, the quality of land, the supply of reasonably cheap food, and access to fresh water are at stake. Because of this, they will face much economic uncertainty linked to climate change. This doesn't only apply to very poor countries, such as Bangladesh, or regions such as Sub Sahara Africa and the Middle East, but also to China and India, where the incidence of and stress from flooding and drought is already rising. Even today's or tomorrow's higher income emerging countries, therefore, are vulnerable to negative, climate change-related economic shocks, which might easily spill over into threats to social and political stability.

Second, because the causes and consequences of climate change do not lie solely within their jurisdiction, they have to negotiate with richer nations about how to share the responsibilities for preventing global warming, and the costs of moving to a low-carbon economy.

Third, emerging markets face a climate change Catch 22, or 'no-win' situation. If they pursue rapid economic growth, their emissions of climate-destabilising greenhouse gases (GHG) will continue to rise rapidly, aggravating damage to the environment and the economic growth outlook everywhere in the process. They would be damned if they grow. But if they opted to follow slower and environmentally friendly economic growth, they might never invest enough to adapt to the consequences of everyone else's GHG emissions. They would not have the economic momentum needed to embrace the green industrial revolution necessary to sustain the global system. Emerging markets would then be damned if they don't grow. This is the main focus of the chapter, and the complex nature of this topic demands that we then look at some of the main issues in the climate debate, the principal consequences for emerging markets, and what they might be able to do, if anything, to break the link between economic growth and GHG emissions.

Damned if you grow, damned if you don't

The 'Stern Review on the Economics of Climate Change', published by the UK Treasury in 2006, found that growth in per capita GDP and growth in per capita emissions of carbon dioxide (CO_2) were highly correlated[1]. This relationship has actually been corroborated by anecdotal evidence since the financial crisis and the recession. The downturn in economic activity in 2007–2009 was accompanied by a flattening out in the growth of emissions. According to the US Energy Information Administration, for example, energy-related CO_2 emissions saw their largest recorded absolute and percentage decline in 2009 (405 million metric tons, and 7%, respectively).

The only way in which the relationship between economic growth and emissions is likely to be broken is if far-reaching structural changes occur in the ways in which we source and use energy and infrastructure. Total man-made CO_2 emissions depend on a number of factors, including global population, per capita GDP, the energy used per unit of GDP, and the carbon intensity of energy, that is, the amount of carbon generated by energy production. Normally, as countries become wealthier, population growth tends to slow down (or reverse), so that over time governments need to focus their environmental policies on energy and carbon intensities, restructuring sectors such as transport, industry, fossil fuel energy, utilities and construction, which generate substantial carbon emissions.

For the vast majority of emerging markets, though, and also for China despite its more stable population size, becoming wealthier is not a question of choice. Rising population size or rising numbers of working age people, and the demand for higher living standards are going to remain the key variables driving future emissions. Consequently, the growth of emissions is likely to be significantly faster in emerging than in richer countries. The outcome is likely to be a much larger focus on the abatement of emissions in larger emerging economies, such as China, India and Brazil.

China and a few other emerging nations have achieved significant reductions in energy intensity already. During the decade to 2002, for example, while per capita GDP grew by 8.5% per year and the population increased by 0.9% per year, China improved its energy efficiency considerably, so that the growth in carbon emissions was limited to 3.7% per year. If gains in Chinese energy efficiency had been as small as, for example, in the rich countries belonging to the OECD, global carbon emissions in 2002 would have been over 10% higher[2]. India and other emerging economies also made significant gains in energy efficiency that compensated for increases in population and per capita GDP, but still left carbon emissions growing by 3–3.5% per year, compared to 1.3% per year in OECD countries.

The shift to low carbon energy activities will be important in breaking the Catch 22 for emerging countries, so they have strong vested interests to pursue the acquisition of technologies that realise this goal. Energy innovation will help emerging countries as they seek to sustain the quest for economic growth. But, at best and for the time being, reduced energy and carbon intensities will only offset the aggregate rise in emissions, which depend on the simpler matters of population and lifestyle.

Emerging markets complain, quite reasonably, that it is unfair for rich countries to lecture them about how they must curb their aspirations to higher living standards. They think the bulk of the burden of policy change should rest with the rich world, which is more culpable for emissions, and better able to finance the shift from a carbon-intensive growth model to a 'green' industrial revolution from which the whole world will benefit. The advanced countries throw the issue back by arguing that their own actions to mitigate climate change would be completely undermined if emerging markets didn't pursue similar policies.

The case for high levels of coordination, rather than confrontation, as a way of improving the quality of the environment is clear, but the enormity of the task is evident from the close association of CO_2 emissions with the level of economic development. Consider, for example, Figure 7.1, which shows GDP per head on the bottom axis and GDP growth on the vertical axis. Economic development is an imaginary line that goes from the bottom left-hand corner to the top right.

Now, each bubble in the chart belongs to a country, where the size of the bubble represents the level of 2005 GHG emissions (the

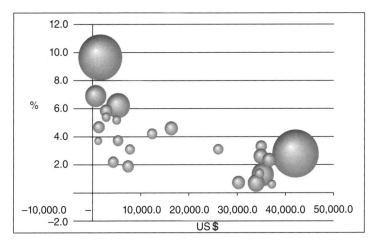

Figure 7.1 GDP per head, GDP growth and emission bubbles.
Source: World Development Reports, World Bank, Washington DC

most recently available data). But in fact, only two bubbles really matter. China is top left, growing very rapidly (close to 10% per year), but still with a low level of GDP per person. The US is bottom right, growing at a more sedate rate as befits a mature economy, but boasting extremely high levels of GDP per head.

The US and Chinese CO_2 bubbles are about the same size, representing roughly 6 billion tonnes of CO_2 equivalent per year, each amounting to about 20% of the global total. While all countries represented on the chart have a stake in the climate change issue, the significance of the US and China means that the whole issue takes on a distinctly geopolitical character.

As emerging countries pursue their economic catching up, we should expect China's bubble to move down a slope in the direction of the US but, from a climate change perspective, the crucial questions are whether China can move along this path without creating an even bigger CO_2 bubble, and whether the US can reduce its CO_2 bubble, moving away from the fossil-fuel dependent model without moving to the left.

It is no coincidence that this chart looks rather like a boxing-ring with two economic heavyweights in opposite corners. The less-than-friendly exchanges between the US and China at the Copenhagen climate change conference in 2009 were an interesting test for international relations. In some ways, climate change behaviour is a sort of economic game, where actions by one side may be taken or rejected on the basis of expected reactions by the other side. The US and USSR engaged in this game during the Cold War, under the philosophy of 'mutually assured destruction (MAD)'. The idea was that no one would launch a nuclear strike for fear that the other side would retaliate. This time though, the situation is less immediately threatening but more complex, because there is no clearly identifiable trigger for conflict. Yet if climate scientists are even approximately right, there might well be. Rich and poor nations, championed by the US and China respectively, cannot duck this essential issue forever.

The bottom line for emerging markets, though, is that economic growth is not a negotiable option, but a necessity. Economic development leads to wealth creation, which finances better infrastructure, higher spending on education and scientific research, and a greater capacity to adapt when structural change is needed, specifically to confront the perils of global warming. The rational decision for emerging markets should be to continue with the 'dash for growth'. A unilateral sacrifice of economic growth could backfire politically, and faster wealth and capital accumulation will underpin their capacity to buttress their own ecosystems and adapt to the negative consequences of other nations' emissions.

But this is, of course, a paradox, because if all emerging markets think like this, then the sooner they will bring on the consequences of global warming, which it is in all their interests to avoid. I shall consider the options for emerging markets again later, but before that it is important to look a little more closely at the climate debate, and especially as it affects emerging markets now and in the future.

Climate debate

After a century and a half of industrial development, but particularly since emerging markets joined the fray in the last 20–30 years, evidence has grown that sustained economic and population growth causes society to become more dependent on the environment, while at the same time depleting and polluting it. Growth increases the demands on planetary resources, such as energy, water and protein, and generates a stream of waste products emitted into the environment.

One of the big differences between the industrial revolutions in rich countries in the past and emerging markets today is that there is now a lot less environmental wiggle room. The environment is a global, rather than a local, problem. Degradation has effects that are far bigger in all dimensions than in the past, including square miles of land, cubic metres of air, water or waste, and numbers of people involved. It is self-evident that the prevention of environmental degradation is better and, in the long run, decidedly cheaper than the cure, but that doesn't mean that nations or societies see eye-to-eye about what to do.

Some GHG, in particular carbon dioxide (CO_2), are by-products of almost everything human beings do. But the debate about how much humans are responsible is often like the debate about religion. It includes both zealots and heretics, who question one another's credibility. In 2009–2010, these rivals clashed over a series of incidents. These included email scandals, suggesting the manipulation of climate change data[3]; the so-called 'glacier gate' controversy, alleging that estimates of the rate at which glaciers would recede in the future had been made without the proper checks and balances of scientific process[4]; attacks on a UN study that said 40% of the Amazon rainforest was at risk from global warming, called 'rainforestgate'[5]; and research suggesting temperature variability in the 1990s and after 2000 may have been attributable to changes in the amount of water vapour high up in the atmosphere. These spats countered, to some extent, the growing conviction in man-made climate change professed by large numbers of people, for example, in the wake of large weather events, such as Hurricane Katrina in 2005, which caused about $80 billion of damage[6].

Scientists and politicians, though, have different interests. The former postulate hypotheses and are supposed to test them to destruction, or until better ideas come along. Categorical assertion is not normally in the scientist's toolkit. Politicians, however, and most of us in our information- and numbers-obsessed age, demand conclusive evidence of climate change, and 'yes' or 'no' answers in order to justify the 'inconvenience' of spending taxpayers' money on climate change mitigation, and of implementing radical policy measures to become greener.

We tend to focus on anecdotal evidence or stories that we can read about or watch on TV or the Internet. We tend to forget that the climate in the expression 'climate change' refers to the long-run average, or trend, in climatic conditions such as temperature and humidity, whereas weather (of which we are more aware) refers to something that is much more random and short term. Weather is the equivalent of statistical 'noise', which is what extreme events like Hurricane Katrina in 2005 may turn out to have been, even though the popular response is to see them as a harbinger of global warming.

Experts care about both trend and noise. They care about what drives the trend, because observing it can help to identify aspects of human behaviour that might change temperatures in the long run. They also care about the noise because global warming is likely to make the weather 'noisier', that is, more Katrinas, more environmental deterioration, and more urgent demands to build the appropriate infrastructure, such as sea and flood defences for protection.

Essence of climate change science

GHG in the atmosphere, such as water vapour, carbon dioxide, methane and ozone absorb and emit radiation. The 'greenhouse effect' refers to the effect these gases have in making the Earth warmer than it otherwise would be, and therefore uninhabitable. Global warming, on the scale now envisaged by climate scientists, arises from the accumulation and continuous increase in those gases, notably CO_2. Each person's 'carbon footprint' can barely be reduced significantly by one simple action. GHG put into the air today join those that have been accumulating in the atmosphere for many decades, and will affect all countries for decades to come, whether they are the large emitters or not. The bellwether for environmental impact is the recognised proxy for GHG emissions, or so-called CO_2 'equivalent', which translates the different effects of several greenhouse gases into a single index.

CO_2 concentration in the atmosphere is measured in parts per million (ppm), and climate scientists have demonstrated that, after holding steady in a range of 180–300 ppm for a couple of million years until the Industrial Revolution, concentrations have increased to about 400 ppm (350 ppm for CO_2 alone) at the end of March 2010. To get back to what is regarded as the safe side of 350 ppm in total concentration in the next few decades, global carbon emissions would have to stop right now. So what climate scientists are trying to define is how to limit the growth in carbon emissions, now growing at the fastest ever rate of about 2% per year, so as to limit the rise in average temperature to about 2 degrees centigrade.

In order to restrict the rise in global average temperatures to 2–3 degrees, they think that concentration of CO_2 equivalents in the atmosphere, broadly speaking, needs to be held at around current levels of 430–500 ppm[7]. This corresponds to about 400 ppm of CO_2 alone. Clearly, the consequences of climate change could be significantly larger if average temperatures were to rise more than this. Even if they didn't, these average temperature changes will mask significant variability between countries and within regions. If things carry on as they are, however, global emissions are expected to take GHG concentrations to over 550 ppm of CO_2 equivalent by 2050 and over 650–700 ppm by the end of the 21st century[8].

No one is sure if stemming the emissions tide can be done, or what the costs of mitigation might be, let alone the costs of not acting to mitigate. When you also take account of other, but no less important, climate change phenomena, such as water stress, species loss, deforestation, and pollutants emitted into the air, land and water, you can see why climate change is at the forefront of the environmental debate. But it's incredibly complex for two reasons.

First, there is a generational problem. According to the World Bank's World Development Report data, the cumulative GHG emissions between 1850 and 2005 from the US were three times as large as the next largest emitters at the latter date, comprising Germany, Russia and China. The US accounts for 18.5% of cumulative emissions over the entire period, compared with China's 5.8%, Russia's 5.7%, India's 1.8% and Brazil's 0.5%, given the gulf in economic size between the US and the BRICs.

Similarly, GHG put into the atmosphere today – and attributable more to emerging markets than in the past – will still be warming the Earth several decades from now. Human beings and their political representatives tend not to care too much about vaguely-defined risks 'down the road' when the demands of everyday life occur on much shorter rhythms: the next meal, the next pay packet, the next year, and the next election. These are important constraints on the willingness to act on climate change all over the world, but especially in emerging countries, where per capita incomes are low.

Second, GHG cannot be easily contained. Think of the poet Edmund Lear's 'Jumblies', who went to sea in a sieve and very cleverly kept the damp out with blotting paper. This unlikely feat of engineering belies their name, for this was no 'jumble' but cooperation in the face of an impossible task. Slowing down GHG emissions, similarly, is going to require hitherto unachieved levels of cooperation between countries and groups of people who, unlike

Lear's colourful creatures, sometimes do not like or respect one another very much.

The biggest CO_2 emitters are split roughly 50:50 between rich countries on the one hand, and poor and middle income countries on the other. In terms of total individual emissions, the largest countries are China, the US and Russia, and then India, Brazil, Germany, the UK and Canada. China accounts for about 16% of global energy demand, or more than twice its weight in the global economy. And as yet, China's voracious demand for energy has less to do with rising consumer preferences for cars and air conditioners than with the investment surge in heavy industry, which accounts for about two-thirds of national energy consumption. That said, automobile demand is bound to speed up as per capita incomes grow towards around $5000, a level associated with rising demand for cars. Car ownership could rise by about 500 million in China and 300 million in India by the middle of the century.

But on a per capita basis, the pecking order of emitters looks quite different, headed by the US, Australia, Canada, and followed by Saudi Arabia, Russia, Japan, Germany and the UK. The distinction between total and per capita emissions is important, because it is the basis of a lot of the friction between richer and poorer nations over climate change and what to do about it.

Bare necessities for emerging markets

The literature on climate change nowadays is vast, and highlights the particularly adverse effects on emerging nations, many of which depend on their agricultural, forest, fishing and tourism industries. Unchecked, sea levels are expected to rise by 15 and 34 centimetres, respectively, by 2050 and 2100. Deforestation is expected to account for 15% of CO_2 (carbon dioxide) emissions in the atmosphere by 2050, mostly from the Amazon. Water shortages are developing rapidly, causing stress for hundreds of millions of individuals, and for fast-growing populations that share rivers, such as the Nile, Ganges, Jordan River, and the Tigris-Euphrates. Desertification is already affecting China, Brazil, Nigeria, and the countries of North Africa. In fact, taking changes in land use and deforestation into account, the responsibility of emerging markets for CO_2 emissions is now probably bigger than that of the advanced economies.

Other consequences include growing threats to the quantity and quality of agricultural land, crop yields and fish stocks, and the greater incidence and ferocity of tropical storms and catastrophic weather events. Health experts fear the spread of diseases, such as Lyme disease, malaria, asthma, lung and gastrointestinal ailments and skin cancer. The effects of climate change are expected to lead to disruptive patterns of migration. According to the United Nations, there are now about 215 million migrants worldwide, just over half living in rich countries, and about a quarter classified as 'environmental refugees'. Total migration is growing at just under 2% per year, but the number of environmental refugees is expected to quadruple by 2050.

The precise effects of climate change on individual emerging countries cannot be predicted as such, but they will reflect both initial temperatures and the level of economic development. Initial temperatures are important. The cooler the climate is to start with, the greater the capacity to withstand, or even benefit from, modest increases in average temperatures. And the converse holds, of course. The level of economic development is pivotal, since poorer countries or regions are more likely to be heavily exposed to a large agricultural sector, low per capita incomes, sparse public services and weak public governance. Sub Sahara Africa, which has high temperatures and is poor, is clearly highly vulnerable to climate change. But large swathes of the emerging world beyond are also at risk, including the Indian subcontinent and Southeast Asia, parts of China, the Middle East, Brazil and small islands in the Pacific and Caribbean.

An average rise of 2°C may not sound significant, but a higher average also means that the range of variability shifts up, leading to intolerable levels at the top end of the range. The 2003 heat wave and drought in Europe, for example, is thought to have contributed to over 37,000 deaths, of which two-fifths were in France. Although some areas, such as the Indo-Gangetic plain, are already very hot, others such as Russia could gain significant economic benefits from a milder climate[9]. Siberia could benefit as it opens up to greater cultivation and resource discovery.

For most of the emerging world, however, changes in the environment and global resource and biosystems brought about by climate change will be of great concern. They will affect the availability of and access to natural resources, including food, which will be increasingly demanded as they chase higher levels of per capita income. The availability of freshwater and of water for the survival of humans, animals and crops is expected to come under increasing pressure. The adverse effects of climate change on biodiversity, which determines what lives and grows where, and the survival of habitats for birds, fish and animals, including elephants, polar bears, emperor penguins and koala bears, are becoming a matter of increasing concern. Changes in temperature variability in the context of rising overall temperatures will bring with it a greater incidence of disease and illness. And the ability of land and soil to support life will be at risk from flooding, desiccation – that is, the long-term process in which land dries out and becomes arid – and desertification – the permanent degradation of dry and already water-stressed lands.

Desertification is estimated to affect a third of the world's population, or roughly 2 billion people, and is associated with overexploitation of land, overgrazing, the widespread displacement of indigenous people, and the expansion of deserts such as the Sahara, Gobi and Sahel. It is rampant in Sub-Saharan Africa and central Asia, but is present also in China, Chile, and even parts of the Amazon rainforest in Brazil.

Water

The issue of water availability and quality has already made it to the top of the agenda of climate change concerns and effects[10]. The World Bank says that there are already 21 countries, home to 600 million people, with significant water scarcity. By 2025, it thinks there will 36 such countries with 1.4 billion inhabitants.

Water is fluid in an obvious sense, but also less obviously through the inter-connectedness of the water cycle. It begins when rainfall hits the earth, and ends up where it started, after passing through soil filters, aquifers, lakes, plants, human beings, rivers and seas, feeding, recycling, cleansing and being cleansed at different stages in the cycle. Human beings come into contact with water in many different ways. They drink it to sustain life, and use it in cooking, for washing, to irrigate crops, and as a waste sink. But we interfere with this cycle. We throw waste into the water in one place, but compromise other activities, such as food production, in another. We cut down trees to clear land for agriculture in one place, but cause water in wells in another to become undrinkable due to rising salt levels.

Precipitation patterns are expected to change with less water in already relatively arid parts and more in more temperate ones. Scientists also expect a higher incidence of flash floods, posing risks to physical infrastructure, a deterioration in water quality, and even social unrest. Increased water temperatures will affect the physical, chemical and biological properties of freshwater, with adverse consequences for biodiversity and food stocks. In coastal areas, a rise in sea levels would not only put the infrastructure at risk but also exacerbate water resource constraints due to increased salinisation of groundwater supplies. Water stress and more arid land will become more widespread, lowering agricultural productivity and exacerbating poverty.

Water and food are inseparable. Changes to water availability, along with changes in average temperatures and weather variability, will inevitably affect agriculture. At mid to high latitudes, crop productivity may rise for local mean temperature increases of up to 1 to 3°C[11]. But lower-lying land in seasonally dry regions would undoubtedly suffer, with crop productivity projected to decrease for even small local temperature increases of 1–2°C. Climate change will therefore affect agricultural yields and agricultural output directly, but it will also have other indirect but significant effects. As the Stern Review on the Economics of Climate Change states, 'In some tropical regions, the combined effects of loss of native pollinators, greater risk of pest outbreaks, reduced water supply, and greater incidence of heat-waves could lead to much greater declines in food production than through the individual effects themselves'[12].

Water and land are also inseparable. Human settlement tends to be driven by water availability, for consumption and as a key part of food and transportation chains. Urban and agricultural land alike will be affected by the proximity of coastal areas to increasing physical risks. According to the Intergovernmental Panel on Climate Change (IPCC), we should expect many additional millions of people to experience floods every year due to sea level rise over the next 50 years or so. In economic terms the costs could be significant, when you consider that currently more than 200 million people live in coastal floodplains around the world, with 2 million square kilometres of land and $1000 billion worth of assets less than 1 metre above sea-level. Some of the largest cities in the world are in low-lying areas with great risk of flooding: Tokyo, Shanghai, Hong Kong, Mumbai, Calcutta, Karachi, Buenos Aires, St Petersburg, New York, Miami and London[13].

Climate change will affect health, both as a consequence of deterioration in the quantity and quality of water, food and land, but also as a result of a rising temperature itself. The World Health Organisation has calculated that climate change caused a loss of 5.5 million disability-adjusted life years in 2000, mostly in Africa and Asia. Several factors contributed to this development, including flimsy housing, poor public health, inadequate insurance possibilities and affordability, and a range of communicable diseases including malaria, meningitis, diarrhoea and dengue fever. This underscores the central role played by stronger incomes and infrastructure as one of the main defences against climate change.

China has become increasingly aware of its vulnerability to climate change, becoming involved in the global debate as a champion of the emerging countries. It is just about on target to realise reductions in carbon emissions announced in the current five-year plan (2006–2010). Like many nations, China craves energy security and, if possible one day, energy independence through the massive expansion of renewable energy sources, from which it wants to get 15% of its energy consumption by 2020. It has big plans for electric cars and trucks, and gives large subsidies to purchasers. That said, China's big leap into solar panel production has run into problems of oversupply and overcapacity, and the strides made in wind turbines with generous subsidies haven't yet pushed the wind-driven share of electricity consumption past 0.5%. China also has economic interests in climate change mitigation. It sees green and clean energy as a potential new source of economic growth, and it earns a few billion dollars a year in credits in a United Nations' scheme to help finance clean energy.

But China's principal interests arise from climate change itself. The weakening of the monsoon means it is not moving inland as far nowadays, instead dumping rainfall and causing floods in coastal areas. Melting glaciers on the Tibetan plateau and loss of snow cover in the winter threaten to increase flooding during the wet season, and aggravate the shortages of dry-season water supplies. Moreover, economically significant cities such as Shanghai sit in low-lying areas that are potentially vulnerable to flooding in the event of a rise in sea levels. China is already water stressed. It accounts for 20% of the world's population but has only 7% of the world's water supply. Most of the water is in the south of the country, but 50% of the population lives in the north. China uses about 40 billion cubic metres more water each year – that's about six times the water consumption of Southern California – than its natural endowment can sustain over the medium to longer term.

To help compensate for the effects of water scarcity on factories, farmers and even in causing social unrest, China completed a major geo-engineering project in 2006, when it 'opened' the Three Gorges Dam spanning the Yangtze River. The idea had been proposed originally in 1919, but it wasn't taken seriously until the 1980s, and only after some appalling flood-related deaths and environmental damage. In 1954, flooding killed 30,000 people and left over 1 million people homeless, after which Mao Zedong wrote a poem called 'Swimming' in which he envisioned how the river might be brought under control. In the end, the work didn't start until 1994. It is the largest hydroelectric dam in the world, designed to limit the risk of dangerous flooding, generate significant increases in electricity output, and increase navigational capacity. China is also now constructing canals to take water to the north of the country and will doubtless move mountains, literally, to conserve and strengthen its water supplies. Still, China's water problem is likely to become increasingly demanding and dangerous.

Many key water resources are shared, and so increased water stress is likely to lead to increased tensions arising from shared water resources, particularly if mitigation efforts impact other users. For example, the Chinese South-North Water Transfer Project, overdue but expected to be in full operation by 2014, includes controversial plans that could affect the Ganges-Bumiputra River system in India. Reductions in the flow of meltwater from glaciers could also generate disruptive migration patterns within and between China and India as a result of a higher and wider incidence of drought and more arid climactic conditions. Notwithstanding the admission by scientists in 2010 that they could have overestimated the speed of the disappearance of glaciers, they remain largely confident that the phenomenon itself remains real. This could affect not just the Himalayan glaciers between China and India, but also those in the Andes in Latin America

The Indian Sub-Continent is also likely to be at great risk from climate change. The stability of the monsoon in India is almost the lifeblood of the economy. It provides 80% of the annual rainfall normally, and is vital for drinking water, agriculture and hydro-electric power. Greater fluctuations in the strength and timing of the monsoon both year to year and within a single season have already led to significant flooding or drought.

Tropical areas of India are already subject to volatile weather conditions. The potential economic impact of any sort of regular monsoon failure was hinted at in 2002, when monsoon rains did not fall as expected. The resulting seasonal rainfall deficit was 19%. The significant losses of agricultural production caused a drop of just over 3% in India's GDP[14]. In 2005, unusually heavy rains flooded Mumbai and, in 2009, a very late monsoon caused serious drought and social unrest in northern India. India is also vulnerable to the retreat of glaciers in the Himalayan Hindu-Kush region, where meltwater from the glaciers feeds seven of Asia's largest rivers, including 70% of the summer flow in the Ganges which provides water to around 500 million people. Scientists fear that glacial retreat could reduce the flow to about 30% over the next 50 years.

South and Central America also face significant risks. South America is already quite dry, and therefore particularly vulnerable to any reduction in rainfall. Melting glaciers and loss of snow in the Andes are projected by the IPCC to increase flooding during the wet season, and threaten dry-season supplies in some regions. Many large cities such as Lima, La Paz and Quito and 40% of the agriculture in Andean valleys depends on meltwater supplies. Up to 50 million people will be affected by the loss of dry-season supplies. Africa, including economically important areas such as South Africa, is vulnerable to climate change because it is already dry. Climate change is expected to reduce water resources further, a situation hardly helped by the continent's low capacity to adapt because of relative or absolute poverty. Similar to Asia, the African mega-deltas and coastlines support large populations and are potentially exposed to rising sea levels, storm surges and river flooding, as well as to the risk of food shortages and increased exposure to diseases such as malaria.

Some countries already suffer from an inability to balance fresh-water supply and demand. In Mexico, for example, 104 of 653 aquifers, which provide half the water consumed in the country, are being drained faster than they can replenish themselves. The IPCC has also noted that many semi-arid areas such as north-eastern Brazil will suffer a decrease in water resources due to climate change, with adverse impacts on multiple sectors, including agriculture, water supply, energy production and health. It also fears that, for Latin America, the increases in temperature and associated decreases in soil water by mid-century will lead to gradual replacement of tropical forest by savanna in eastern Amazonia.

Deforestation is a significant cause of both GHG emissions and environmental degradation that contributes additional emissions. Independent sources cited in the Stern Review suggest that emissions from deforestation amount to more than 18% of total GHG emissions. Countries losing forest cover most rapidly include

Brazil, Indonesia, Sudan, Myanmar and Zambia. The greatest amount of CO_2 is emitted when land is converted from forest to agricultural land, a shift which threatens the survival of native inhabitants but also exacerbates the deforestation cycle.

It does this partly as a result of the unintended consequences of economic growth. Higher growth leads to stronger demand for energy and natural resources, and higher global commodity prices. The latter encourage governments and companies to intensify land use, which leads to further deforestation, exacerbating GHG emissions. As much as three-quarters of deforested land in Brazil ends up as pastureland, and in Indonesia the cultivation of oil palm is a significant driver of deforestation.

Brazil, like many other emerging markets, has struggled and will continue to wrestle with the unintended emissions consequences of economic growth. It needs to generate ever-larger volumes of power and energy to fuel economic development and satisfy the demands of its working age citizens, who are expected to increase by 15%, or roughly 20 million, by 2030. In 2010, Brazil's courts gave approval to dam the Xingu river at Belo Monte in eastern Amazonia, and construct a massive $11 billion hydroelectric station. But environmental groups, already opposed to nuclear and coal-fired power, fear that the project will give rise to both flooding and desiccation in different regions of the rainforest, along with large displacements of local inhabitants. In other words, more power could cause more damage to the rainforest, and even more GHG emissions and economic and social stress.

Deforestation is not irreversible, as China has shown by restoring 18 million hectares of forestland in the 1990s, raising the share of forests in land use from 16% to 18%. These efforts did not stop

GHG emissions from growing but they would almost certainly have been higher otherwise. And deforestation was at least one bright note to the less-than-spectacular Copenhagen climate talks in December 2009. An agreement on the need to prevent deforestation, to nurture forest as carbon sink, and to provide for the mobilization of financial resources from richer nations was widely welcomed. And not least, perhaps, because, according to a report commissioned by the Stern Review, the elimination of annual forest loss in eight countries (Brazil, Indonesia, Papua New Guinea, Cameroon, Congo, Ghana, Bolivia and Malaysia) would result in a 46% reduction in global deforestation[15].

Breaking the link between growth and emissions

If climate change were gradual and wholly predictable, the Catch-22 problem would be much less significant. But environmental degradation is unstable and liable to run into tipping points, beyond which catastrophic consequences could follow. Jared Diamond's well-known book, *Collapse*, identifies five 'strands' leading to collapse. These comprise rapid population growth that puts pressure on resources; environmental degradation – such as deforestation – caused by human activity, that leads to a decline in the productivity of agricultural land; increased conflict over access to and ownership of resources; climate-change induced drought; and a focus on short-run 'coping' problems rather than the more important management of longer-term risks, which is basically about money, skills and investment. These phenomena all loom large in the emerging world today with the one silver lining that the management of longer-term risks is gradually gaining in importance. What can countries do about tipping points they can't predict?

In everyday life, think about the parallel of insurance. People take out fire insurance on their properties, not because they expect disaster to strike but because, should it do so, a financial payout would help them to recover relatively quickly. Insurance costs can be contained by requiring policyholders to adopt small changes in behaviour, like the installation of smoke alarms, and by charging higher premiums for customers who fail to do so. In the sphere of climate change, such insurance-based thinking should be a no-brainer, but unfortunately there are too many cases where it isn't.

One well-known example of such myopia was the city of New Orleans, and the impact of Hurricane Katrina. While this occurred in the most economically advanced nation on Earth, it represented the potential consequences for emerging markets of being caught in the Catch 22. Hurricane Katrina exposed the myopia of not investing adequately in infrastructure, and the inevitable helplessness of mostly poorer citizens. In its own way, it can be seen as a microcosm of the situation facing the BRICs and other emerging nations.

New Orleans is three metres below sea level, protected by a system of levees and pumps, but it had inadequate levels of investment in the flood protection and lacked a 'just-in-case' recovery plan. In their absence, people had to make their own judgements about risk, but their ability to do so cut strongly across income and racial lines. Over the years, wealthier and mostly white residents and businesses had moved away from the most vulnerable areas of the city, while poorer mostly black people occupied the lower, more dangerous ground. In 2005, 36% of the residents in an area known as the 'Lower 9' (the Lower 9th Ward), lived below sea level and the poverty line, with limited access to transportation. They were to find themselves all over the newspapers, in desperate straits, stranded in the Superdome and clinging to the rooftops.

Even though Katrina cannot be said to have been the result of climate change, the increase in the incidence and severity of natural disasters around the world has captured the attention of meteorologists and climate scientists alike. The Indian Ocean Tsunami in December 2004 caused 230,000 deaths in 14 countries from South East Asia to India, Bangladesh and the east coast of Africa, deprived over half a million people of their homes, and led to widespread environmental damage to mangroves, coral reefs, forests and coastal wetlands, as well as significant pollution. Like Katrina, it couldn't be linked directly to climate change, but it demonstrated the tragic costs of being ill-prepared, and the particular plight of poor people, especially those living in low-lying areas that are vulnerable to rising sea levels. It also showed the possible dangers of significant submarine land slippage and movement that some scientists think could be exacerbated by the release of methane gas compounds in the oceans.

Between 1987 and 2006, the number of reported natural disasters due to drought, floods, tropical storms and wild fires rose from 195 per year in the first 10 years to 365 per year in the subsequent period. By 2007, more than 230 million people per year in emerging countries were the victims of natural disasters. Hurricanes in the Caribbean are annual events, but in recent years they have seemed to grow in ferocity. In 2004, Brazil experienced its first ever hurricane, and a year later Hurricane Wilma wrought devastation in parts of Mexico, Cuba and Florida.

Bangladesh floods regularly and frequently. Three-quarters of the country is less than a metre above sea level, and four-fifths of the land is classified as flood plain, as the country's 800 rivers, including the Ganges and the Brahmaputra, meander into the world's largest delta. Moreover, Bangladesh has a monsoon climate, falls victim every year to tropical cyclones, and experiences spring flooding as the Himalayan snow melts. Large-scale loss of life and way of life is common in this country, whose GDP is a mere $80 billion, and where per capita income is just shy of $500. But since chronic flooding is a long-standing and enduring phenomenon, it begs the question as to why the same questions about the lack of cyclone shelters, poor building construction and land use, deforestation and overexploited agriculture arise every time disaster strikes.

China, too, is prone to increasingly severe flooding and drought. Over 100 people died and nearly 15 million in 13 provinces in southern China were affected by floods in May 2010, following one of the worst droughts in a century. Sadly, hundreds of people are killed or made homeless every year in the June to August rainy season, and climate experts believe the problem is being made worse by the effects of deforestation and soil erosion, which means that large parts of the country are increasingly vulnerable to flash floods and landslides because of the disappearance of trees, plants and bushes that would normally absorb water while the land structure remained intact.

These examples demonstrate clearly why emerging markets cannot take environmental risk lightly in the pursuit of rapid economic growth. They illuminate the significance of social, ethnic and political divisions, and the inability of poor people to cope. These factors will be of still greater significance, bearing in mind the widening gulf in coping ability between richer and poorer nations and regions, assuming the IPCC climate change scenarios are anywhere near right. Cities, regions and countries where per capita GDP is less than $2000–4000 will be especially badly affected. While emerging countries with strong export surpluses and high levels of foreign exchange reserves, such as China and Russia, should be able to afford the infrastructure needed to mitigate climate change, many others will need substantial financial and technical assistance to lessen their vulnerability to the damage that climate change is expected to cause, let alone to adopt new green and clean technologies. But how much is this all expected to cost? And would faster growth pay for it?

The IPCC has examined a number of scenarios, leading it to conclude that GHG mitigation should begin as soon as possible, meaning the reduction in carbon emissions from economic activities in key sectors, including power generation, transport, agriculture, housing, infrastructure and consumer goods. In other words, we have to try to break the links between carbon intensity and economic growth. The corollary, of course, is that if this cannot be done effectively or if it is prohibitively expensive, then economic growth should be constrained or redefined. This is where climate change ceases to be a purely scientific matter, and encroaches deeply into international relations and politics. If population, economic growth and the demand for rising living standards are to be managed better or controlled, the crucial questions are 'whose' are to be managed better, who is going to tell who that they need to do so, how will conformity or deviation be monitored, and will there be penalties in the case of the latter? These are highly sensitive issues, and ones around which politicians have to tread very carefully.

Constraining growth as we understand it today means suppressing wellbeing, that is, fewer jobs, less food to go around, and a lower quality of life. That is never going to be much of a runner for most politicians, especially in emerging markets, or indeed in countries, such as China, where the legitimacy of the political elite depends on sustained and rapid growth. The idea of changing the nature and measurement of economic growth by following a new and untried economic model, based around low carbon systems, entails enormous risk. A new and rising awareness about environmental damage, to be fair, is spurring changes, which are welcome. But the process is slow and lacks full commitment, not least because of the costs involved.

And we can't get a handle on the costs unless they can be properly measured. The trouble is that conventional economic measures, such as GDP, tell us about national output, derived from making and using more energy and, for example, plastics, chemicals and pesticides. But they don't tell us anything about the costs of environmental degradation and making good, and about the costs associated with the depletion of natural resources. Consequently, until we sew the benefits and costs of economic growth on the environment together, progress towards a greener planet is likely to be slower and much less complete than we'd like.

The Stern Review did mark the first serious attempt to quantify the costs of climate change. Stern suggested that, unless climate change mitigation measures were adopted, the economic costs of climate change would be devastating – the equivalent of losing at least 5% of global GDP each year and for the foreseeable future. But with investment to reduce GHG emissions, so that the worst of the effects of climate change were avoided, the economic cost of climate change could be limited to about 1% of global GDP per year. Subsequently, and as suggested earlier, economists and scientists have debated the numbers at length, and reckon the costs may be significantly higher.

The costs will not be evenly distributed; some of the poorest countries may not even be able to afford to make any headway in climate change mitigation, and the net costs and benefits of mitigation measures are bound to vary from country to country. So the issues of responsibility and equity are significant in this debate, making climate change an extremely hot political potato. Green or clean energy investment will most likely become a big driver of economic growth, but this raises many questions about affordability, how costs are distributed between countries specifically, and the 'free-rider' problem – that is, the extent to which the benefits of energy innovation in one country are shared by others who pay few of the costs.

In the absence of significant policy measures to deal with climate change soon, economists reckon the economic losses could amount to up to 3% of GDP for a rise of 3 degrees Centigrade in average global temperature. This is almost certainly an underestimate, not least because it allows only for the things that economists think they can measure and predict over time in markets for goods and services. We also need to add on the costs of cleaning up or making good environmental and weather damage, a deterioration in public health, lost leisure pursuits, and the damage to and rebuilding of ecosystems and human settlements. It's only guesswork, but for some countries, such as India, Bangladesh and several in Africa, the cost of global warming limited to 2 degrees centigrade could be as high as 4–6% of GDP. How can these costs be offset or managed?

Setting GHG emission targets for the global community is a self-evident means to try and restrain their growth, and the associated costs. But targets alone won't really work without at the same time putting in place mechanisms that distinguish individual national obligations, taking account of specific circumstances. Resource conservation, energy efficiency and new technology can all contribute towards a reduction of global GHG emissions but only if there is a universal behavioural change in the way resources are used, as the world's population rises towards 9 billion by 2050. As noted earlier, most of these extra citizens will be born in and live in emerging markets and other developing countries.

Emerging markets must play a full role in climate change mitigation, and are in an ideal situation to do so. While the traditional forces of economics, markets and trade in carbon credits, for example, can help to slow GHG emissions, global mechanisms are required to channel strategic investment funds into long-term projects, designed to change consumption and production patterns. And locally, emerging markets can pursue GHG emission reduction targets for key sectors, build a low carbon economy, conserve key resources, particularly forests, and provide funding for new green technologies.

The Stern Review emphasised that it is cheaper to pursue emission cuts in lower income countries that are in the process of building up their infrastructure through significant capital investments, because, through low emissions technologies, carbon savings can be locked in for the long run. This creates a great opportunity for emerging countries, and larger ones – such as China and India – are in an ideal position to exploit this advantage. But there are also substantial barriers. Apart from the fact that progress is slow, expensive and not accorded top priority, significant economic inertia exists. Sustained and continuous economic growth continues to be based largely around the use of coal-fired power, and most emerging markets are a long way from the establishment of low carbon energy systems to heat and light major cities, and power industry. It is easy to say that a green industrial revolution would strengthen existing economic growth in the long term, but because such an enormous shift in energy utilisation and efficiency entails taking risks with short-term economic performance and job creation, this is largely a political decision.

Some countries could cut emissions and lower those risks by building cleaner energy infrastructure, such as solar power, wind turbines and biofuel systems in countries where the local topography is well suited[16]. For example, Brazil scaled up the share of biofuels in total road transport fuel from 1% to 25% from 1975 to 2002. On the other hand, because biofuel is still a hydrocarbon burned by an engine, the growth of road transport emissions slowed down but did not decline. Nevertheless, Brazil, China and India have the wherewithal to produce relatively abundant amounts of clean energy. Countries that are just starting to build up transportation systems can focus on efficient urban public transport infrastructure, and on facilities to support the broad use of electric vehicles. Success would be much to the envy of cities, such as London, which is constrained by an ancient underground railway system and congested urban roads that were built before anyone worried about the size of modern conurbations, and the need for integrated, clean energy transportation infrastructure.

Emerging countries can also use new mechanisms designed to limit carbon emissions. The so-called 'Clean Development Mechanism' (CDM), set up in 2008 by the United Nations Framework Convention on Climate Change (UNFCCC), isn't yet as convincing as its name suggests, but it points to some interesting opportunities. According to this scheme, an energy investment project in a developing country that can be proved to prevent GHG emissions can earn one Certified Emission Reduction certificate (CER) per tonne of CO_2 equivalent. CERs can be traded, and can be used by developed country entities to meet emission reductions targets under the Kyoto Protocol[17]. In January 2010, less than two years after it was set up, the CDM registered its 2000th project.

Cumulatively, China has registered 37% of all projects, India 23% and Brazil 8% as at January 2010[18]. Of the 397 million CERs issued, China accounts for 48%, India 20%, South Korea 13%, and Brazil 10%. These numbers suggest significant demand, and since the United Nations CDM is the only such scheme of its kind, the potential for wider use is significant. CDM can also help get round the problem of companies in rich countries simply outsourcing their emissions, as well as other environmental damage, to developing countries by setting up production facilities abroad. The CDM offers a means of evaluating the costs of emissions in different locations, and facilitating the necessary investment to mitigate climate change effects.

Since outsourcing of industry is a form of CO_2 arbitrage, where companies move manufacturing from a location where emissions are more tightly controlled to one where they are not, the CDM could allow low carbon businesses to compete in outsourcing locations, and make it less attractive to export emissions, as now. In the future, countries could become more selective about which companies they admit and which they don't, depending on the payments companies might make to fund the mitigation of GHG exported, as it were, from one location to another.

In a way, emerging markets are well positioned to act on climate change. They can build infrastructure for protection against the worst and most likely effects. They can invest in green and clean technologies to wean themselves away from fossil fuel dependency, not only because of the risks to the environment, but also because of existing concerns over unstable politics in the main oil-producing areas, the security of supply routes, and the risks of escalating prices because of production limits. They have an opportunity, at relatively low levels of economic and infrastructure development, to invest in a low carbon economy 'from scratch', and steal a march on their richer competitors and rivals, who are saddled with a lot of high carbon infrastructure built much longer ago. Establishing a consensus to limit pollution and waste, preserve forests, and strengthen water conservation and supplies is hardly rocket science. But it's costly, and quite hard to 'sell' to citizens who are absolutely or relatively poor.

Dash for growth and be damned

The big improvements in energy efficiency in the US and Europe over the last 50 years have not been spurred mainly by environmental concerns, but by political and geopolitical issues related to the cost and availability of crude oil. To be fair, the environment has been a more significant factor in inducing companies and governments to look for clean and green energy in more recent years. But will China and India act any differently from the West, putting the environment before economic growth? Can they be green and grow?

There's little question that Western observers and politicians will want to shift the focus in the next few years to new – that is emerging market – GHG emissions, as opposed to the accumulated emissions for which they have been largely responsible. China's current and next prospective five-year plans lean firmly towards a reduction in carbon intensity but the big problem for China, and other emerging countries, is whether they will succeed in moderating their emissions as they become richer. The last thing we want is for the BRICs to become American in this regard, that is, increasingly rich but increasingly negligent of emissions. In view of China's 1.3 billion population, its low level of GDP per head, and its aspirations to modernise, there is little question that the country will want to compromise much, if at all, when it comes to economic growth. The same goes for India and its 1.2 billion people.

If China's economic and energy policies don't change, emissions will resemble those of the US in due course. But perhaps China has to keep going for the moment – that is, continue with its dash for growth – so as to be in a stronger position to lower them in the future. The trouble is that the costs of reducing GHG emissions in China are only going to increase. They are expected to reach $438 billion a year over the next 20 years, which is the equivalent of 10% of 2009 GDP[19].

It is small wonder, then, that China's demand that rich countries pay 0.5–1% of their own GDP to help poorer countries reduce emissions finds many sympathisers. In the meantime, emerging countries are likely to pursue GHG-intensive growth strategies partly because they claim to have the moral high ground – cumulative emissions are not their fault – and partly because it is precisely the dash for growth that should allow them to develop new sustainable energy technologies.

Large-scale energy innovation could, indeed, break the Catch 22 for emerging nations. Countries like China, India and Brazil could then really lay claim to be global leaders. They would be the ones with sustainable resources under their control, energy independence, and shaping possibly a new industrial revolution and global economy. That at least is a very long-term and laudable goal. In the meantime, the jockeying for global leadership and geopolitical advantage will take place and in broader and more complex ways.

Chapter Eight

Who Will Inherit the Earth?

Europeans built the first truly global geopolitical system, upsetting what was once a global system of sorts centred around China and the rise and fall of other Asian powers. The world order over which they presided disintegrated during the tumultuous period from 1914–1945, and leadership passed to the United States, which became the undisputed global hegemon after the collapse of the USSR in 1989. A mere 20 years or so later, is the baton of global power in the process of being passed on again?

Most people believe that the financial crisis is intensifying the trend towards a shift in global power and a new world order that favours China and other major emerging nations. So is this the moment when the much-heralded decline of the United States is accelerating and the Chinese century is beginning – or, to put another way, who will inherit the Earth?

I have examined the role that the BRICs and other emerging nations play in the world economy, noting the economic and financial stresses between them and the advanced economies in a global context, and emphasising the demographic, technological and climate change challenges that will shape their future. In this final chapter, I want to speculate about where all this may be leading, especially as so many of us in the West seem resigned to the idea that the old order is now decaying quickly. This latter sentiment, of course, is feeding off the current economic and financial crisis, and the frustration at the enormity of the wrenching changes that Western societies have to make.

We can begin by asserting that the world order that may be emerging from the crisis is, as yet, quite disorderly. Our global institutions and the embryonic G20 governance structure have vital functions, but what's missing is effective leadership, around which the rest of us can fall into line. The only major players that can provide it, China and the United States, are unwilling or unable to provide what is needed, partly because of the new economic and political insecurity arising from the financial crisis and its consequences. Although the European Union has significant economic weight, it lacks both a clear and unified approach to policy making, and a firmness of purpose to make a big difference in the world, except in matters of trade. If anything, the European sovereign debt crisis has amplified these shortcomings.

I will argue that, while China is well suited in terms of its size and geography to be a major global power, its economic dynamism is going to expose important deficiencies in its institutional and legal systems that may have significant domestic social and political implications in the next 20 years. Together with China's poor demographics, these are highly relevant to the country's ability to sustain rapid growth without running into financial, inflationary and economic shocks that could easily threaten the legitimacy of the Communist Party. In turn, they could even make China's weakness a bigger problem than the strength that is visible in a contemporary context.

By contrast, while the demise of the United States and the relative, if not absolute, decline in its status is a popularly held theme for many reasons that resonate nowadays, it also has the attributes of renewal. If exploited, and the only thing we can say is that the United Sates has done so before, it is likely to sustain itself as the most prominent, if not the overwhelmingly dominant, power in the world for a very long time to come.

Contours of power

China's claims to being a global power rest on five important planks. It is the world's largest creditor nation. Its economy is sufficiently large to have a material impact on the global economy. It is dynamic. It has engaged forcefully with global trade and capital markets in ways that impact its own welfare and that of other nations. And it is a major consumer and participant in global energy markets. But as I noted early in the book, demographics, geography, and institutions play important roles in the ability to command and project economic and political power.

The concluding focus is on the last two factors, since the demographic issues have already been laid out. It remains only to add that, on current projections, China will be inferior to the United States by 2050 on every demographic count except total population size. In most other respects, including median age, life expectancy, fertility rates, gender mix, old age dependency and immigration, the United States' demographic structure is expected to be stronger.

Notwithstanding China's current growth surge, therefore, it will be unable to sustain anything like it for any length of time. The imminent reversal in the growth of China's labour supply, together with the exhaustion of migrant and cheap labour and the inevitable decline in productivity growth that accompanies economic maturity will render China's growth rate quite pedestrian over the coming decade or two. Moreover, the enormous economic and social changes needed to accommodate ageing populations tend to favour the United States, for the simple reason that it has a superior starting position when it comes to wealth, innovation and flexibility.

The geography of power is often overlooked but it is an essential facet, and here, China and the United States both have strong claims. In the case of the latter, they have been self-evident for a long time. China, though, has been exploiting its geography much more recently. Napoleon, who knew a thing or two about continental power, once wrote to the King of Prussia in 1804 that 'La politique de toutes les puissances est dans leur géographie', or, 'The politics of all powers lies in their geography'[1]. The geography of power is important because it transcends the 'news' to which our attention is drawn on a daily basis concerning individual politicians and their reactions to events. This is not to say that presidents and prime ministers don't matter, but even the less memorable and effective ones tend not to derail the strategic interests of their countries dictated by geography. The United States and China, with large landmasses, populations, resources, and long temperate coastlines are both favoured by their geography. But they are quite separate physically, and while they vie for influence and access to resources in Asia and many other parts of the world, there is no equivalent of the battleground of Europe that polarised American and Soviet Russian interests until 1989.

The internal geographic coherence of the United States was resolved late in the 19th century in the wake of the Civil War and with the conclusion of the Indian wars. American economic, military and naval power evolved naturally thereafter as the country exploited the advantages of a steadily more integrated and flexible economy. China's internal coherence is a much more recent phenomenon. Even though it has a 9000-mile stretch of coastline to the east and south that dominates East Asia and could link up via railways and roads to the Indian Ocean, the rest of China is land-locked. To the west, Tibet and the province of Xinjiang border India and central Asia. To the north, Mongolia lies as a buffer next to the Russian Far East. Consolidating these regions was always going to be a priority.

As Robert Kaplan has noted, China had to assimilate Tibet and Xinjiang by force in order to integrate them into the state. Periodically, trouble flares up[2]. In 2009, the Uighurs, descendants of the Turks who once ruled Mongolia and who make up 45% of Xianjing's population, rioted for several days against Han (ethnic Chinese). Over 170 people were killed and over 1700 were injured. And in Tibet, where the prospect of local autonomy is anathema to China, the most serious riots in 50 years erupted in the same year. These western areas are strategically vital to the integrity of the Chinese state, lying as they do between China and central Asia, in a broader region that possesses oil and gas, iron ore and copper, and carries vital energy pipelines from the Caspian Sea and the former Soviet republics in Asia into China. Mongolia is also important to China, not only as a buffer province, but also because of its oil, coal, uranium and rich grasslands. To the south, Vietnam, Laos, Mynamar and North Korea are all natural spheres of influence for China, while further afield China's trade and investment relationships with Japan and the countries of south-east Asia have been growing for many years.

Kaplan argues that now China feels more secure and economically strong within its own expanded borders, it is free to move on to the next project, namely to build a stronger naval capability, not least to protect shipping and supply routes. He notes that China still lags a long way behind the United States as a naval power but that it is at least in a position now to thwart or check US naval dominance in the Pacific Ocean and South China Sea. Nowhere is this more important, perhaps, than in Taiwan, a mere 100 miles from the Chinese coast. Keeping the US Navy in distant waters is certainly one way of trying to exert subtle dominance over the island. If ever Taiwan became an integral part of mainland China, it would send the strongest of geopolitical signals. It would signify to Japan, India, Australia, South Korea and the whole of Southeast Asia that the United States was in retreat. The Pacific Rim would belong to China and, as noted in Chapter 2, this would signify a real and far-reaching geopolitical shift, marked by China's ability to project power throughout Eurasia and perhaps beyond. Conscious of this, there is no question that Japan, South Korea and India, as well as the United States, will all attempt to build stronger navies and naval capabilities.

The consolidation and integration of the internal economy in pursuit of economic power, and the ability to project external strategic commercial interests have been driving China's global role forwards in the last several years. In 2001, China, along with Russia, Kazakhstan, Tajikistan and Uzbekistan founded the

Shanghai Cooperation Organisation ostensibly to deal with disputes, terrorism and separatist threats. But it has become a forum to spur energy and economic cooperation and to deter or contain US presence and influence in central Asia. In 2005, India, Iran, Pakistan and Mongolia were admitted as observers, and Iran and Pakistan have applied for full membership.

China has also worked with Asian, Arab and OPEC countries to establish regular consultations on economic and political interactions, but it is China's bonds with Iran, Saudi Arabia and Africa that have grabbed recent attention. Saudi Arabia is China's principal source of oil, and receives investment in oil production and refining and railway construction in return. It does extensive energy and infrastructure trade with Iran, from which it gets 14% of its oil imports. It is developing oil reserves in Africa, which now accounts for a third of total oil imports, as well as access to other raw materials and seaports in several other nations, including Angola, Niger, Mali and Senegal, Sudan, Tanzania, Zambia and Mauritius. In exchange for strategic access to natural resources and for political support, China offers a pot-pourri of goodies that include aid on attractive terms, preferential trade agreements, large-scale investment, infrastructure, and labour and materials.

Rule of law and enduring economic power

Population, natural resources, capital accumulation and technology figure among the biggest drivers of economic growth and success over time, but the quality of institutions is the essential and often neglected attribute that binds them all together to deliver the results. Earlier, when considering China's global dominance and subsequent decline in the face of the European Age, I suggested that the weakness of China's institutions trumped its other strengths that resided in a more authoritarian and rigid state. The weakness of the legal system has always been the Achilles' heel, and remains so to this day, although for reasons I will explain China has been able to overcome it so far. But as China becomes a more complex, modern, ever more consumer-oriented, economy, this lacuna will become increasingly evident giving rise to political tensions.

I am not saying that the rule of law means China, or other countries, has to be democratic as we understand the term in the West. The noted economist, Milton Friedman, argued 30 years ago that economic performance, civil liberties and economic freedoms were highly correlated, but this didn't necessarily apply as much when it came to political rights. And so, as we explore the argument, bear in mind that this is not, *per se*, a pitch to say that China can only succeed if it turns into a democracy.

Law is about rules that govern contracts, property rights and human rights, as well as being the bedrock of criminal, constitutional and administrative structures. All of these are important for economic development, but the rule of law, contracts and property rights, and neutral third party enforcement institutions such as courts, top the list because these are crucial to the sustained accumulation of capital over generations, which is the source of durable economic strength and power.

In Anglo-Saxon countries, primacy is accorded to the judiciary over the state and then political parties. In continental European countries, the roles of the judiciary and the state are reversed, reflecting a different legal evolution; this was captured by the French king, Louis XIV's, alleged declaration that 'L'etat, c'est moi', or 'I am the State'. In much of Asia, variants or aspects of these two models have been imported over time, but in China (and also Japan and other countries with strong central authorities), the party is the principal source of authority, to which the state and then the judiciary are subservient.

The most significant difference in this last model is the lack of an independent judicial system. It is in this context that we can say that in China, for example, there is rule *by* law, rather than rule *of* law. In other words, instead of a creative and innovative process of court-administered laws that change continuously to reflect changing political and social values, change grows not out of the legal system but only as a result of government and diktat. This tends to lead to ambiguity, unpredictability, the protection of vested interests, and corruption.

I should point out that lawyers and economists have mixed views about the significance of strong formal versus informal contract law and enforcement mechanisms. For example, countries and communities that are small, poor or at primitive levels of development are likely to have a preponderance of cash and barter-type arrangements, where a formal legal system may have little relevance. Even richer countries, including many in Asia, may have tightly knit, ethnically- and family-based business communities that are normally characterised by a high degree of mutual trust. I referred earlier to the Chinese term *guanxi*, which comprises business relationships based on informal relationships among families or close associates. A formal legal system may not be necessary if the members can negotiate and mediate long-term relationships among themselves. Further, contract law and a stable and long-settled legal system are not so significant in societies dominated by oligopolies, that is, a relatively small number of large and powerful companies that can effectively make up their own rules and can depend on the largesse and favours of the state. The former USSR, and even modern Russia, could fall into this category, as indeed would many energy- and raw material-producing nations.

But there comes a point in the development cycle when more robust and formal legal institutions are essential to economic sustainability. The speed with which the BRICs have developed in the last 20 years makes this highly relevant and of rather pressing significance. As the economy becomes large, more modern and more complex, important changes take place that require good institutions to govern relationships and adjudicate in disputes. Trade in goods and services becomes bigger, more complex, more irregular, and more impersonal. Numerous enterprises emerge, each relatively small in relation to the economy, but collectively the agent of billions of transactions and source of widespread competition. Governments and companies spend large amounts of money on large, long-life investments, especially social and economic infrastructure, usually involving complicated financial arrangements between the operators and the creditors. Technological progress, as I pointed out earlier, needs a sound legal system to protect and nurture innovation. The financial system comes under growing pressure to create credit, to innovate new products to gather the savings of households and companies, and to channel them efficiently into both financial and physical assets – the creation of capital and equity – that drive future growth. It is no accident that economic development is marked by the development of sophisticated capital markets that do just this, if sometimes – as recently – with a Wild West abandon. If the doors to foreign investment are open, arriving companies need to have confidence they will get paid, not have their property confiscated or otherwise stolen, and be able to send profits back home.

These developments make the fulfilment of promises and predictability even more important to success and stability. But these promises have no meaning in the absence of a stable and trusted legal system. Some promises are quite short-term – for example, if I deliver components to you, I want to know you'll pay me in 60 or 90 days without fail. Or, if I lend you money for working capital or to fund a project, I want to know your collateral and ability to repay your debt are good, but that I have legal recourse in case you fail. If my local authority plans to build a highway through my house, or a dam above my village, I ought to be able to object, bring a case and, if necessary, get compensation.

Other promises are absolutely fundamental to the fabric of economic growth, and are embodied in the equities and in bonds issued by enterprises. In other words, if I give you capital today, I want to be assured that you will either pay me back in 10 or 20 years along with annual interest, or pay me a share of the profits for as long as I own my shares or equity. If I give you capital and you are a start-up technology geek, or you run a distribution business with next to no assets to which I might have recourse, the force of contract law would be additionally important for my comfort.

The bottom line is that more complexity in the economy gives rise to more uncertainty, and you can't build strong, sustainable economic power on the back of rules and laws that are unpredictable and open to change at the whim of politicians. You need an independent judiciary, and judge-made law, providing for rules that are clearly understood, and that can be enforced or challenged. That, at least, is the fundamental belief in Western societies that insist that contract law, property rights, and neutral third party enforcement contribute to accountability, political stability, regulatory quality and the control of corruption. In their own ways, we could point to Russia and Vietnam as examples of countries that changed or introduced new legal systems in the 1990s, based around these precepts, and that unquestionably derived economic benefit from so doing.

But if that's the case, how come China seems to be tearing the 'rule book' apart?

China has a legal system, of course, and changes to establish forms of property rights have been introduced in the last 25 years. More recently, it has established special courts to adjudicate over intellectual property rights, for example, but sometimes under pressure from the United States for change, it has made concessions as part of institutional reform but to head off foreign pressure. The real problem is that it has no consistently enforced legal framework that allows the judicial system to be a credible third party enforcer of contracts. Its courts are constitutionally subservient to the Communist Party and therefore to political whim. And they have a reputation for lack of competence and independence, are prone to political interference and judicial corruption, and get 'protection' from local governments in the adjudication of judgements. It has a weak to non-existent system of intellectual property rights and software and other product piracy is widespread. In the European Chamber of Commerce Business Confidence Survey 2010, covering 500 European companies operating in China, most companies expressed continuing optimism about China's economic growth, but also rising concern about the discretionary enforcement of laws and regulations, opaque processes for registering products, and the weakness of intellectual property rights. Only two-thirds of those companies that had prioritised China as their top investment location thought this would be the case in five years.

But, as these companies know, the economy is growing like gangbusters, investing nearly half its GDP, and attracting large volumes of foreign investment, admittedly with much emanating from Hong Kong, Taiwan, Macao, Singapore and other parts of the Chinese Diaspora. There are basically two explanations for this apparent conundrum, both of which are likely to be challenged in the future.

First, instead of there being a formal and stable contracts system, there is an informal social contract that is based around the reputation and ability of the leadership to deliver 8% per annum GDP growth and rising prosperity year in, year out – and from which the Communist Party derives its legitimacy. Hence, the single-mindedness of the authorities in prioritising economic growth and investment, and stressing domestic interests, almost at whatever cost. From this standpoint, it is understandable that investors see the Communist Party, not the courts, as providing the certainty that their investments will be protected and kept largely free from political encroachment. But within the next 10–20 years, China's economy is going to slow down on a permanent basis, and before then it is likely to encounter more temporary economic shocks as it seeks to fend off rising inflationary pressures.

Second, local governments have significant economic powers and are the principal agents in delivering annual growth of 8–9%, tax revenues, and employment. Their job would be impossible if they weren't able to provide some property rights to local businesses and individuals, assuring them that their property is free from confiscation or interference. Local governments also have substantial administrative power, along with strong and favourable access to local social and business networks, and this makes local officials key players in the trade and transactions of both local businesses and those that expand geographically. Seen one way, this can be seen as a system of trust and promise that substitutes for a formal contract framework. Seen another, it says 'crony capitalism'.

And given the rapid accumulation of local governments' real estate and debt as part of China's 2008 mega-stimulus programme, the chances are quite high that their fingerprints will be somewhere in the next bout of economic and financial turbulence.

A formal and stable system of contracts won't protect China from boom and bust in the economy, but it is going to become more important as the country becomes more sophisticated, reliant on the sustainable accumulation of private capital, populated by a rising middle class, and anxious about social cohesion during a time of rapid economic change. Whether and how China's legal institutions change are matters for conjecture. But it is incumbent on futurologists to ask if an autocratic China with weak legal institutions can avoid the likely clash between accelerating economic development and the rising demands for commercial and political freedoms, especially as the growth momentum in the economy mellows. It could be that nothing less than this will determine whether, in the longer run, China will continue to develop as an economic power or succumb to mediocrity. China is, and will doubtless continue to be the dominant power in Asia, provided it doesn't succumb to unrest and weakness. But more than that is a matter for debate.

America RIP?

Nothing succeeds like success, and if China is basking in this light today, how do we know that RIP is not so much Rest In Peace on America's epitaph, as Renewal In Progress on its shell?

If American power and its capacity to shape the world are in irreversible decline, you could argue that it's been going on for almost the whole of the six decades since the end of the Second World War[3]. It may have started at a seemingly unimportant reception at the Soviet Union's Embassy in Washington in October 1957, when a *New York Times* journalist received a phone call from his bureau chief to say 'it's up'. What he meant was Sputnik 1, the first earth-orbiting artificial satellite, launched by Moscow to the evident discomfort and embarrassment of the US.

In the same year, Senator John F. Kennedy warned, wrongly as it later turned out, that the US was losing the ballistic missile race with the USSR and that this would prove highly damaging to America's struggle against communism. A decade later, the US had lost its bearings, fighting a major war in Southeast Asia, and confronting civil rights unrest and immense pressure for social change at home. In the 1970s, it presided over the collapse of the Bretton Woods system and high inflation, fell victim to a deep industrial malaise, and to more expensive oil, and became involved in a hopeless and humiliating confrontation with Iran.

In the 1980s, the inevitability of Japanese economic power captured new notions of decline. The historian Paul Kennedy wrote in his book, *The Rise and Fall of the Great Powers*, that the US was succumbing to imperial over-stretch. Kennedy's timing was unfortunate because the US was in the process of turning decline into renewal, courtesy of the fall of communism in the USSR and eastern Europe, the acceleration in globalisation, and the information and communications technology revolution in the 1990s. Even though the economy returned to boom after the dotcom bubble burst and the accountancy scandals in the early 2000s, the pendulum swung back to decline again during the two presidential terms of George W. Bush from 2000–2008. However else this period is remembered, it will be for the terrorist attacks in

September 2001, the wars in Afghanistan and Iraq, America's alienation of both its Western allies and the Islamic world, and the worst
banking, debt and economic crisis for 80 years.

In 2004, the historian, Niall Ferguson wrote *Colossus*, with a UK
subtitle that read 'The Rise and Fall of the American Empire', in
which he alleged that the US was succumbing to increasingly problematic deficits in its manpower, finances, and attention (to empire
building). In 2008, Kishore Mahbubani, a Professor of Public Policy
at the National University of Singapore, published *The New Asian
Hemisphere: The irresistible shift in global power to the East*, in which he
asserted what many had been contemplating, namely that China
would take over the mantle of global leadership from America.

Echoing the theme, Martin Jacques, senior visiting fellow at the
London School of Economics, and former editor of *Marxism Today*,
published *When China Rules The World* in 2009. He argued that the
financial crisis had simply hastened an on-going shift in the balance
of power from the US to China that was as much about America's
relative decline as it was about the renaissance and triumph of
China's civilisation. And in 2010, in an article in *Foreign Affairs*
called 'Decline and Fall', Niall Ferguson was unrepentant, now
post-crisis, warning that America's decline was liable to be sudden,
and then extraordinarily rapid.

These authors have generated a debate that has been joined by
many others, who seem undeterred by the last 60 years, at least, in
which the US has often been caught napping, or worse, fallen off
some economic or political precipice, but responded by reinvent-
ing itself, or rebooting, as we might say today. It is still the largest
economic and military power in the world by far, accounting for a
'healthier' 25% of world GDP than the more sclerotic European
Union, and for about 42% of global military spending, 53% of the

world's combat aircraft and a naval tonnage that is larger than the fleets of the next 17 countries together. It has essentially robust institutions and legal systems, which are not free from abuse or inertia as the financial crisis demonstrated, and which the budgetary crisis is exposing. But these institutions exist to challenge and to change in ways that few countries can emulate. Politicians can always be criticised for a failure to act or behave responsibly, but the self-evident quality of America's institutions is more enduring and fundamental.

So are the sceptics right to assert that 'this time, it is different' and that American decline is now unstoppable and irreversible? The idea that the US has become overstretched, at least economically and financially, certainly stands up to scrutiny. This could generate social and economic instability at home, compromise the country's appetite for global security duties, give policies a markedly more nationalistic hew, and undermine America's place in the world.

Between 2000 and late 2009, the total debt owed by the government, households and companies rose from 180% to about 240% of GDP. In addition, during this time debt owed by financial companies rose from 65% to 120% of GDP. In less than a decade, US national debt rose by as much as it had done in the previous two decades. Total government debt, including that owned by other government departments, stood at $12,900 billion at the end of 2009, or roughly 90% of GDP. According to the non-partisan Congressional Budget Office, accumulated deficits in coming years could push public debt to over $22,000 billion by 2020, at which point it would represent considerably more than 100% of GDP. There is little question that the US government is confronting a budgetary black hole, partly because of the impact of the crisis, but most importantly because of the substantial unfunded future costs of healthcare. If the government had to make a cheque out today for all the costs associated with ageing until 2050, it would amount to about $70,000 billion, or five times today's GDP. This is not going to occur, because long before these forecasts are realised, the US will succumb to a new financial crisis, unless it acts voluntarily and soon to bring the budget back under control.

Budgetary issues will spill over into America's external economic relations. The US is already the world's largest debtor nation, with gross external liabilities of $13.8 trillion at the end of 2009. Because the US also owns a lot of assets in, and lends to, other countries, the net liabilities are much lower, standing at $3.5 trillion at the end of 2008. It is often forgotten that the US was a creditor nation until 1985, but it took 15 years for its net foreign debt to grow to $1000 billion, and a mere eight years to increase by a further $2500 billion. Foreigners own about $3600 billion of US government bonds, notes and money market instruments, and almost $4000 billion of other bonds. As noted earlier, China, with about $1 trillion of US Treasury bonds is America's largest single creditor.

These economic and financial developments predate the financial crisis, of course, but the crisis has exposed the economic frailty of the US economy, its sensitivity to volatile credit and asset market conditions, and its financial dependence on 'the kindness of strangers', as Blanche DuBois says at the end of the Tennessee Williams play, *A Streetcar Named Desire*. Foreign nations fund America's balance of payments deficit, which is the difference between what Americans save and what they invest. The US budget deficit acts to reduce national savings. Now, many nations, including not only China but others such as India, Russia and Mexico, have become more vocal about what they see as fundamental weaknesses in the global financial system built around the US dollar.

America is clearly vulnerable to any decision that China or other large holders of foreign currency reserves may make to sell US dollars and diversify significantly into other currencies or precious metals. Countries with sovereign wealth funds that have broader investment mandates than central banks are already acquiring gold and commodities and physical investments abroad. So far, this has occurred without destabilising currency and financial markets, and the extent of the switch out of US dollars has probably been relatively modest. In any event, countries such as China, that intervene regularly to prevent their currencies rising too far, are condemned to buy US dollars and investing a sizeable proportion of them in America's capital markets, which retain an unparalleled depth and breadth. It is hard to see China or other major economies opting to dump US dollars, except in the event of a major deterioration in international relations. Nevertheless, emerging nations will doubtless continue to press for global action to 'fade' the US dollar in the global monetary system in favour of other instruments, such as the IMF's Special Drawing Rights, and eventually perhaps, a Chinese Yuan that is fully convertible. The United States would be loathe to see the US dollar downgraded, in effect, and cannot take the threat lightly.

Away from money and finance, the US still has a lot going for it. Its geography, size, natural resource endowments and economic and technological prowess will underpin its status as a dominant power for a long time. Its higher education system is the best in the world, and its potential to succeed based around sound institutions, the exploitation of innovation, and the encouragement of imagination is undiminished. These qualities are less visible and harder to appreciate than the harsh facts thrown up by unemployment rolls, a fragile banking system, and massive budget deficits and public debt in Washington and in the states. But they are the decisive factors that, in the end, will determine how the United States regains control over its public finances and the economy, harnesses its demographic and technological advantages and, as a result, restores its reputation.

Current bones of contention

China's complex economic and financial relationship with the United States is an important source of friction, especially since the financial crisis. Despite the constructive roles played by both China and the US in the G20 in the immediate aftermath of the crisis, the impetus for cooperation has floundered. China's exchange rate policy, for example, is likely to remain the source of regular dispute and misunderstanding, not just vis-à-vis the United States, but also in relation to other major emerging markets. The United States and others see a major change in China's exchange rate regime as a fundamental issue in global monetary reform, but China sees it as a vital matter of national sovereignty, over which the Communist Party holds sway, and responds only weakly for diplomatic reasons to what it regards as unjustified pressure to change it. Conflicting views have become even more polarised. For example, it was reported in March 2010 that five prominent members of the G20 – the US, the UK, France, Canada and the Republic of Korea – had written a formal rebuke to China about what they saw as the country's backsliding on several important issues related to global imbalances, including its exchange rate policy[4]. And, as noted earlier, the decision in June 2010 to restore tightly managed 'flexibility' to the RMB's links to a basket of currencies – the way the basket is structured is not known – was almost certainly timed and designed to avert the world's attention at the G20 summit a week later.

The US and China will continue to cross swords on the RMB, as well as on global imbalances and global financial governance, largely because they see the causes and consequences of the financial crisis differently. Consequently, it is hard for them to agree on shared solutions and policies. The US sees the crisis as the product of poor banking regulation, which it is trying to do something about, and of global imbalances, which – alone – it can't. Accordingly, it believes that China's reluctance to revalue the RMB significantly and embrace domestic reforms to give a more marked domestic character to the economy are obstructing progress. China sees the crisis principally as the product of America's tolerance of excessive consumption and borrowing, and now sees high US public borrowing, and the Federal Reserve's monetary policies as undermining the stability of the world's reserve currency, in which it just happens to own most of its foreign assets.

Although the exact composition of China's holdings of foreign securities is not known, its direct ownership of US assets amounts to about $1500 billion, including nearly $1000 billion of US Treasury bonds. On the face of it, this gives China extraordinary financial muscle, and many financial commentators have drawn attention to what they see as a sort of financial sword of Damocles that China holds over the United States. Financial markets get weak knees every now and then when they think China may be on the verge of dumping large amounts of US dollars, and precipitating a sharp fall in the US dollar and in global financial markets.

I said the US–China relationship is complex because China's 'leverage' over the United States is nowhere nearly as simple for three reasons. First, China's exchange rate regime and an excess of savings over investment mean that it will continue to run big trade surpluses and earn US dollars. There simply isn't anything else that China can do but to plough most of these US dollars back into US assets. It is likely to channel a growing proportion of new investments into Euros and other tradable currencies, and it is quite conceivable that a greater proportion of the official reserves will be allocated towards foreign equities. But US dollar assets dominate global capital markets and this is where the bulk of China's holdings will continue to reside.

Second, China still has a rather backward financial economy. Its exchange rate is not fully convertible, and Chinese residents face strict controls on the amount of money they can send or take abroad. It does not yet possess deep and sophisticated financial markets for saving and lending, and although it has foreign currency swap and exchange arrangements with Brazil, Argentina, Indonesia, South Korea and Malaysia, it certainly does not yet command global trust in and acceptance of its own currency.

Third, and most people don't think about this much, China's worries about a weak US dollar tend to a vicious circle in which the longer it waits to revalue the currency significantly, the bigger the problem becomes, which leads to greater inertia and so on. The problem is that if the RMB were ever revalued by a significant amount, say 15–25%, anyone in China that owned more US dollars than they owed, would lose out. The biggest losers would be the Peoples' Bank of China with $2500 billion of reserves, China's companies that tend to own substantial US dollar assets, and some banks with large US dollar holdings.

China's foreign exchange reserves are a hot populist issue, with many Chinese seeing them as an emblem of national pride and the reward for years of hard work. Threats to the reserves, including from a possible collapse in the US dollar, are viewed in strongly nationalistic terms. A popular (and overtly anti-semitic) book, *Currency Wars*, written in 2007 by Song Hongbing, surged in popularity in 2009, was discussed widely in blogs and supposedly caught the attention of top government and political leaders. It sees China as the victim of a clique of Western banks and foreign currency manipulators, and warns insistently that China should resist any appreciation of its currency against the US dollar.

In any event, if there were a major appreciation, the central bank's capital, which is only about RMB 22 billion, or not much more than about $3 billion, would be wiped out at a stroke, and the government would need to inject new capital into the central bank, and probably step in to stabilise any banks or banking networks that were at risk of large losses. The loss at the central bank alone, which would translate into a sudden increase in public debt, is the equivalent of about 7–8% of GDP currently, but the longer that China accumulates US dollar reserves, the bigger the losses will become.

This is not all bad news, because Chinese households would be enormous winners from a big change in the currency. And, I would submit, the world economy would be a better place for it. But in the end, someone always has to pay for losses, and it is quite likely that Chinese consumers would pay, either through higher taxes and charges, or via lower interest rates, further delaying the needed rebalancing of the Chinese economy.

In effect then, China seems to have considerable financial leverage over the US, but in the absence of wanting to commit a financial act of war, it is stuck with its US dollar reserves and owns all the problems that go along with managing them. The perceived China threat to the US dollar and to the United States is hollow, but this is neither a reason for inaction by China on changing the exchange rate regime, nor one for inertia by the United States on reducing its financial dependence on China.

Trade is a related issue, where political competition and nationalism have replaced a long-standing convention whereby the US and China downplayed the precise legalities of certain types of trade. More difficult economic, financial and political circumstances resulting from the economic turbulence after 2008 have shifted the two governments towards more nationalistic rhetoric and actions. Incidences of trade protectionism have risen. In September 2009, President Obama approved a 35% tariff on Chinese tyre imports. In November, he agreed to hefty tariffs on Chinese steel pipes. In February 2010, China announced it was imposing tariffs on $700 million of imports of US poultry. Even though such incidents were random rather than systematic, and affected a relatively small share of total trade, they pointed nonetheless to the increasingly difficult environment for trade when jobs are at stake.

Moreover, there has been no breakthrough in kick-starting the stalled Doha Round of trade liberalisation negotiations. The rather esoteric nature of world trade negotiations means that they are often seen as a 'side show'. But global agreements to open up the world to trade are very important. And 2010–2011 could well be a pivotal time for the world trade system and for the WTO. The G20 nations have pledged to complete the Doha Round this year but this comes after similar pledges made at the meetings held in the last few years in Cancun, Geneva (three times), Hong Kong and Potsdam.

These economic spats have joined those over human rights and freedom of information, and spilled over into geopolitical issues too. In 2010, the US angered China by approving the sale of $6 billion of weapons to Taiwan and, much to China's chagrin, President Obama hosted the Dalai Lama at the White House. Waiting in the wings, of course, is the sensitive matter of China's evolving position vis-à-vis Iran's nuclear ambitions.

Perhaps the RMB, trade disputes and geopolitical matters, taken individually, amount to much ado about nothing. It is quite possible that the politically sensitive issues of Taiwan and Tibet were preceded by official background communications to avoid too much misunderstanding in private. They were certainly discussed by President Obama and President Hu in April 2010, as part of a bilateral attempt to rebuild confidence after several months of growing acrimony. Hu also agreed to attend Obama's nuclear non-proliferation summit in Washington in the same month and, in a shift in policy, advised the US that Chinese diplomats would participate in United Nations Security Council discussions about sanctions against Iran. China agreed to these, though in more diluted form than favoured by the United States, in June 2010.

For its part, the United States Treasury agreed to postpone a mandated annual report to Congress, which had been expected to label China a 'currency manipulator', and which, if approved, would almost certainly have resulted in the US hauling China to the WTO, and possibly in the imposition of new tariffs on Chinese imports. The Americans clearly didn't want this and may have themselves been concerned about a humiliating climb down in the event that the case before the WTO failed. Both sides said in Washington that they looked forward to the annual bilateral discussions under the Strategic and Economic Dialogue. Perhaps initiatives such as these can succeed from time to time in restoring cordial relations, but ultimately, small-scale measures designed to buy time will not substitute for substantive negotiation and compromise.

China and the US clearly have high levels of economic and financial interdependence, and share concerns about global security and foreign policy. But it is equally true that the issues that divide them are far from trivial. They reflect an antagonism that can be attributed partly to a change in the way they see each other, and partly to the impact of the financial crisis, which is spawning much debate in Beijing and Washington about far-reaching changes in the global economy, but one that has been joined in both countries by domestic political or party factions and pressure groups which have much more nationalistic agendas.

If these and other bones of contention are to remain manageable for the moment, but sorted out in due course, America and China have to engage in a different way. America has to see China not as a new appendage to the global status quo but as a power with which to partner and compromise. Similarly, China has to persuade itself that it is a big power, and needs a big power mentality and willingness to assume global responsibilities. This means that it has to try and reconcile its domestic and global economic, and importantly, political interests. We will return to the latter in a moment.

Leading to a new world order?

Creating a new world order in the current environment is a complex and protracted task, involving leadership and the establishment of rules and processes. In the past, the building of a new world order has been associated with periods in history when there is an existential challenge. The world's major powers tried to do it after the First World War when German and Japanese militarism was on the rise, and failed. They tried again after the Second World War as they sought to contain the USSR, and succeeded. Now, in the wake of the financial crisis, they have to do it again.

After 1918, it proved impossible to put the global system back together again, despite a renaissance of economic optimism in the 1920s, based then – as now on rapid industrialisation and the discovery of new technologies. Most attempts at building effective global institutions and a new global order came to nothing or were ineffective. The League of Nations, established at the Treaty of Versailles in 1919–1920 (and the forerunner of the United Nations) lacked political commitment from its members, and the power to forge and implement international agreements. The US, the UK, Germany and France could not agree about how to rebuild a stable economic system. The UK was too weak, and economically unable to lead. The US was unwilling, and France and Germany continued to fight the European war, in effect, without major recourse to arms, until 1939.

They did stage a World Economic Conference in London in June 1933 under not dissimilar circumstances to the G20 meeting in London in April 2009. London was supposed to be an opportunity for nations to come together and fix the world.

The conference got off to a bad start with delegates arguing vociferously about which country should supply the chairman, and with the US, the UK, and France focusing on different issues. US President Roosevelt instructed his delegation to concentrate on plans for economic recovery. Britain wanted to talk about war debts arising from the First World War. France and other European countries, which were still on the Gold Standard, thought the only issue of substance was currency stabilisation, that is, how to arrest the fall in the US dollar and British pound, and get the US and the UK back on to gold at some point in the future. The conference achieved nothing except a display of acrimony and indecision, and closed with a whimper within a month.

President Roosevelt probably torpedoed what little chance there was of reaching even a weak agreement. Referring to and condemning the proposals for currency stabilisation as 'the old fetishes of so-called international bankers', he had sent a cable reading 'I would regard it as a catastrophe amounting to a world tragedy if the greatest conference of nations, called to bring about a real and permanent financial stability ... allowed itself a purely artificial and temporary expedient'[5]. His principal concern was to secure US economic and financial recovery, and the conquest of falling prices at home. There was no chance he would be deflected from these pursuits by an attempt to bolster the exchange rate system that contributed to the economic trauma of the time. In the end, no country was in a position to act as, or be regarded as, a leader, and although the US had strong claims, it felt weakened by the Depression and unwilling to take on the leadership role vacated by the Europeans.

It was a different story after the Second World War. In fact, amid ongoing destruction at the end of the war, the US and its allies convened a United Nations Monetary and Financial Conference in 1944 at Bretton Woods in New Hampshire. The global system to which the location gave its name proved to be remarkably successful for about 30 years. It recognised that government had important obligations to social welfare and income redistribution, as well as to global economic integration. This new world order was built around a rules- and regulations-based system, providing for compromises and procedures affecting policies towards trade, international investment, capital flows, and currencies. Bretton Woods is still feted for its role in post-war reconstruction and for the creation of global institutions, such as the IMF and the World Bank, both of which carry out vital functions to this day. But it was about much more than institutions.

It came to emphasise a genuine global reordering. The US committed politically to the rebuilding of Japan, Germany and the rest of Europe, the dismantling of trade barriers, and the purchase at low rates of duty of the exports of the 'free' world. In exchange, the US acquired a key role in the determination of security and foreign policies. Gradually, the system expanded to incorporate the Asian Tigers and other developing countries. These arrangements did not preclude recessions, conflicts and wars and, for many years, France within the Western world had a nagging discomfort about US-centric power. For the most part, though, the system proved to be beneficial, at least economically.

By the late 1960s and early 1970s, the Bretton Woods financial system and the US dollar peg at its core were in trouble. The system of rules and regulations, especially those involving capital transactions, came under growing pressure from financial globalisation and innovation, and from America's attempts to have both 'guns and butter', that is, it succumbed to financial overstretch as it attempted to fight the Vietnam War (1964–1973) and implement new social welfare and civil rights programmes. The Bretton Woods currency arrangement collapsed in 1973, just as the first oil price shock rumbled through the world economy, the two events contributing to rising inflation and a temporary lurch towards protectionism.

The spirit of Bretton Woods, however, and its important institutions survived and, from the 1980s, new beliefs in deregulation and the primacy of markets breathed new life into the global economy, and the collapse of communism in Europe, accelerated globalisation and new technologies drove the world forward in the 1990s and early 2000s. Talk about a new world order at the time was coloured by feelings of a sort of victory. Francis Fukuyama, who wrote *The End of History and the Last Man* in 1992, had already claimed in the summer of 1989, when he was the deputy director of the US State Department's policy planning staff, that the 'total exhaustion of viable systematic alternatives to Western liberalism' meant that the West had emerged triumphant from the Cold War. And so it seemed for a decade or so, during which the US drove the world-changing information and communications technology revolution, market capitalism erupted in much of the emerging world, including notably in China, Asia, Russia and Eastern Europe, and economic reforms began in earnest in India and Brazil.

But the terrorist attacks on the US in September 2001 shattered that triumphalist spirit, and not just because they exposed the vulnerability of Western societies to disaffected and violent opponents. In a broader sense, they also undermined confidence. Some analysts and commentators have identified the terrorist threat and security implications as a catalyst, inhibiting the ability of the United States and the West to resist the shift in tectonic plates of economic and political power that had started a few years before. A few weeks after the attacks, former UK Prime Minister Tony Blair told the Labour Party Conference, 'the kaleidoscope has been shaken. The pieces are in flux. Soon they will settle again. Before they do, let us reorder this world around us.'

But the pieces didn't settle, and the reordering never happened. The fastest global economic growth since the Second World War, and the breakneck speed of Chinese economic expansion made political leaders complacent. Everyone was too busy milking the economic boom to worry much about building a new world order or strengthening global institutions. The party went on, until the financial crisis erupted in 2007–08.

After the collapse of Lehman Brothers, Blair's successor, former UK Prime Minister Gordon Brown, writing in the *Washington Post*, said that 'This is a defining moment for the world economy. We are living through the first financial crisis of this new global age. And the decisions we make will affect us over not just the next few weeks but for years to come'[6]. A few months later, at the G20 Summit in London in April 2009, he said, 'I think the new world order is emerging, and with it the foundations of a new progressive area of international cooperation.'

The trouble is that, while he was right about a defining moment, there isn't a lot of evidence to suggest a new world order is taking shape. The rise to prominence of the G20, including both advanced and emerging markets, as the world's top 'talking shop' on global economic and political matters, is an important step. The London Summit in 2009 lifted spirits around the world, demonstrating the integration of the world's richest and rapidly emerging nations into the G20 forum, and a display of shared concerns and intents. It endorsed the coordinated expenditure of $5 trillion to boost business and create jobs, reconstituted the existing Financial Stability Forum as the Financial Stability Board to accommodate all G20 members and pledged to take action on financial reform and governance, boosted the financial resources and lending facilities of the

IMF, and committed to an open system for world trade and capital flows, and to climate change policy cooperation. But the spirit of cooperation and integration faded even as economic recovery began. The G20 forum can draw up agreed communiqués and agendas, but it has no executive power. While the participants acted in unison to good effect in 2009, it is also true that they acted in their blatant self-interest too. China had already announced its stimulus programme the prior November, and the US stimulus had been proposed in February. Subsequently, the G20's clarion calls for action over banking regulations and practices, economic and financial reform, and climate change, for example, have become bogged down in arguments and ended up in unilateral, sometimes blatantly nationalistic, actions.

Western nations are fixated on the complex tasks of banking reform, restoring stability to public finances, and doing what they can to spur economic growth and safeguard employment. Even so, they disagree among themselves. They are struggling to find the 'right' balance between free markets on the one hand, and governments and rules on the other, in delivering positive social and economic outcomes. The US and Europe have different agendas, much as they did in the 1930s, with the former emphasising the need to sustain economic growth and strengthen the banking system, and the latter preoccupied by fiscal orthodoxy and currency stability.

They worry about political instability, arising from the strains and stresses of the crisis. In the wake of the crisis, Americans turned against the Republicans, electing a Democratic President, and returning Democratic majorities to both Houses of Congress. Japanese voters ended 54 years of single party rule by the Liberal Democratic Party, voting into office the Democratic Party of Japan.

Governments in the UK and some smaller countries, such as Iceland, Latvia and Hungary, were overturned. Political shock-waves inside the Eurozone, that included violence on the streets of Athens and widespread protests elsewhere, also raised serious questions for the first time about the viability of the Euro-system and the Euro itself.

Meanwhile, the political standing and reputation of govern-ments in China, India, Brazil and many other emerging markets have increased not just locally, but on the world stage too. The old 'Washington Consensus' emphasis on market-oriented values and economic policies is being challenged by a 'Beijing Consensus'. This idea, first mooted by the former editor of *Time Magazine*, Joshua Ramo, in 2004, is based around a different and authoritarian form of capitalism, in which China's goal is to reach out to nations in the emerging and developing world to challenge the West, not through force of arms, but by resisting it ideologically and politically.

A lot of countries in Africa and the Middle East have opened up to Chinese financial aid, exports and investment. China's govern-ment has offered over $10 billion in concessionary loans to African countries in the period up to 2012, and 1600 Chinese companies have made over $8 billion of investments in infrastructure projects, including highways in Algeria and Kenya, ports in Angola, hydo-electric power in Ghana and Gabon, and a new airport in Mauritius. For many countries, the big pull of China is that they don't have to listen to or conform to the standard Western lectures about governance and human rights.

It is worth emphasising, though, that China's ability to forge geopolitical alliances to counter those of the United States is not as strong or predictable as many assume on the basis that emerging and poorer nations will naturally fall into line behind a rising China. For some countries, the issues revolve around trade and governance, which go to the heart of the 'quality of institutions' argument. For a few, others, they are about China's reliability and legitimacy as an ally.

Several emerging nations, including Brazil and many in Asia, for example, are as unhappy as, if less vocal than, the United States over China's reticence to reform its exchange rate regime, arguing that China is effectively engaging in unfair competition and 'stealing' their export markets. In Africa, the welcoming of Chinese aid and investment is also giving rise to resentment about the political strings and economic baggage that come attached. Already in 2006, former President of South Africa Thabo Mbeki had warned that African countries should be on their guard against the risk of creeping Chinese colonialism, and there is a continuing flow of stories that reflect local concerns about China's commercial and political practices. Cases include China's military support for Sudan in exchange for oil, alleged corruption against a Chinese company's dubiously legal deals in Namibia, a trade deal with Guinea that ignored the latter's poor human rights record, and the blatant discharge of untreated effluents by a Chinese company into the Cross River in southeast Nigeria. More generally, many Africans fret about the Chinese practice of importing its own workers to Africa rather than offering jobs to unemployed local youth, and about the contravention of health and safety standards by Chinese companies.

More serious, from a geopolitical angle, was the Cheonan incident in March 2010, in which North Korea allegedly torpedoed a South Korean navy ship causing the death of 46 sailors. China's response to the incident was slow, and when it came, it was half-hearted in its criticism of North Korea. China's interests in, and support for, North Korea may be less motivated by goodwill and friendship than to prevent the destabilising consequences of an economic collapse in a country with nuclear weapons. Regardless, northern Asia countries, at least, especially South Korea and Japan, had a vivid reminder of why they retain an underlying suspicion of China. As the respected and ever-insightful economist, Simon Ogus, has noted, 'Despite ever growing trade, investment and population engagements, historical rivalries, resentment and distrust ensure the foundations of regional political relations remain as shallow as ever'[7].

The pieces of the global system are indeed in flux. We know that the world is becoming multipolar, centred around the US and China, but involving also Germany, France, the UK and Japan in the advanced world, and Brazil, India and Russia in the emerging world. But many countries are beoming more vocal and assertive, including Indonesia, Iran, Saudi Arabia, Mexico and Turkey. This developing multipolar system is very unlikely to be stable or effective unless one or two conditions hold. First, there has to be a system of rules and obligations, such as those of the Bretton Woods system, designed to moderate behaviour and strengthen cooperation. Second, and more controversially, a stable system probably requires, by way of precondition, a benign global hegemon, that is, a single large state that has the ability to marry its own interests with those of others by exercising soft power to enlist their voluntary support or acquiescence.

The US and China are the only two candidates. Japan's sun has set. Its declining and ageing population, burgeoning public debt, and deep-seated resistance to change the structure of the economy, leave it as an important, rich but fading Asian power. The European

Union shows all too many signs of going the same way and for similar reasons. Further, the European sovereign debt crisis has cast a huge existential cloud over the whole Euro project, which is going to keep Europeans introverted on the global stage for the foreseeable future.

In the emerging world, many countries apart from China are now strong enough, and able to step into a vacuum and demand to be heard and respected. These include Brazil, Russia and India, but also countries such as Saudi Arabia, Iran and Turkey, which are by no means in the same economic league. Yet, all of them have predominantly local or regional agendas, or very specific global interests, for example, energy and climate change in the case of the world's major oil producers.

But if the United Sates and China are the only candidates, neither seems to be able or willing to offer the kind of leadership that would establish an international consensus for changing the way the global economy works. This would have to involve the role and functions of global institutions such as the IMF, but also new ones whose purpose would be to help resolve global imbalances, the explosion of public debt, dysfunction in the financial system and financial, including foreign exchange, markets, and global programmes to address food and energy security, and to expand investment and infrastructure. In the absence of such leadership, this new world order is actually quite disorderly, and 'winging it' is about as good as it's likely to get.

The US and China have good reasons to cooperate, not least because they depend on one another in many areas of economics and finance, and have many mutual interests besides. Presidents Obama and Hu, for example, established a unique forum in April 2009, the 'US–China Strategic and Economic Dialogue', as a top-level bilateral structure to discuss a broad range of issues of mutual interest spanning ten areas of government policy. And yet both countries have domestic issues that often militate against cooperation.

The Obama Administration understands the need for a *modus vivendi* with China, and the shift towards Asia and the BRICs in the world economy, but the United States also has other pressing concerns, ranging from the perception at least of America's faltering global status to a weak economy, high unemployment and bloated government debt. In fact, America's biggest enemy is not China or anyone else, but the fear of its own decline. This could quite easily push the United States into a different sort of bilateral relationship with China, marked by suspicion, lack of trust and 'China-bashing'. Festering resentment about China's currency regime, and angst about its rising economic power and political ambitions could get the upper hand, leading to more trade barriers and a more hostile attitude towards Chinese goals and policies.

For its part, China denies it is a power with global significance, despite the fact that it is. It prefers to be a global partner to and drafter of rules along with like-minded nations especially in the emerging world, rather than locking horns with the United States. It subordinates its global responsibilities to domestic concerns about economic stability, the demand for 8% annual growth, and social tranquillity as it endeavours to lift China's per capita incomes to loftier levels.

But some sort of change in China is inevitable. The Communist Party will lead the reform agenda for the foreseeable future and, most likely, along a hesitant, incremental and idiosyncratic path rather than one embracing major, institutional and political reform.

Over time, it could evolve a model of soft authoritarianism and more democracy, similar to that of Japan's Liberal Democratic Party or to Singapore. Or it could retain a firm grip on the state, with no recognisable democracy and few institutional reforms. But sooner or later, rising living standards and the spread of modernity through the country are going to generate a growing public clamour for political participation and institutional reform.

China's biggest enemy isn't the United States, but comprises the hubris that comes from economic success, the nationalism that is endemic, and the contradictions between rising levels of wealth and the intolerance of political dissent and involvement. Whether and how the Communist Party responds to these challenges will say more about China's ability to be a global leader than any amount of GDP.

Conclusions

The existential challenge we face today and for the foreseeable future is not, as far as we can see, one that involves military adversaries at the global level. Instead, it arises from the fragility of our economic and financial systems, and various non-economic issues such as climate change, the spread of nuclear weapons and terrorism. No one country, not even a benign global hegemon, can confront these alone, and no one doubts we need an effective multilateral system to manage and resolve these issues if an open global economy is to be preserved.

In 2008 as the Lehman Brothers shock rumbled through the world, the UK Labour politician, former EU Commissioner of Trade, and Business Secretary of State, Peter Mandelson, wrote in the *Guardian* newspaper under the heading 'It is time for a Bretton Woods for this century', that 'States and effective governance are what makes globalisation possible … But the networks that make up globalisation will keep transmitting the shocks along with the benefits unless we take a tougher line with excessive risk, and strengthen the multilateral instruments that govern the global financial system'[8].

His focus was on economic and financial governance, and the same can be said about other matters too. Without an effective multilateral system, where the voices of smaller countries can be heard but where powerful countries are incentivised to act and take responsibility, protectionist and nationalistic reflexes have a strong tendency to spring into action all too easily. The only outcome of arbitrary decision-making, bilateral trade and investment deals, and informal – and most likely, ineffective – alliances will be rising tensions, risks of misunderstanding, and a stall, if not reversal, in globalisation.

The G20 is a good forum, but it's too big, cumbersome and toothless to translate communiqués into actions effectively. The IMF, with a stronger emerging market voice – it is planned to reallocate 5% of the voting rights from advanced and emerging nations to make them roughly equal – could be given additional responsibilities to govern the global financial system, to pool and manage foreign currency reserves, and to establish economic and financial strategies, including naming and shaming in the event of noncompliance, designed to promote global economic growth and stability. But the IMF can only be given this mandate by its shareholders, which are its members. The United States and China are going to have to lead other G20 nations towards such radical reform.

Without big power leadership within a multilateral system, there's little chance of building a stable new order. The Bretton Woods system might never have happened without the leadership from the United States and the United Kingdom, and the extensive benefits of trade liberalisation under the auspices of the WTO, and its predecessor, the General Agreement on Tariffs and Trade, would never have happened without leadership from the United States and a small group of other advanced economies.

When it comes, therefore, to the trappings of global power and leadership, I submit that, as far as we can see, there is only one candidate, the United States. Singapore's former Prime Minister and architect of the modern city-state, Lee Kuan Yew, told an audience in Singapore in April 2008 that 'After the crisis, the United States is most likely to remain at the top of every key index of national power for decades ... No major issue and no country or grouping can yet replace America as the dominant global power'. Let's go a little further.

Lee is right. He didn't mention it specifically, but the world will do business with China, while balking at its authoritarian and nationalistic nature. But it is also implicit in this passage that the United States will forever be willing and able to engage with friends and foes in the creation of order and the settlement of disputes. No one can say with certainty that it will, in view of America's own domestic issues and a tendency towards isolationism at times of crisis.

There is no doubt that China has made enormous strides towards being a great power by adopting enterprise capitalism, demonstrating high achievement levels in scientific, engineering and human endeavour, and building commercial and political alliances. It has become a major industrial power, partly at America's expense, and will shift to a more consumer-oriented society will happen eventually. Further, it cannot have minded the damage to America's reputation for financial leadership as a result of the financial crisis. It hasn't profited directly, for no other country has such sophisticated and broad capital markets, but it can certainly join the debate about the virtues of tightly regulated financial systems, for now at least.

The United States will clearly have to fix its industrial and financial sector weaknesses in the coming decade. A new government focus on technological advances in energy and biotechnology and the laborious process of financial reform have at least started. In other areas, including the exercise of soft power, the possession of military power and the ability to be a technological power, it is and will remain dominant, though there is no case for sitting on laurels. The United States will have to live up to its reputation and capacity for technological leadership and innovation by ensuring that financial weakness and the need to lower public debt does not strangle the education and research systems that feed it.

Ultimately, the United States has what China lacks when it comes to the ability to change and adapt, and that is a legal, political and institutional system based around private property rights, independent adjudication, contract law, and above all, the rule of law. This system was an essential part of the Western ascendancy five centuries ago, and remains as a pillar of Western societies and American power. Even though large, populous economies can choose many routes to play in the higher income leagues, once they get there, individuals and business people start to get politically restive and demanding. The last 20 years in China tell us nothing about how this process will evolve over the next 20 years and, in the end, we could still be wondering for how long the United States might remain the world's most prominent, if not dominant, power for a very long time to come.

This book asks whether, in the wake of the financial crisis, emerging markets will shape or shake the world. There's no question they, and China in particular, are shaping it economically, and in ways that will hopefully spur richer nations also to respond in mutually beneficial ways as the economic and financial turbulence fades.

But there is no room for complacency. The rise of emerging markets could just as easily shake the world if there is a persistent failure of political leadership to address the problem of globally unbalanced trade and destabilising financial flows.

This is not to deny the self-evident responsibilities of richer nations to fix the causes of the financial crisis and pursue responsible and sustainable growth-oriented economic policies. The global economic system, however, binds together debtor nations, such as the United States, and creditor countries, notably China, in relationships that require both sides to support its well-being. If the latter are unable or unwilling to change direction, new economic crises and politically divisive policies that would threaten the efficient working of the global system are assured.

To change direction means to implement political and institutional reforms designed to address home-grown economic imbalances that have evolved during the last 20 years. These include the discrepancies between domestic demand and foreign trade, consumption and savings, rural and urban conditions, and wealth- versus waste-generating GDP. Failure to change would run the risk of social and political instability, and much slower economic progress. The world's eyes will be on emerging markets as they confront these challenges, and nowhere more so than on China.

Notes

Introduction

1. The term 'BRIC' was first coined by economists at the US investment bank, Goldman Sachs, in a research note in 2001. Throughout the book, the terms 'emerging markets or countries' and 'developing countries' are used interchangeably. The latter refer to the generic group of countries as opposed to, for example, advanced or industrialised economies. The former refer to the BRICs and to other large developing countries.

2. See a detailed speech on the topic by Professor Yu Jianrong, Chairman of the Social Issues Research Centre of the Rural Development Institute of the China Academy of Social Sciences at www.chinadigitaltimes.net, 20 February 2010.

3. IMF, Fiscal Implications of the Global Economic and Financial Crisis, IMF Staff Position Note, SPN/09/13, IMF, Washington DC, 9 June 2009. The full costs will be smaller as temporary financial support is withdrawn or repaid and, eventually, if governments can turn a profit by selling assets back to the private sector.

4. Thomas Friedman, Advice from Grandma, *New York Times*, 21 November 2009.

5. The G20 was established in 1999 as an informal forum for advanced and emerging country finance ministers and central bank governors

to discuss and assess matters related to global economic stability. The member countries comprise Argentina, Australia, Brazil, Canada, China, France, Germany, India, Indonesia, Italy, Japan, Mexico, Russia, Saudi Arabia, South Africa, South Korea, Turkey, the UK, the US, and the EU, represented now by the President of the EU and the Governor of the European Central Bank.

6. George Magnus, Capital Flows and the World Economy: Petrodollars, Asia and the Gulf, Economic Insights – By George, UBS Investment Research, November 2006.

7. Danny Leipziger and William O'Boyle, The New Economic Powers, *World Economics*, Volume 10, No 3, July–September 2009.

Chapter One   Back to the Future?

1. Justin Yifu Lin, The Needham Puzzle, the Weber Question, and China's Miracle: Long-term performance since the Sung Dynasty, *China Economic Journal*, Volume 1, Issue 1, 2008.

2. Andre Gunder Frank, *Re-Orient*, University of California Press: Berkeley and Los Angeles, 1998.

3. See historical data at www.ggdc.net/maddison

4. Thomas Malthus, an English economist and demographer, asserted in his book, *An Essay on the Principle of Population* (1798) that world resources, notably food, would not be able to keep up with population growth, and that this would result in war and famine, which would then check population growth again.

5. See comprehensive literature surveys, for example, Gale Stokes, The Fates of Human Societies: A Review of Recent Macrohistories, *The American Historical Review*, Volume 106, No 2, April 2001, and Christer Gunnarsson and Jonas Ljungberg, China in the Global Economy: Failure and Success, Lund University, Sweden, 2007.

6. See www.ggdc.net/maddison

7. Paul Kennedy, *The Rise And Fall of the Great Powers*, Fontana Press: London, 1989.

8. Paul Kennedy, op. cit.

9. Louise Levathes, *When China Ruled The Seas: The Treasure Fleet of the Dragon Throne 1405–1433*, Simon and Schuster: New York, 1994.

10. Jared Diamond, *Guns, Germs and Steel: The Fates of Human Societies*, W. W. Norton & Company: New York and London, 1997.

11. J. M. Roberts, *The Penguin History of the World*, Penguin Books: London, 1990.

12. Jared Diamond, op. cit.

13. Jared Diamond, op. cit.

14. Adam Smith (1776), *The Wealth of Nations*, New York: Random House, 1937.

15. Jared Diamond, op. cit.

16. Davide Cantoni, The Economic Effects of the Protestant Reformation: Testing the Weber Hypothesis in the German Lands, Harvard University, Boston, 10 November 2009.

17. Justin Yifu Lin, op. cit.

18. Francis Fukuyama, *The End of History and The Last Man*, New York: Free Press, 1992.

19. Paul Kennedy, op. cit.

Chapter Two   Who Are Those Guys?

1. Reported in Guandong's Wang Checks Growth Sums, *Asia Times*, 23 July 2009.

2. Cited in Brian P. Klein and Kenneth Neil Cukier, Tamed Tigers, Distressed Dragon, *Foreign Affairs*, Volume 88, No 4, July/August 2009, Washington DC.

3. The 26,000 or so rural communes that were the backbone of Mao's China gave way to a family farming system and agricultural prices

were liberalised. Banks were created to replace budgetary financing of enterprises, operational control was eventually switched away from Communist Party secretariats to commercially-incentivised factory managers and state-owned enterprises were relieved progressively from their obligations to provide lifetime employment and social welfare.

4. Ben Bernanke, Global Economic Integration: What's New and What's Not?, remarks at the Federal Reserve Bank of Kansas City's 30th Annual Economic Symposium, Jackson Hole, Wyoming, 25 August 2006.

5. Global Economic Prospects 2007, Managing the Next Wave of Globalisation, World Bank, Washington DC 2007. The measures of per capita income are in US dollars, based on 2000 prices and exchange rates.

6. Jonathan Anderson, Toothless?, UBS Investment Research, Emerging Market Comment, 24 November 2009.

7. Jonathan Anderson, Bad Rules of Thumb, UBS Investment Research, Emerging Economic Comment, 18 February 2010.

Chapter Three   To Armageddon and Back

1. Reported in *China Daily*, 18 February 2010.

2. Nicholas Watt, Blue-eyed Bankers to Blame for Crash, Lula tells Brown, *Guardian Online*, 26 March 2009.

3. Have We Arrived at a Minsky Moment?, George Magnus, Economic Insights By George, UBS Investment Research, London, March 2007.

4. Shadow banks were financial intermediaries that existed within or as subsidiaries of deposit taking banking institutions, but also comprised non-bank financial entities, such as structured investment vehicles and hedge funds. Their distinguishing feature was the ability to engage in essentially unsupervised and opaque lending and borrowing activities,

and free from capital requirements designed to restrain just such behaviour.

5. The phrase 'atomic cloud of footloose funds' was used originally by UK Chancellor of the Exchequer Dennis Healey, who, in answer to a parliamentary question about monetary speculation said, 'I certainly agree that the atomic cloud of footloose funds that is liable to search for easy targets for speculation, either upwards or downwards, has had a destabilising effect on the international monetary scene', Oral answers to questions, House of Commons, 10 November 1977.

6. Meryck Chapman, *Don't Be Fooled Again*, FT Prentice Hall: Great Britain, 2010.

7. Ben Bernanke, The Global Savings Glut and the US Current Account Deficit, remarks to the Virginia Economics Association, Richmond, 10 March 2005.

8. Meyrick Chapman, op. cit.

9. Emerging Markets and Recession, *The Economist*, 2 January 2010.

10. *Asian Economic Monitor*, July 2009, Asian Development Bank, Manila.

Chapter Four   Atomic Clouds of Footloose Funds

1. C. Fred Bergsten, The Dollar and Deficits, *Foreign Affairs*, Volume 88, No 6, November–December 2009.

2. Financial Globalisation and Emerging Market Capital Flows, BIS, Paper No 44, Basel, December 2008.

3. The difference between savings and investment in an economy is equivalent to the current account surplus or deficit, which is broader than just trade in goods and services. Crudely, whatever isn't consumed or spent out of national income today is saved. If a country's national savings are greater (less than) than its national investment, it will have a surplus (deficit) on its balance of payments. Global external

imbalances, therefore, reflect global imbalances between savings and investment.

4. Alan Greenspan, Gold and Economic Freedom, in Ayn Rand, *Capitalism, the Unknown Ideal*, New American Library: New York, 1967.

5. For a full discussion, see Morris Goldstein and Nicholas Lardy, The Future of China's Exchange Rate Policy, Peterson Institute for International Economics: Washington DC, July 2009.

6. The SDR is a reserve asset and accounting unit, introduced and used by the International Monetary Fund since 1969. It is a basket of fixed amounts of US dollars, Japanese Yen, Euros and British pounds, and its value changes daily. While not a currency as such, it is a claim on usable and tradable currencies.

Chapter Five   After the Crisis: Catharsis or Chaos?

1. Carmen M. Reinhart and Kenneth S. Rogoff, This Time Is Different: A Panoramic View of Eight Centuries of Financial Crises, National Bureau of Economic Research, Working Paper 13882, Cambridge, Mass., March 2008.

2. Bill Emmott, *The Sun Also Sets*, Simon and Schuster: London, 1989.

3. Uri Dadush, The G20 in 2050, *International Economic Bulletin*, Carnegie Endowment for International Peace, Washington DC, November 2009.

4. Catch-up refers to a process by which poorer countries with low levels of capital per worker will tend to grow faster than richer countries for any given level of investment, and hence that per capita incomes in the former will catch up those in the latter. The process works via the higher productivity growth that results when capital is relatively scarce.

5. My colleague at UBS, Andrew Cates, has explored these at length in The Shifting Face of Global Growth, UBS Investment Research, 13 August 2009.

6. See George Magnus, *The Age of Aging: How global demographics are changing the global economy and our world* (Singapore: John Wiley and Sons, 2008) for a detailed account of the consequences of ageing societies in both richer and poorer nations.

7. Deepak Lal, Driving Forces Behind Acceleration of Indian Growth and the Outlook to 2030. Paper delivered In Honour of Angus Maddison, University of Queensland, Brisbane, 5–6 December 2006.

8. On Deaf Ears, *The Economist*, 6 March 2010.

9. Yu Yongding, China Needs to Stimulate Reform, not only the Economy, *Financial Times*, 26 August 2009.

10. Will Hutton, New China. New Crisis, *The Observer*, 7 January 2007.

11. Simon Ogus, Combobulating Capital Stocks, *DSG Asia*, 22 March 2010.

12. China's Investment Boom: The Great Leap into the Unknown, Pivot Capital Management, 21 August 2009.

13. Tao Wang, Local Government Finances and Land Revenues, China Focus, UBS Investment Research, 24 February 2010.

14. Tao Wang, op. cit.

15. Robert Ash, Give Me Land, Lots of Land, *DSG Asia*, 17 September 2009.

16. Hung Ho-fung, America's Head Servant, *New Left Review* No 60, November–December 2009.

Chapter Six   Older and Wiser: Demographic and Technological Challenges

1. See George Magnus, *The Age of Aging: How global demographics are changing the global economy and our world* (Singapore: John Wiley and Sons, 2008) for a detailed account of the consequences of ageing societies in both richer and poorer nations.

2. See Donella H. Meadows et al., *The Limits to Growth*, Universe Books, 1972, for the concerns that were expressed at the time.

3. Matthew R. Simmons, *Twilight in the Desert*, Hoboken, NJ: John Wiley and Sons, 2005.

4. Global Economic Prospects 2010, World Bank, Washington DC, 2010.

5. Global Trends 2025: A Transformed World, National Intelligence Council, Washington DC, November 2008.

6. The State of Public Finances: Outlook and Medium-Term Policies After the 2008 Crisis, International Monetary Fund, Washington DC, 6 March 2009.

7. The Worldwide War On Baby Girls, *The Economist*, 6–12 March, 2010.

8. Nicholas Eberstadt, China's Family Planning Goes Awry, *Far Eastern Economic Review*, 4 December 2009.

9. Succeeding in the Family Business can be a Hazardous Affair, *China Daily*, 3 March 2010.

10. China Mismanages its Rural Exodus, *Financial Times*, 11 March 2010.

11. Alan Wheatley, Party Needs to Loosen its Grip in China, *International Herald Tribune*, 11 March 2010.

12. T.S. Papola, Employment Challenge and Strategy in India, International Labour Office, Working Paper Series, Delhi, January 2008.

13. The World Turned Upside Down, *The Economist*, 17 April 2010.

14. Peter F. Drucker, The Way Ahead, *The Economist*, 1 November 2001.

15. Technology Diffusion in the Developing World, Global Economic Prospects 2008, World Bank, Washington DC, 2008.

16. World Bank, op. cit.

17. Andrew Cates, Productivity Perspectives, Tectonic Economics, UBS Investment Research, 14 October 2009.

18. India: The Impact of Mobile Phones, Vodafone Group PLC, The Policy Paper Series Number 9, January 2009.

19. Rising Tigers, Sleeping Giant, The Breakthrough Institute, and The Information Technology and Innovation Foundation, Oakland, California, January 2010.

20. Will China Achieve Science Supremacy?, Room For Debate, *New York Times*, 18 January 2010.

21. New York Times, op. cit.

22. Richard Silberglitt et al., The Global Technology Revolution 2020, In-Depth Analyses, The Rand Corporation, Santa Monica, California, 2006.

23. China Shuts Out GE as Homegrown Rivals Pushed Up Economic Chain Over West, *Bloomberg Business Week*, 26 March 2010.

Chapter Seven   The Climate Change Catch–22

1. The Stern Review on the Economics of Climate Change, HM Treasury, London, 2006, p. 205.

2. Stern Review, op. cit., p. 205.

3. University of East Anglia. CRU Update 2. Press Release dated 24 November 2009. See www.uea.ac.uk/mac/comm/media/press/2009/ nov/CRUupdate

4. See the IPCC statement on the melting of Himalayan glaciers at www. ipcc.ch/pdf/presentations/himalaya-statement-20january2010.pdf. This statement confirms the validity of the broad conclusion, which was that 'Widespread mass losses from glaciers and reductions in snow cover over recent decades are projected to accelerate through the 21st century, reducing water availability, hydropower potential and changing seasonality of flows in regions supplied by melt-water from major mountain ranges (e.g. Hindu-Kush, Himalaya, Andes) where more than one-sixth of the population currently lives'. The controversial statement, suggesting disappearance of Himalayan glaciers 'in 2035 and perhaps sooner' without supporting evidence is found in section 10.6.2 of the report on Impacts, Adaptation and Vulnerability written by Working Group II. See www.ipcc.ch/publications_and_data/ar4/ wg2/en/ch10s10-6-2.html

5. Gene Koprowski, UN's Global Warming Report Under Fresh Attack for Rainforest Claims, Fox News, 28 January 2010.

6. Gabrielle Walker and Sir David King, *The Hot Topic*, p. 49, Bloomsbury Publishing, London: January 2009.

7. Winning the Battle against Global Climate Change, European Commission, Brussels, 2005.

8. The Stern Review on the Economics of Climate Change, HM Treasury, London, 2006 concludes that this interpretation is robust to a wide range of assumptions.

9. Stern Review, op. cit., p. 87.

10. Stern Review. See Chapter 3, and the Intergovernmental Panel on Climate Change (IPCC), Fourth Assessment Report (AR4), 2007, p. 27.

11. See IPCC AR4 p. 26 and the Stern Review p. 83.

12. Stern Review, op. cit., p. 70.

13. Stern Review, op. cit., p. 90.

14. Stern Review, op. cit., p. 107.

15. Maryanne Grieg-Gran, The Cost of Avoiding Deforestation, Report prepared for the Stern Review, International Institute for Environment and Development, p. 2, October 2006.

16. T. Barker, Economic Theory and the Transition to Sustainability, Tyndall Centre for Climate Change Research, Working Paper 62: Norwich, 2004.

17. For this definition and further information see the website of the UNFCCC at http://cdm.unfccc.int/about/index.html

18. http://cdm.unfccc/statistics

19. China's High Price for Cuts in Emissions, *Financial Times*, 2 September, 2009.

Chapter Eight   Who Will Inherit the Earth?

1. Robert Kaplan, The Geography of Chinese Power, *Foreign Affairs*, Vol 89, No 3, May/June 2010.

2. Kaplan, op. cit.

3. Josef Joffe, The Default Power, *Foreign Affairs*, September/October 2009, Volume 88, Number 5: New York.

4. Beijing Reprimanded by G20 Leaders, *Financial Times*, 31 March 2010.

5. Liaquat Ahmed, *Lords of Finance*, William Heinemann: London, 2009.

6. Gordon Brown, Out of the Ashes, *Washington Post*, 17 October 2008.

7. Simon Ogus, 'Is it About to Kick Off ... And We Don't Mean the World Cup', *DSG Asia*, 11 June 2010.

8. Peter Mandelson, In Defence of Globalisation, *The Guardian*, 3 October 2008.

Index